Possession & Exorcism

Hans Naegeli-Osjord

Foreword by Martin Ebon

Translated by Sigrid & David Coats

1988
NEW FRONTIERS CENTER
Oregon, Wisconsin

COLIN SMYTHE, LTD.
Gerrards Cross, Bucks
England

English translation copyright © 1988 New Frontiers Center

First Published in 1983 under the title *Besessenheit und Exorzismus* by Otto Reichel Verlag, D-5357 Buschhoven, West Germany

All rights reserved. No part of this book, either in part or in whole, may be reproduced, transmitted or utilized in any form or by any means, electronic, photographic, or mechanical, including photocopying, recording, or by any information storage and retrieval system, without permission in writing from the Publisher, except for brief quotations embodied in literary articles and reviews.

Any variations from the original German text are a result of the author's wishes and are not the responsibility of the translators.

For permissions, or for serialization, condensation, or for adaptations, write the Publisher.

First published in the United States of America in 1988 by the New Frontiers Center, Oregon, Wisconsin 53575

Library of Congress Catalog Card No. 88-60521

Naegeli-Osjord, Hans.
  Possession and exorcism.

  Translation of: Besessenheit und Exorzismus.
  Bibliography: p.
  Includes index.
  1. Demoniac possession. 2. Spirit possession.
3. Exorcism. I. Title.
  BF1555.N3413   1988   133.4'2   88-60521
  ISBN 0-945831-01-3 (pbk.)

First Published in Great Britain in 1988 by Colin Smythe Limited, Gerrards Cross, Buckinghamshire

British Library Cataloguing in Publication Data

Naegeli-Osjord, Hans
  Possession and exorcism

  ISBN 0-86140-298-7 (pbk.)

Produced in the United States of America
Printed and Bound by Bolger Publications, Inc.
3301 Como Avenue Southeast, Minneapolis, Minnesota 55414

Dedicated to Katherina Nager
My friend and collaborator of many years

TABLE OF CONTENTS

Foreword by Martin Ebon viii

Preface by Walter and Mary Jo Uphoff. xi

1 **Introduction** 1

2 **Present Day Views of Possession** 3
The Author's View of Possession; The "Creed" of
Rationalism; The Importance of Experience

3 **Natural Philosophy and Natural Science** 10

4 **Good and Evil** 20

5 **The Demonic (Evil)** 23
The Demonic as Qualitative Reality; The Demonic in the
Ancient World View; The Ethereal Embodiment of
Demons; The Demonic in Theology; Western Man's
View of the Demonic; Manifestations of the Demonic;
Need for Expanded Thinking; Religious Aspect of the
Human Soul

6 **Possession** 31
General Observations Concerning Possession; Forms of
Possession; Causes of Possession; Psychic Prerequisites;
Nature of Possession; Characteristics of Possession

7 **Positive Possession** 40

8 **The Exorcism** 45
Major Exorcism; Minor Exorcism; Exorcism Within the
Protestant Church

9 **Types of Exorcism** 54
By Martin Luther; In the Christian Philippines;
Baptismal Exorcism; Non-Christian Exorcism

10 **Medical Exorcism** 62
In Brazil; The Author's Method; Dr. Carl Wickland's
Method; Observations by Wilson Van Dusen, Ph.D.

11 **The Case History of Gottliebin Dittus** 71
The Course of Events; Pastor Blumhardt's Personal
Opinions Compared With Contemporary Viewpoints in
Parapsychology; The Case History of Gottliebin Dittus
from the Viewpoint of Modern Psychiatry

12 **Other Cases of Possession** 89
The Possession of Mrs. P. 1952; The Possessed M.M.;
The Possessed Mrs. C.

13 **Unusual Cases of Possession** 95
The Lads of Illfurt; Jeanne Ferry; A Possessed Girl in
Löwenberg; The Nut-Eating Bewitched Woman; Several
Possessed Boys; The Possessed Youth; About a Possessed
Girl; The Possessed Nuns in the Convent of Kentorff;
The Possessed Servant; Agnes Katherina Schleicher;
Germana Cele; The Possessed Cat

14 **Cults and Charismatics** 117
Cultic Possession; Similarities Between Charismatics and
the Possessed

15 **Anneliese Michel** 125
A Case that Went to Court; Expiatory Suffering

16 **Harassment and Multiple Personality** 135
Multiple Personality Disorder; Harassment Differs from
Possession; Treatment of a Non-Schizophrenic Patient
Suffering from Harassment

17 **The Electronic Voice Phenomenon** 143
The Potential Risk of Intense Preoccupation with
Paranormal Taped Voices; The "Spiricom" Experiments

18 **Infestation: The Mildest Form of Possession** 150
Mrs. L. in B.; Events Surrounding Mrs. F.; Mrs. M.G.;
Miss H. N.; Mr. R.; Miss O.

19 **Witchcraft and Possession** 173

20 **Summary and Conclusions** 175

Bibliography 179

Index 183

FOREWORD

By Martin Ebon

The concept of possession is as old as recorded history. Ancient China and Babylon furnish evidence of pre-biblical exorcism practices; cuneiform tablets and scrolls contain accounts of efforts to defy extra-personal interference in physical and emotional well-being. Today, possession and exorcism, in a variety of forms, create a world-wide and cross-cultural pattern. On the following pages, Dr. Hans Naegeli-Osjord, a Swiss psychiatrist of unique experience, provides case histories and sharply defined analyses of possession data, past and present.

The special contribution that Dr. Naegeli is able to provide is based on his own extensive work as a physician, his background in the natural sciences, his long services as president of the Swiss Society for Parapsychology, and extensive travels to centers of paranormal practices, including the Philippines and Brazil.

The author does not, however, restrict himself to a mere mustering of the striking and varied evidence he has assembled over a period of more than four decades; he advances his own conclusions with vigor and conviction. Essentially, Dr. Naegeli calls for fresh approaches to the phenomena of possession, with all their ramifications, and for rejection of a purely materialistic or neuro-physiological approach to the diagnosis and treatment of cases that might otherwise be categorized as merely subjective aberrations or as paranoid schizophrenia. On the one hand, the author advocates a reexamination of earlier concepts, such as that of "subtle" bodies and influences that play a role in possession phenomena; on the other hand, he looks to future insights that will combine the findings of psychosomatic medicine with traditional as well as modern parapsychological research.

To this reader, Dr. Naegeli's work is particularly appealing for the author's own experiences — his personal encounters with possession-type elements, as well as his day-to-day work as a psychiatrist who uses exorcistic techniques to supplement or replace more widely used methods. He feels that academic parapsychologists lack the personal experience with the paranormal that placed him on the path toward his current insights. I am inclined to the belief that many prominent academic parapsychologists have, in fact, encountered the paranormal in their own early life, but have been impelled either to encase such experiences in acceptable academic structures or have, retroactively, come to downgrade or even deny the validity of such experiences.

Naegeli, by contrast, takes the reader into his confidence, thereby answering immediately the questions of his own motivations for extensive studies in a field that is as esoteric and — let's be candid — often as fear-inducing and repulsive as possession. Traditionally, exorcists have often found their tasks not only, as Naegeli states, to be emotionally and physically draining, but actually contagious; the powers of evil that seem to control the affected person seem capable of turning on the exorcist, even "rubbing off" on him. Being an exorcist is not an easy or risk-less undertaking.

World-wide public interest in exorcism was aroused in the mid- 1970's, by the motion picture *The Exorcist,* which combined a multitude of traditional possession phenomena into a single, sensationalist film. Since then, numerous novels and films have provided even more unrealistic images of the possession-cum-exorcism processes. Yet, this is not an area of scholarly or public knowledge that needs any kind of exaggeration — the most factual presentation of events, such as the author provides, is in itself quite arresting; no fictional scenario-writing is required!

By combining historical case histories with his own findings, in private practice and far-away places, Dr. Naegeli offers data providing variety but also an overall pattern. By stating his own independent position clearly, he enables the reader to approach this challenging field of inquiry with equal freshness and openness. Above all, links between possession phenomena and other seeming paranormal elements call for further examination. Possession phenomena have a kinship with mediumistic phenomena generally, such as apparent spirit manifestation during trance states, automatic writing, the manifestation of multiple personalities, and the apparent control of mediumistic personalities who create works of art, writings and musical compositions that seem to exceed their own creative capacities.

It is to Dr. Naegeli's credit that he does not ignore the risks involved in certain practices, such as the virtual addiction to seeming spirit communications that have afflicted several researchers engaged in tape recording apparent incorporeal voices. Such emotional over-involvement in occult practices, including the use of "Ouija" boards, has long been frowned upon by serious investigators. As to the actual practice of diagnosing possession and engaging in exorcism — Naegeli's caveats are clear.

Above all, I think, readers should not look in this book either for total confirmation of their own views nor for something with which they enjoy being in disagreement. For all the strength of his convictions, the author makes it clear that the border areas between various mental states defy easy definition. He does not replace one dogmatism with another; rather, he points up rigidities in prevalent approaches and stimulates the reader toward independent thinking.

Dr. Naegeli's *oeuvre,* including his writings about the "psychic surgeons" of the Philippines, invites the attention of the mental health profession, because it stimulates novel concepts in related fields. Physicians can surely benefit from the author's foray into areas they are not likely to encounter during their own professional career. The general public needs a counterbalance to the over-rich diet of sensational fiction, motion pictures and television shows that equate possession with horror and violence, rather than with exceedingly rare and complex individual experiences.

The author notes the world-wide crisis in the field of religion, weakening traditional denominations and bolstering fundamentalist and cultist extremes. He feels that the churches have abandoned much of their healing functions, such as exorcism. And yet, healing services would seem to proliferate in an increasing number of mainline houses of worship. Trends are mixed. Some doors close, while others open. There is always a time, it seems, for defiance of current dogma, for a new clearing of the air.

Martin Ebon

Mr. Ebon, for twelve years Administrative Secretary of the Parapsychology Foundation, is the author of *The Devil's Bride; Exorcism Past and Present,* editor of *Exorcism: Fact, Not Fiction* and translator of *Demonic Possession Today,* by Adolf Rodewyk, S.J.

PREFACE

This book should interest everyone who has wondered about reports of "possession" and whether there is good evidence to support the concept that the so-called "dead" and also non-human "demonic forces" can invade or displace the personality of an individual in times of emotional crises or extreme stress or openness. The widespread revival of interest in "exorcism," no doubt increased by the sensational treatment the phenomenon has received from some of the media and in such recent films as *The Exorcist,* suggests that there is an element of truth behind the experiences of persons who behaved "as though they were possessed."

There may never be agreement about the extent to which events have been exaggerated, and in some cases fabricated, but a residue of cases remains which cannot be explained away as fiction and which should not categorically have some psychiatric label attached to them without also considering the possession hypothesis. It is these cases which warrant the serious attention of all those interested in exploring the mysteries of the psyche and the human mind.

Hans Naegeli-Osjord, M.D., a Swiss psychiatrist who has practiced in Zürich for half a century and has had extensive clinical experience with the mentally ill, found that in some cases the concept of possession and its treatment by exorcism has proved more appropriate and effective than traditional therapies. Dr. Naegeli has travelled extensively in many parts of the world. During his long career in psychiatry, he has also investigated paranormal phenomena which have provided insights into strange or inadequately-understood behavior.

The predominant contemporary view of mental illness, which does not seriously consider the possibility or likelihood of survival of human personality after death, leaves no room for considering the hypothesis that, in *some* cases, "possession" might provide a more accurate explanation for bizarre personality disorders than other labels which categorize some extreme forms of deviant behavior.

Mental health professionals who cannot conceive the possibility of disturbed, discarnate entities expressing themselves through another body, may thereby limit their own effectiveness, and thus unwittingly ignore or prevent more effective therapies in cases where "exorcism" should at least be considered. Mental health care professionals, lawyers, judges, social workers and religious leaders as well as educators and those in the media, should be aware of the entire range of views — including possession and exorcism — recorded in psychiatric literature. Dr. Naegeli's book should help broaden perspectives of human experiences too often unfamiliar or misunderstood.

Dr. Naegeli's perspective reflects his personal involvement with cases severe enough to be brought to him for help as well as his familiarity with much of the literature on possession and exorcism. He recognized that the beliefs and motives of the possessing entities should be considered when deciding which exorcistic approach is most likely to be effective. Exorcists with a strong religious orientation may consider most, if not all, possessions as demonic when in fact many are much more likely to be confused, lost or embittered discarnate entities. Viewed in its broadest terms, possession can involve both willing and unwilling individuals, human and non-human, living and deceased, and "thought forms."

Dr. Naegeli cites many cases and a variety of methods for treating the possessed. He has developed his own concepts and methods, based on his many years in his profession, but he also includes examples of exorcism practices used by religious leaders and others. Our own exploration of this area of human experience provides impressive evidence that the views persons hold before their death may have a significant role in whether a particular form of exorcism will be effective. A person who during life was anti-religious is less likely to respond or yield to exorcism couched in a religious terminology. Dr. Naegeli agrees that the negative or demonic aspects of possession are often over-emphasized by church-associated exorcists, but he recognizes this as another dimension of existing belief systems or "realities" of which practitioners should be aware.

Dr. Naegeli's extensive clinical experience and scholarly background make this a challenging book. Parts of this book may stretch the reader's view of what is possible or likely; some sections delve into accounts of reported phenomena and experiences of other eras and cultures, and deal with belief systems and mythology which may be unfamiliar to readers. These can be a stimulus to re-examine the validity of commonly-held concepts. Each reader, obviously, will incorporate into his view of reality only those phenomena and views which provide insight for an expanded view of the range and complexity of human experience.

We realize that at the materialistic end of the belief spectrum, there are many who dismiss possession as a superstitious concept of a by-gone era; at the other extreme there are those who quickly label all such cases as "demonic" or "devil" possession. More than likely, most genuine cases are merely lost or confused "souls" or those seeking vicarious satisfactions for the real satisfactions they missed or enjoyed while still "in the flesh." Dr. Naegeli discusses positive as well as negative states of possession and also partial possession (harassment) to acquaint the reader with the range of recorded experiences involving such phenomena. Obviously positive cases (viewed as positive manifestations) do not call for exorcism and thus receive less space in this book than the distressing cases that have plagued some through the ages. As an example of a positive "takeover" Dr. Naegeli describes the well-documented case of George Chapman, a fireman from Aylesbury, England, who in trance, as the deceased Dr. William Lang, has successfully treated thousands of patients. Dr. Lang, who died in 1937, was a prominent ophthalmic surgeon at Middlesex Hospital, London. Family members and medical colleagues were convinced that Dr. Lang's medical skill manifests through Chapman, who has had not such training. Investigators of Arigò, a Brazilian peasant who healed thousands and was purported to be the "instrument" for Dr. Adolfo Fritz, a German physician who died during World War I, were also impressed by his skill in healing the sick. After Arigò's death in 1972 at the age of 49, *Time* magazine (10/16/72) reported:

> *"A few years ago, reports on the exploits of such miracle workers would have drawn little more than derision from the scientifically-oriented. Now, however, many medical researchers are showing a new open-mindedness toward so-called psychic healing and other methods not taught in medical schools."*

Today, a Brazilian physician, Dr. Edson Quieroz, in trance, also treats patients in the same manner as Arigò did. Luis Gasparetto, a Brazilian psychologist, has become known internationally for portraits and paintings he produces in trance, in styles of famous deceased artists — Picasso, Van Gogh, Monet, Renoir and others.

Long-term negative possession, when correctly identified as distinct from personality disorders, requires treatment with skill and understanding if the patient is to avoid a life of severe disorientation and even incarceration — shunned and misunderstood.

Numerous documented cases of haunting and poltergeists, as well as possession, are making people aware how much is still to be learned about these aspects of life. Dr. Naegeli's book presents a perspective which includes beliefs and practices from other times and other parts of the world, some of which may seem too bizarre for the "modern" person to accept. Yet these are a part of human experience and should not be dismissed just because these cultures are (or were) different from our own.

Possession can be long-term, or only one or several brief episodes in the person's life. Frequently the phenomenon is associated with adolescents whose personality and character structure are not yet stabilized to be resistant to entities seeking expression and which find "openings" when ouija boards and automatic writing are dabbled with for frivolous purposes. Some years ago, four high school students in Boulder, Colorado, came to us to discuss a frightening experience while playing with a ouija board. One of the girls had suddenly become hysterical and her face transfigured. When she came out of her trauma, she explained that she had experienced seeing her five-year-old child trampled to death by cavalry horses during the Civil War and then committing suicide in her grief. During the following week, she experienced the same episode two more times.

Knowing about our interest in parapsychology, and not feeling free to discuss the experience with her parents, she and three of her high school classmates came to talk with us, hoping to find some insight into her terrifying experience. To us, it appeared that this might be a case of temporary possession, because there is considerable evidence that when a person is murdered, commits suicide or dies suddenly, the surviving entity may be confused, earthbound and for some reason attracted to an emotionally susceptible person. If she were to experience another episode, we suggested she consult Robert A. Bradley, M. D. in Denver, who is also a hypnotist and familiar with paranormal phenomena. Apparently the insight gained during our discussion was enough to help her resist further invasion. (That episode might also have been a flashback to past life experiences.)

An early classic on possession, *Thirty Years Among the Dead* by Dr. Carl Wickland, an American psychiatrist, first published in 1924, contains transcripts and actual dialogues which took place with "possessing entities" through the doctor's clairvoyant wife, after he had "dislodged" them by the use of an electrostatic generator from some of the patients under his care in hospitals in Chicago and California. Wickland's experiences convinced him that possessing "spirits" were speaking through Mrs. Wickland in trance. He persuaded these "entities" to give their names and places of residence and with patient arguments proceeded to convince them that they had invaded another person's psyche. What often clinched the argument that it would be better for the entity to leave was to point out that they were in a body and clothing of the opposite sex (when this was the case), which brought about the realization that they were indeed "dead" and the acceptance of the suggestion that it would be better to move on to other dimensions of existence.

Naegeli's and Wickland's books will provide insights for those interested in or professionally involved with cases of extreme aberrant behavior, so that they may be aware that there are alternative explanations for such cases.

As a sequel to this book, or for additional reading on the subject, we suggest the book *Multiple Man — Explorations in Possession and Multiple Personality* (Toronto: Collins, 1985, and New York: Praeger, 1985) by Adam Crabtree, a former Benedictine monk, who has been a practicing psychiatrist for the past 18 years. His experiences provide additional information and insights for understanding behavior which is often misdiagnosed.

Another excellent book on this subject, *Minds in Many Pieces* (New York: Rawson, Wade Publishers, Inc, 1980), by Ralph Allison, M.D., a California psychiatrist, describes how the author learned to treat multiple personality disorders, most of which he felt were dissociated or splintered parts of the primary personality. He discovered in his clinical practice that some cases could not be explained by considering multiple personality a product of a disturbed person's creation for coping with stressful situations, but were more likely to be possession by disoriented discarnate spirits with an identity of their own.

There may never be agreement as to what proportion of cases are "demonic" rather than merely possession by confused or lost, "earthbound" spirits, but the concept that there are external influences at work in some mentally ill persons should no longer be automatically dismissed. There should always be a thorough clinical examination and case history and a consideration of all possible explanations, including possession. When using various psychotherapeutic techniques, including hypnosis, mental health professionals should be primarily concerned with what is most likely to benefit the patient. Dr. Allison states:

> *"In my own case this has often entailed the utilization of techniques that are bizarre, unorthodox and even religious in nature. But, these methods have cured many patients, and the patient's welfare must be the only concern."*

Edith Fiore, Ph.D., a clinical psychologist in Saratoga, California, has also written a challenging book, *The Unquiet Dead: A Psychologist Treats Spirit Possession — Detecting and Removing Earthbound Spirits* (Dolphin-Doubleday, 1987). She estimates that in her practice, roughly seventy percent of her patients suffer from spirit possession, not always of the extreme or long-term kind to which this concept is frequently restricted, but also to lighter but real forms she is able to treat with hypnosis.

With the growing awareness and acceptance of MPD (Multiple Personality Disorder) as a concept to describe some types of aberrant psychiatric behavior, the question undoubtedly will be raised more frequently: "Are all these multiple personalities generated within the subconscious and only reflect suppressed traumatic experiences? OR are there also cases in which external "entities" play a role in dominating or controlling disturbed individuals? If so, what is the best and most effective treatment?"

A widely-read book, *People of the Lie,* by M. Scott Peck, M.D. (New York: Simon & Schuster, 1983) deals with human evil he has encountered in his psychiatric practice. His clinical experience led him to view some cases of psychiatric disorders as demonic possession. His 30-page chapter on possession and exorcism is followed by a discussion of "insane" behavior of political leaders who use the lie to gratify their intense narcissism, while they unleash terror and violence. Can it be said with certainty that all wholesale violence stems from internal hatreds? Or may there also be cases of "possession by invisible evil forces" expressing themselves through emotionally unstable individuals?

In reading this book it should be kept in mind that the author's use of the word MAGIC is *not* in the sense of sleight-of- hand or deception employed by stage magicians, but as "magic" in the sense of sorcery or witchcraft.

Names, references and cases cited by Dr. Naegeli may be unfamiliar to readers in other countries. This in no way detracts from the genuineness of these experiences. Even those who have considered "possession" unlikely or impossible will be challenged by some of the cases he describes. At times, his views reflect an impatience with 20th century materialism which leaves no room for alternative hypotheses. It is hoped these views will not keep objective persons from seriously considering his important work.

We are pleased that Martin Ebon, an internationally-known author on many aspects of the paranormal, agreed to write the forward to this book. He has known Dr. Naegeli for years and can attest to his extensive knowledge and experience and his basic integrity. We also wish to express appreciation to David and Sigrid Coats of the Coats Translation Service, Minneapolis, Minnesota for an excellent translation loyal to the German edition. We have been authorized by Dr. Naegeli to make whatever additions and modifications we deemed appropriate, as long as these did not interfere with the basic theme of the book.

Frank Farrelly, a Madison, Wisconsin psychotherapist, who has been in demand for presenting numerous workshops in Europe, as well as Australia and Hawaii, made the following comment about the book:

"For those psychotherapists, researchers and academicians who increasingly suspect that the totality of human experiencing is not explained by

the DSM III (Diagnostic and Statistical Manual, 3rd Edition), *Naegeli's book may well become an important pioneering effort and source book in the history of psychotherapy."*

Our thanks also to Frances E. Ehrlich, M.D., psychiatrist; Frank Farrelly, A.C.S.W., psychotherapist; psychiatrist-neurologist Marshall Gilula, M.D.; and Roger Severson, Ph.D., psychologist, for reading the manuscript and making suggestions to clarify concepts and expressions for readers of English.

Walter & Mary Jo Uphoff
The New Frontiers Center

1. INTRODUCTION

It is not possible to understand the phenomenon of possession within the framework of natural science or the psychological views derived from natural science. The basic principles of natural science are based on a materialistic view of the universe. According to these principles, all life, including soul and mind, is said to have material roots (causes), and the pre-Cartesian division into mind and matter — which even Descartes did not abolish — becomes superfluous. Ancient sacred writings refer to a dual but also parallel creation of God — the immaterial and spiritual, and the material. Indian philosophy even classifies mind and soul as matter, and considers matter merely a concentration of mind and soul.

It is obvious that the phenomenon of possession is not causally anchored in the material sector. Research into ultimate cause was never able to comprehend the *essence* of the soul's forms of manifestations. Even today, what cannot be fitted into a materialistic framework is referred to as miracles. Walter Nigg[1] rightly asks: "Has ostensibly sound human reason ever recognized a miracle?" On the contrary, man constantly tries to attribute everything that is incomprehensible, or that does not fit into his conception of the world, to a physical-chemical construct, even when such an explanation is totally inadequate. While writing these lines, I read in the parapsychological monthly *Esotera*[2] an article with the oversimplified title: "Walking on fire turns out not to be a paranormal phenomenon!" The article asserts that fire walkers in northern Greece perform a dance that brings the feet into contact with the carpet of fire for only four-tenths of a second, an interval found to be so brief that the human skin suffers no damage. With this, the investigator considers the problem solved. All spiritual potential is happily excluded by the author. With this exclamation of *eureka!,* all further considerations seem superfluous, including the fact that, among the many fire walkers who appear every year, there have been many instances when the fire-walker remained in contact with the carpet of fire for much longer than four-tenths of a second. Their clothing also remained undamaged. In 1981, I myself observed the Indian avatar, Sri Ganapathy Sachchidananda, stand in the fire pit at Mysore for 13½ minutes. That phenomenon has frequently been filmed, and was also documented on film on that occasion.

The notion that the rational and the irrational can co-exist, as C.G. Jung postulated, is alien to the orthodox natural scientist, who is unable to comprehend the fact that there are energies emanating from the human soul which control matter. Still less is he willing to admit that there are beings of a

---

[1] Walter Nigg, *Große Heilige* (Zürich: Artemis Verlag).

[2] August, 1982.

non-corporeal or, more precisely, of an ethereal nature which also act on and influence the physical environment.

Although Jung's view is entirely comprehensible to me, there are few teachers in Western universities who present this view. Courageous teachers who dare support views deviating from orthodox beliefs usually remain on the periphery and may be subjected to discrimination. Anyone who has not spent decades in research on parapsychology and the philosophy of nature, as I have, may have difficulty understanding the phenomenon of possession. Exorcism, too, will remain inexplicable when examined merely within the current "scientific" framework of psychiatry and psychology. The genuine, successful exorcist is still a part — often unconsciously — of the magical in life, and still has a sense of the mystifying aspects of the world. By being open to the transcendent, he succeeds in making contact with those spirits which have invaded the mental and spiritual sphere of the possessed. Only then does a dialogue occur, and a bitter battle may develop.

Through the years I have been through all stages of belief in natural science. My lively interest in fairy tales and the paranormal in my youth challenged me, in the next five decades, to explore many phenomena which most adults reject without questioning. However, gates seldom open without crises and experiences of one's own. My gratitude extends to all those persons who sought me out for advice and became involved in the adventure of attempts at exorcism, even though they scarcely dared inform their closest companions of their activity without risk of being categorically considered insane. An additional fact is that most of the people who sought help from me were uncertain about matters of faith or were atheists. In these cases, religious preparations, preferably not of the orthodox school, necessarily preceded the exorcistic efforts. A number of them, although endowed with strong religious leanings, were *de facto* heretics, no longer able to relate to the orthodox dogmas supported by the church. What was needed, therefore, was a non-sectarian religious viewpoint. Moreover, it is my conviction that a religious orientation is far more effective than intellectual brilliance in engendering understanding for the human soul. This is apparent in the already-mentioned description of the Pastor of Ars by Walter Nigg, as well as the activities of Saint Josef von Copertino.

Every intellectual perception rests on the critical evaluation of external and internal realities; but in order to achieve *complete* insight, we need also to rely as well on the three functions of human knowledge: feeling, perception and intuition. That has been my objective in writing this book, and it is my hope that it may succeed in helping expand the often constricted perspective of those who are unfamiliar with experiences such as those presented in this book.

I am indebted to Harold Sherman for suggesting that the German edition of this book be translated into English. He had promised to actively support such a project but the state of his health did not permit this. Therefore, our friend in common, Professor W. H. Uphoff of the New Frontiers Center, Route 1, Oregon, WI 53575, spontaneously and generously sprang into the breach. Without his exceptional initiative, this edition would never have become a reality. He and his wife Mary Jo Uphoff deserve all my gratitude.

2. PRESENT DAY VIEWS
OF POSSESSION

The desire to understand possession and its related spiritual forms of manifestation in a broader medical-scientific context may alienate some persons, including some of my colleagues in the field of psychiatry. Many are eager to categorize or dismiss possession as a part of theology, even though it clearly deals with psychic manifestations. Still others consider my involvement in this area as an anachronism, irrelevant to a so-called enlightened world in which there is no longer any place for the demonic. They maintain that the word and the concept of demonism are inimical to contemporary thought.

The well-known theological tract, *Farewell to the Devil,* was widely read, but was repudiated in 1972 by Pope Paul VI. And quite rightly, for modern psychology considers the devil the archetype of evil that is the polar opposite of good. Precisely that fact, however, of having grown into a new dimension — namely, the ethical dimension — is a characteristic of being human, and in accordance with the highest development to date within the animal kingdom. *Eritis sicut deus, scientes bonum et malum* (you will become like God, knowing good and evil), promised the serpent. The promise was fulfilled, but the achieved resemblance to God was paid for with the loss of the "ethical paradise," a place beyond good and evil. Within this supreme act of Providence concerning man, the *d*evil (N.) can perhaps be ignored — which would be comparable to a fool's ignoring acute danger — but it can never be eliminated.

There is hardly a more visible and unusual phenomenology of evil than some form of possession. Through it, we become aware of everything mean and repugnant; the pleasure of destruction celebrates triumphs, and the most unaesthetic cannot be avoided.

Protestant theology is no longer concerned with this interesting complex of questions, despite the fact that we have an impressive description of the incident concerning the possessed Gottliebin Dittus (Chapter 11). That description was written in 1844 by the well-known, righteous Pietist minister, Johann Christoph Blumhardt.

Let us also keep in mind the fact that in the sixteenth and seventeenth centuries, Protestant clergymen, Luther among them, frequently and often successfully engaged in exorcism.[1] Unfortunately, exorcism is only rarely practiced today. Although there is a growing minority among psychiatrists, psychotherapists, parapsychologists and theologians, both Catholic and Protestant, who recognize possession as a genuine phenomenon, the majority still view human behavior from either a more traditional natural science or theological perspective.

---

[1] Johannis Bodini, *Daemonomania* (Hamburg, 1968).

Catholic theology has made particularly valuable contributions to the classification and treatment of possession. The *Rituale Romanum,* from the year 1614, seems to me even today to provide direction and insights. Historically, the cure of the possessed was mainly entrusted to the Capuchins. The two works by the Jesuit priest, Adolf Rodewyk, about the suffering of a possessed person[2] and the entire evaluation of the problem,[3] can provide important insights.

Although the Catholic Church did not forbid exorcism in 1978, following the attention attracted by the exorcism trial of the possessed Anneliese Michel in Aschaffenburg, Germany (Chapter 15), it seems that there is no longer much consideration given to training in exorcism. To the best of my knowledge, Capuchin priests are increasingly reluctant to accept people who feel bewitched or possessed. I shall later return to this topic.

At present, many Catholics and Protestants prefer to view possession from the perspective of rationalist thinking. Many who were educated outside these traditions increasingly accept the concept that it may be manifestations of religious and related psychic phenomena. This is a curious enantiodromy (counter-trend). Academic psychology still adheres strongly to rationalism, leaving little room for transcendent explanations. It is largely dominated by Freud's teaching, dedicated to rationalism and causal research. The conceptual structure of C. G. Jung, which is directed toward the transcendent, is only slowly gaining ground. Psychology is increasingly focused on psychiatry, influenced very little by theological thought, and even less by the wisdom of the East.

Psychiatry does not recognize possession as a specific disease, but classifies it along with various illnesses such as epilepsy, hysteria, and schizophrenia. Eugen Bleuler[4] makes only a single reference to possession in his textbook, as does his son, Manfred Bleuler, a successor in the field. Both define the experiences of the possessed and those who believe themselves to be bewitched as the expression of schizophrenic or illusionary phenomena. Eugen Bleuler, the ingenious investigator of schizophrenia, then and now set the stage for the definition of possession. As a rationalist and natural scientist, neither he nor his successors had any doubt about the accuracy of his conception. Therefore the initiative for loosening the dogmatic attitude of scientific psychiatry toward possession and to question basic assumptions about the phenomenon — in fact, to question it in its entirety — must come from within our own ranks.

The Author's Personal Experiences and View of Possession

As a board-certified psychiatrist (FMH [Medical Association of Switzerland]) I received three-and-a-half years of training at the Bleuler Research Center at

---

[2] A. Rodewyk, *Dämonische Besessenheit heute* ["Demonic Possession Today"] (Pattloch Verlag, 1966).

[3] A. Rodewyk, *Die dämonische Besessenheit* ["Demonic Possession"] (Pattloch Verlag, 1963).

[4] E. Bleuler, *Lehrbuch der Psychiatrie* ["Textbook of Psychiatry"] (Berlin: Verlag Jul. Springer, 1929).

Burghölzli, Zürich, and at the Bleuler polyclinic. I also worked as an assistant physician at the neurological clinic (Salpétrière) in Paris, at the university surgical clinic of Lausanne, the medical department of the Canton Hospital of St. Gallen, and served two years as a military physician. Since 1940, I have been in private practice as a psychiatrist, working not only as an analyst but also seeing as broad a clientele as if I were active at a polyclinic. I am familiar with the entire spectrum of psychiatric diseases. As the son of an internationally known physician and natural scientist, I was trained in the scientific method by him and by all my teachers, and am thus familiar with the premises of natural science. For fifty years I observed the successes of medicine based on these premises. I recognize its triumphant conquest of former scourges of the people, but I also know about the other side of laboratory research, the alienation from man, and the treatment of animals as if they had no souls. In addition, there must be consideration for the unfortunate effect on the demographic balance within the Third World.

As far back as my last years in medical school, I developed an interest in parapsychology and began giving lectures on that subject. I took part in the founding of the Swiss Parapsychological Society in Zürich, and served as its president from 1958 until 1980. Primarily, I was involved with research into ghosts and collaborated with K. Nager in investigating instances of poltergeists. Along with other researchers of the Swiss Parapsychological Society, I experienced striking manifestations of a ghost bound to a certain locality. In 1957 I was summoned to a castle in central Germany that for decades, perhaps even centuries, had been plagued by appearances of a ghost. I described my experiences in the parapsychological Journal, *Neue Wissenschaft,* published by P. Ringger.[5]

The following is an abbreviated description of those experiences:

> *After spending a pleasant evening at the castle, I went to the music room, the main scene for the ghostly incidents. Shortly after 3:00 a.m., I awoke from a dreamless sleep. All my limbs were paralyzed, and I had a feeling of oppression in my chest that I had never before experienced. I cried aloud, not from fear but spontaneously, as if an alien being were screaming out of me. For a short period of time, I and the whole bed were shaken vigorously. I cannot accept the argument of colleagues who make light of the incident, who maintain that I had dreamed it or that unconsciously I had been expecting such an event. After all, no one is more suited to accurately distinguish between real life and dream life than an experienced psychiatrist. Since there had been no activity for three hours, I had given up any expectation of experiencing ghosts.*

Although phenomenological in nature, that incident was so clearly differentiated from, and independent of, my own on-going psychic experiences that I

---

[5] H. Naegeli, "Ein selbsterlebter Spuk" ["A Ghost I Experienced"], *Neue Wissenschaft* (7/2, 1957).

neither can nor wish to exclude a transcendent origin as the likely cause.

Even prior to that time, less significant experiences and careful study of the literature had made me skeptical of an exclusively animistic interpretation of ghost phenomena. My personal conviction of a transcendent influence on the world of our reality was strengthened. On the other hand, much of the literature about paranormal phenomena by university scholars adheres almost entirely to the precepts of philosophical materialism. The basic hypothesis of this orientation has already become an axiom, according to which all parapsychological phenomena, as well as the world of human experience, derive from one's own psychic potential (animistic direction).

This theory is considered to represent the most advanced knowledge, and there are attempts to claim *sole* validity for it. The majority of parapsychologists are now oriented toward the scholastic principle of parsimony and to John Stuart Mills' principle of simplicity. Both principles require that the researcher, if confronted with two possibilities of interpretation, should align himself with the established, already existing conclusions — in other words, accommodate to what is already familiar and recognized. It is argued that any other view complicates the situation, and is therefore not parsimonious. This, however, leads to blocking off any vital, dynamic research. William Herschel was an exception who took a more progressive view. He coined the maxim: *"The complete observer will keep his eyes open in all aspects of knowledge, in order that they be immediately struck by any event which, according to the theories already accepted, should not occur, for these are precisely the facts that lead to new discoveries."*[6] Another exorcist of the sixteenth century considered the intrusion of the spiritual and transcendent dimensions into our reality to be self-evident. He based his ideas on Theophrastus Paracelsus, the great philosopher and reformer of medicine, who is again held in high esteem by the medical profession today. A hypothesis based on the principles of parsimony and simplicity, explaining the reality of transcendent beings or of possession, if it were to follow the mental orientation of science at that time, would have resulted in conclusions opposite to those of today.

Although the philosophical materialists within the field of science fundamentally base their views on the teachings of Descartes,[7] especially on his "first reality," the *res extensae* (matter), they ignore his posited "second reality," the *res cogitans* (spirit). Such a reduction of the world view to matter alone and to philosophical abstractions and deductions (conclusions), must be considered a backward step for a unified conception of the world.

The "Creed" of Rationalism

The *Weltanschauung* (world view) of rationalism adopted by scientists, most academics, and contemporary persons of average education, resembles a religion — its binding creed is generated not by religious reformers, but by

---

[6] *Einleitung in das Studium der Naturwissenschaften* ["Introduction to the Study of the Natural Sciences"], William Herschel (1738-1822).

[7] Descartes = (lat.) Cartesius

zealous scientists who, although deserving the recognition they are accorded, promulgated but one part of the dynamic heritage of Descartes. Notable in this respect are I. Kant,[8] I. Newton, H. von Helmholtz, R. Virchow, & J. P. Sartre. The world view of rationalism today is treated with devout respect, although it represents only a part of reality. Even personal experiences which contradict these teachings are forced into presently held theories.

When describing my own experiences anchored in magic, I have occasionally encountered true indignation. An expansion of the rational view was perceived as an unreasonable demand, and often aroused resistance. No new theory of knowledge and no creed remains unchanged in all of its aspects. This, however, does not apply to the teaching of Jesus Christ or Buddha, both of which reflect the highest intuitive view of the world to date, even though their teachings have been reshaped into various dogmas and creeds.

The Importance of Experience

True insight into the *essence* of psychic phenomena can only be conveyed through direct experience. Personal experience manifests itself as the reaction of our whole personality to an external event. All four functions of cognition are involved: intuition, perception, emotions and intellect; the latter not at the moment of experience, but afterwards as a critical judgement of what was experienced. Experience secures cognition, not just cognizance of singular facts. In that sense, it is more crucial than laboratory experiment and statistics, which should also be taken into account because they provide an objective frame for subjective experience.

As far as I know, only a few of the parapsychologists active in academic positions have had personal experiences which deeply affected their whole being. Evaluating Zener cards,[9] listening to telepathic dreams of others, or reports about poltergeists, and reporting them in a scientifically accurate way, surely has merit, but it is not a substitute for personal experience. The large number of such similar occurrences permits one to point out the high probability of their existence. They, however, do not provide compelling proof. Causation founded in qualitative experiences cannot be demonstrated, nor is the subjective emotional content touched upon thereby. This explains the relatively scant reaction toward parapsychological research by researchers and educated persons who have a natural sciences orientation. Years of professional work, scientific and philosophical endeavor, consideration of the consequences of foreign cultural and religious forms, and especially my own experience, have contributed to a broad perspective of parapsychological phenomena. This is particularly true for the phenomena of possession. One who has not himself experienced, counselled and treated the possessed should refrain from making judgments which only reflect the ivory tower thinking of present-day conventions and dogmas. The rationalistic mentality, with its

---

[8] In his later years, however, Kant agreed completely with Swedenborg's views about metaphysics, and described these views in his little-known work, "Lectures on Psychology."

[9] Five cards with symbols used for statistical evaluation of manifested telepathy, clairvoyance, and precognition (Dr. J. B. Rhine, Duke University, Durham, North Carolina).

focus on material and quantitative causality, does not permit a total illumination of the phenomena of life which are spontaneous and rooted in the spirit. Just as rigid dogma in religion impedes the spontaneous access to the Divine, thinking solely within the methodology of natural science makes the recognition of *spiritual* powers of the psyche and their relationship to the cosmic planes impossible. There will be few gratifying results within the field of psychiatry, which relies so heavily on chemotherapy. There is urgent need to consider thinking which complements natural philosophy.

Before I deal with the differentiation of these two great scientific systems of thought, I would like to direct attention to the fundamental antinomy of the possible interpretations within the range of our subject. Most mental health professionals oriented in the natural sciences along with most psychiatrists explain the manifestations of schizophrenia (hallucinations, delusions, autism and extreme forms of agitation) as a domination of, or the actual overpowering of the patient by one particular part of his psyche. The specific expression for these phenomena is "partial personality." This previously inconspicuous part of the personality was originally capable of fitting harmoniously into the total structure of the psyche, but later it tends to expand — dominating, and at times completely extinguishing, the original center of the personality. With this, the splitting of the whole psyche results, which is the split personality, schizophrenia. This is correct. But *why* the part of the personality gaining power could have won such pathological dominance remains unclear. (We think of exaggerated distrust, or the inflation of the ego — in other words, the overestimation of one's self-concept). Causes such as heredity and environmental factors, according to the hypothesis of animism, contrast with the "spiritualistic" explanation of possession by a transcendent spirit. The first interpretation (animism) merely shifts the problem onto previous generations and hypothetical assumptions; and spiritualism cannot provide valid proof within the framework of scientific precepts.

The actual chain of causes — I believe — can never be found solely in the materialistic, i. e. in the mere physicochemical activities of the brain cells, although the psychiatrists who prescribe chemotherapy think of such causal activity and attempt to counteract it with depressant medication. The latter, however, only leads to a time-limited impediment of psychic thought processes and a temporary suppression of the emotions. Granted, for a certain period of time this can relieve and help. Since the psychiatric manifestations of illness tend to go through rhythmic up and down phases,[10] the turn toward health as a condition of this rhythm can lead to the termination of the medication. Improvement and recovery is then attributed to the medication, even though — and this corresponds with decades of my observations — lasting cures are not effected during a rhythmic downward movement. That is why a majority of schizophrenics and endogenously depressed stay in hospital treatment for months.

---

[10] H. Naegeli, "Probleme um die depressive Verstimmung und die Depressionsforschung," ["Problems of depressed mood and research on depression"], *Praxis,* 59/35 (1970).

8

Today's view, which dominates psychiatric literature, seeks to attribute mental illnesses, including possession, to chemical changes in the brain cells and their fluid chemistry. Among those opposed to this view is Max Thürkauf (professor for physical chemistry in Basel), who points out that up to now, no scientific experiment for the equation Bios = Chemistry and Physics exists. The credibility of science is not enhanced by claiming that everything which cannot be confirmed by experiment is not credible. In that way, it renders itself not credible.

Bios, *life,* is far more than only chemistry and physics and necessarily has its roots not only in the material and its chains of causality, but in a spirituality, which does not — as believed in natural sciences — emanate from matter and cell chemistry, but which is independent; in fact, it is superior to and determinant of matter. Physicochemical activities in the brain merely demonstrate the other (material) part of spirituality to which they are subordinated.

The knowledge of the earlier founders of religions, the Indian teachers of Yoga, and all primitive peoples, was in no way founded on deductive philosophical thinking, but on introspection. Intuitive perceptive consciousness leads from the material existence back into the primal world of spirituality. This is always connected to a change in consciousness, since such introspection requires the blocking of our "Ego." Self-centered goals prevent higher knowledge and make the recognition of transcendental contents and their essence difficult. The change of consciousness can be achieved through rituals or through exceptional mediumistic ability of the individual. Dreams, too, can provide insight into cosmic structures, as we know from the experiences of the German chemist A. Kekulé.[11] The formula for the structure of the benzene ring was revealed to him in a dream. In addition to rational deductive logic and its methods of obtaining knowledge, we also have intuition at our disposal as a means of apprehending knowledge. To me, it appears absolutely necessary to compare the two scientific forms of obtaining knowledge which are available to the seeker, and which, contrary to the prevailing intellectual climate, should complement and stimulate one another.

---

[11] F. A. Kekulé von Stradonitz (1829-96), the German chemist credited with formulating the structure of the benzene ring.

3. Natural Philosophy and Natural Science

In the time of Alkmaion, student of Pythagoras (ca. 550 B.C.) and Heraclitus (540 B.C.), cognition through intuitive, imaginative philosophizing prevailed. Under Aristotle (ca. 380 B.C.), it found its exact opposites in scientific deductive thinking. Consequently, two scientific theories of cognition developed: The inquiry into *concepts* and *essence* by ways of natural *philosophy* and the inquiry into *causation* by natural *science*. Each enjoyed preference depending on the dominant belief (Zeitgeist) of a particular era. However, natural science has predominated ever since Descartes, who, in his book *De Homine*, was the first to attempt to explain all processes in the human body from a purely mechanistic point of view. Although Goethe, Carus, Oken and Schelling opposed this trend, they could not prevent it from becoming the dominant view. At the beginning of this century, Ludwig Klages, who had a doctorate in chemistry, was one of those whose thinking evolved beyond the natural sciences camp. More recently, Wilhelm Blasius, Walter Heitler, Max Thürkauf and Heinrich Zoller joined that camp.

Blasius reminds us that in the way in which natural science understands causality (cause-effect connection), each cause of an effect has to be seen also as the effect of a prior cause. This leads to an infinite chain of causes, to a *regressus in infinitum*, a return into an endless past. No phenomenon can be completely explained with methods of natural science. In the philosophical-rationalistic sense, attempts to achieve a definitive clarification are thus fruitless. Pure research which seeks causality cannot illuminate the essence and meaning of the Universe. This leads necessarily to a narrow view of the Universe. In contrast, natural philosophy can facilitate expression of the essence of events, a dimension which cannot be measured, however. By its very nature, all essence is qualitative, not quantitative.

As far as our subject is concerned, it is of utmost importance to present the significant principles of natural philosophy and compare them with those of natural science. Unfortunately, many educated people have reached the point where only the so-called "exact" sciences (mathematics, physics and chemistry) are considered true sciences, and all other areas of knowledge and experience are downgraded. Walter Heitler, professor emeritus for theoretical physics at the University of Zürich, emphasizes (correctly, in my opinion) that the so-called "exact" natural sciences which subscribe to the principle of causality have become unscientific, because they refer to matter as the *only* aspect of the world.

To show that a large number of life's phenomena, and especially possession, avoid the grip of the dogmatic natural sciences, and thus cannot and should not be judged by it, it is necessary to approach our area of investigation scientifically. For this approach, it is not enough to have a thorough understanding of natural science. One must also understand natural philosophy. The latter, which usually is explored only by departments of philosophy, is practically unknown to most of today's academics. Therefore, the two methods of investigation will be contrasted here, as Walter Blasius, chair of the department of physiology in Gießen (Germany) did in an outstanding work, *Über die Grenzen der naturwissenschaftlichen und der naturphilosophischen Lehre vom Leben,* ["On the Boundaries of the Natural Science and Natural Philosophy Theories of Life"].[1] I agree substantially, and often verbatim, with his exposition. The comparison between the two models of thought illuminates how the intuitive (natural philosophy) and intellectual (natural science) potentialities for perception differ from each other. In fact, they are diametrically opposed but also complementary to one another, and both are necessary for a better understanding of the world.

I would like to point out that each of the four functions of cognition, postulated by C.G. Jung as intellect, emotion, intuition and perception, was able to dominate during its particular era. *Perception* dominated the era of early mankind as a "participation mystique," a total participation in the collective reality of the world; *Intuition* in the early Greek antiquity and throughout the East; *Emotion* during the romantic period; and *Intellect* in times after Descartes and particularly today. However, it appears that there are groups in our society, primarily outside the walls of the university, which are increasingly aware of the limits of rationalism. They are attempting to learn about astrology, parapsychology and mysticism. It is conceivable that future generations may increasingly approach the thinking represented by natural philosophy.

We will now focus on the latter. The teachings of natural philosophy, described by Goethe as morphology and by Klages as ontology, classify and describe the phenomena of life which are experienced as formed and simultaneously *animated.* These teachings perceive the living phenomena in the world as forms or pictures in which souls or essences are expressed. Perception of a *picture,* then, is also the simultaneous perception of the essence of a picture. All of nature is organized for man in a way in which it can be understood by contemplative observation. Therefore, all forceful experimentation appears unnecessary in the face of the obvious readiness of nature to be comprehended in its essential interrelationships. By conclusions drawn from analogies, i.e., by discovering similarities between souls and essences, the world is categorized, and internal and external connections are revealed. Pictures and symbols refer to internal relationships — for example, fire, spring, tree, arrow, circle.

Using three examples, the different methods of comprehending and investigating of the two theories of life will be illustrated in more detail. To the natural philosopher, the circle signifies a symbol of totality. In addition, it contains, on the one hand, a delineation and shielding against the outside, the infinite, and on the other hand, a focusing on a center. For example, the

[1] Walter Blasius, "Erkenntnistheoretische und methodologische Grundlagen der Physiologie" ["Cognitive theoretical and methodological foundations of physiology"] in *Lehrbuch der Physiologie des Menschen,* ed. by Landois-Rosemann (28th edition; Urban-Schwarzenberg, 1962).

11

magician centers his intentions on the spot of the activities where it is also shielded from all detrimental and hostile forces. In contrast, for the natural scientist, the circle becomes a thing which can be measured. The circle is merely a line which at all points has the same distance to its center.

The difference becomes even more clear in the symbol of the hexagram, "Solomon's Seal" or Star of David.

For the natural philosopher, it symbolizes the total harmony within the diametrically opposed forces which gravitate toward the earth or are directed toward heaven. The triangle with its point directed downward characterizes the body, the negative principle, and the element of water, while the triangle with its upward point symbolizes the spirit, the positive principle, and the element of fire.

Goethe portrays Faust's experience observing the symbol of the Hexagram with the following wonderful words:

> How all things interweave to form the Whole,
> Each in another finds its life and goal!
> How each of heaven's powers soars and descends
> And each to each the golden buckets lends;
> On fragrant-blessed wings
> From heaven piercing to earth's core
> Till all the cosmos sweetly rings![2]

But for the natural scientist, the Solomon's Seal is a geometric sign of which the sides, areas and angles are of equal size and can be measured.

To the natural philosopher, the tree reveals similar qualities. The height of its crown reflects the depth of its roots. Prana energy from the cosmos joins with forces from the earth to form a strong living organism. It is rooted in the earth, and contrary to the animal, does not need to change its location. In harmonic balance, its fixed place suffices.

The natural scientist, in contrast, aside from other things, pays attention to the proportions of the tree, investigates its chemical exchange of the gases

---

[2] Johann Wolfgang von Goethe, "Faust, I & II" From the translation by Charles E. Passage (New York: Bobbs-Merrill Co., Inc., 1965), p. 22. Used by permission.

oxygen and carbon dioxide and studies the anatomy of the picture of the plant which for him has become a thing.

Natural philosophy and poetry possess many common roots. A true poet proves himself by being able to condense the essential, the primary relationships, the images of life. For example, a poem, "At Midnight," by the romantic poet Eduard Mörike, which is hardly understandable by pure intellect, is analyzed here in a contrasting of natural philosophical and natural scientific thinking.

At Midnight

Serenely, Night to land did glide,
There, dreaming, she leaned on the mountain side,
The golden scales her eyes now fill
Where time in equal cups lies still.
And bolder the springs appear,
For their mother, the Night, to hear
Of the day,
Of today that was.

Of that lullaby ancient and old,
She wants no more to be told;
To her the sky's sweet blues much sweeter ring,
Than the yoke the fleeting hours bring.
But always the springs carry on,
Into sleep, yet, the waters' song
Of the day,
Of today that was.[3]

If we let Mörike's poem "At Midnight" affect us in quiet contemplation, we become aware of how strangely this world, as viewed by the poet, appears to contradict our accustomed life. We are accustomed to ordering our daily perception of the external world in a concrete, logical and conscious manner. Mörike presents *pictures,* which remain incomprehensible to the intellect. Nevertheless, the vision of the poet deeply moves us — entirely aside from its unsurpassed linguistic musicality — to the core. Thus, this vision is also in accord with a reality, though it is a dreamlike symbolic reality.

Let us bring this poetic view, this look into the deepest secrets of the world, closer to our understanding. Just as Goethe created many parts of his drama "Faust" in a trance state, free from the organizing intellect, Mörike's "At Midnight" appears as a perfect whole, received from lofty spheres. Let us attempt to enter into the spirit of Mörike's dreamlike view:

"Serenely, Night to land did glide,"

---

[3] Translation copyright © 1986 by Sigrid D. Coats. Used by permission.

Night, in the understanding of natural sciences, is nothing but a condition without sunlight. Here it is being personified as "Mother Night." Therefore, night is not only described as a condition minus certain qualities, but it belongs, itself, to the primary forces, and has a polar relationship with day, full of fascinating, interwoven connections. This reminds us of the polarity between male and female!

Mother Night glides "serenely" to land. In analogy to Mörike's poem "Orplid," we may assume that she rises from the waters, the ocean. Even in modern psychological theories, the ocean is considered a symbol of the collective unconscious; in other words, as a spiritual and emotional maternal stratum of cosmic character. Serenely, i.e. completely unruffled, without particular intentions, as a matter of course, she moves into the polar condition, onto firm land, and there, dreaming, she leans on the mountain side. Mountains are concrete, only changing substance slowly. While still in her element, in the depth of night and dreaming, this is equivalent to a first step toward awareness. But this personified Night is still completely immersed in a world beyond, in events *beyond* space and *time.* So the golden scales, at the moment of the reversal of the darkness (Midnight) can be still. The poet sees the scales as golden, i.e. made of the royal metal, which in astrology is associated with Jupiter, the highest ruler and shaper of the worlds. In our material reality, the world could never be "still" but is continuously in motion. Yet in our deepest unconscious — we recognize it in our own dream activity — we cross over into another dimension, in which space and time are relative factors. And Mother Night finds herself for this one moment in a timeless condition, to which eternity, that knows no time, belongs.

But immediately thereafter, the opposite pole appears. In the poem, the rhythm sounds more exciting; lively springs sing of the day, although they arise from the night in the rocks. They do not whisper, they sing, which is an expression of ancient harmony. The natural scientists observe as realistically as possible; in their view of the world, the spring is nothing but overflowing, percolating water. In contrast, natural philosophy sees it in symbolic, spiritual ways. For it, the spring is alive, and its spirituality may crystallize in the form of a water nymph. Out of the world of the night and calm the springs come to light into the world of life, fertilizing all. Here once again we see the relationship of opposites. "Mother Night", belonging to the introverted, passive archetypal, looking into the nocturnal unknown, understands enough of her spiritually opposite side, the active and concrete, and thus tired of the song of the springs:

"She wants no more to be told."

But without her opposite, the day, she could not exist herself, just as without evil, good could not be. In this sense all opposites form a unity. According to conceptions of antiquity (Plato, the Cabala), they separated, but each pair carries within the longing for reunification. That is why any antipodal (diametrically opposed) relationship appears fascinating. Let once again the fascination between male and female be noted. The night appears far more fascinated by the sky's blues than the song of the springs.

"To her the sky's sweet blues much sweeter ring,"

the blues, the bluish colors, which glow most intensely at the zenith of the sun's orbit; poetically, in fact, they "ring." Also, this moment of the clear midday, Night experiences as a yoke; but now within the events of the fleeting hours, therefore time dependent and fitting the conscious.

"But always the springs carry on,"

Theirs is not only the past, but also the coming day; the day as a symbol of awareness and reality, in opposition to the night, the element of the unconscious.

The concept of the fascination between the polarities does not yet explore the complete depths of the poem. While reciting its verses, I was nearly stirred to tears at times. The poem touches on realms of the spirit and the soul which contain the meaning and the evolution of the human race. With Mörike's "At Midnight," a picture of the evolution of our soul arises before our mental eye. "Mother Night" is a metaphor for the soul, which presses toward awakening and strives toward awareness within us. Out of the unconsciousness of the immature soul, depicted as the archetypal ocean, it rises into growing awareness of the developed human. However, this primordial soul *(anima magna) must* encounter the spirit. The spirit is symbolized by the sky's blues, because blue, symbolically speaking, stands for the color of the spirit. Therefore, Mother Night (the soul) considers the sky's blues to be "much sweeter" than the song of the springs, because only the relationship of soul and spirit differentiates the human being from the animal.

Soul and spirit also constitute polarities. Medieval alchemy attempted to draw conclusions about spiritual principles by observing chemical and physical reactions of substances. In this view, *Spiritus* (spirit) lies above and *Anima* (soul) below. All opposites must join together, spirit and soul must form a unity, in order to view the absolute — in biblical terms, "the face of God." However, to accomplish this, one must first become psychically aware. The first step, as we already learned, was taken by Mother Night in stepping onto firm soil, and through her contact with the mountain rock.

By this action, she becomes aware of the polarity of all universal phenomena and sees — which seems to me to be most important — the partner spirit, with which, as a distant development, unity is intended.

This is the highest esoteric objective,[4] aspired toward by all founders of religions. Thus Mörike, with his great vision, saw, intuitively and figuratively, the spiritual evolution of mankind. With the analysis of the poem we realize how a significant succession of images reveal important laws of life, which are recognized by the holistically oriented person.

---

[4] A search for the innermost relationships and secrets of universal phenomena. Goethe, in *Faust:* "So I may learn the things that hold/ The world together at its core,/ So I may potencies and seeds *behold,/* And trade in empty words no more." [Passage, *op. cit.,* pp. 19-20. Used by permission].

From the analysis of the poem we discover something fundamental. Natural philosophical thinking results in the discovery of relationships between phenomena experienced in naturally existing polarities. According to the view of natural philosophy, not only are the female and male principle diametrically opposed to one another, so also are body and soul, as well as the sound of language, which is the body of language, and the meaning, which is the soul of language. Further, the Above and the Below, the microcosm and the macrocosm and many others. Nature is laid out in polarities and only through them maintains its existence. These polarities exist in continuous reciprocal action, although principally they form a unity. Let us remember the concept of harmony of the spheres in Greek thought.

In this respect, the relationship of body and soul, as Klages[5] describes it, is particularly important: the soul does not relate to the body as cause to effect, but as perception to the *appearance* of the perception. Perception and appearance of perception are the archetypal image of all relationships. Thus, Klages does not look for a causal relationship. To him, the simultaneous interaction and mutual dependence are fundamental.

Klages' all-encompassing theory in regard to natural philosophy permits the inclusion of the doctrine of natural science. However, Klages emphasizes that the analytical partial interpretation of the phenomena of life without a philosophical attempt toward understanding the world and life as a whole does not make sense, and, as it were, hangs in the air.

For the natural philosopher, the meaning of the world lies in experiencing true pictures. In order to establish a general picture of the world, observations relating and corresponding to these pictorial impressions are interpreted for their meaning. Since all forms and pictures of this world: the sky, the landscape, human beings, animals, and plants are subject to continuous change and thus appear animated, it is only consistent when natural philosophy concludes that all of nature, the whole cosmos, including all parts of it, are animated and have a soul. For natural philosophy, there is not a fundamental difference between the dead and the living. Thus, natural philosophers categorize the world according to the degree of completeness. Through the experience of the animated cosmos, they arrive at a complete picture of the world, in which all parts are related meaningfully to one another. They are content to experience the world as a beholder and to stand in awe and reverential admiration before the phenomena of life. This explains their reluctance to tamper with nature, to dissect it, or engage in experimental research.

The Natural Science Doctrine of Life

From the background of the principles of natural philosophy, the fundamental difference between them and the natural science principles of life becomes evident. The latter focuses not on a search for pictures and their order, as does the former, but on a search for the *causes* of the manifestations of life.

---

[5] Ludwig Klages, German philosopher, psychologist and graphologist.

Questions about these manifestations begin with "from where," "from which," "from what," and "how". The subject of this doctrine is not the living manifestations of life itself, but their representations, i.e. *abstractions,* such as facts, causes, forces, times, whose conceptual comprehension only takes on meaning through experience.

If nature is dissected in this manner into functioning objects, then it is also inevitably divided into units. Qualities, i.e. properties perceivable by the senses, are thereby treated as quantities and thus countable objects. In the strict sense of natural science, a subject can only be comprehended if it has a property which can be counted. This explains the compulsion of natural science to express all results in numbers. The dissection of nature into functioning objects leads to an evaluation solely of mechanized action within the context of cause-effect relationships. Nietzsche said: *"What provides us [especially the natural scientist — N.] such an extraordinary tenacity in our belief in causality, is the belief that all occurrence is action."* He himself recognized that in reality this is not true. Natural philosophy, in addition, recognizes causation based on primordial rhythms (astrology) and considers also the automatic activation of the polar antithesis in the case of an excessive opposite principle. Such occurrences — according to Greek thinking — happen everywhere in the cosmos, in order to restore harmony, i.e. equilibrium, in the universe. For example, he who experiences too much good luck must, of necessity, expect trouble. I described this at another place,[6] in reference to Schiller's poem "The Ring of Polycrates," as the Polycrates Syndrome. The reversal of the direction of an event happens without mechanical causality; therefore, from the natural scientific perspective, it is uncaused. Influence by sorcery or magic, the influence on matter through the energy of thoughts, occurs in a similar fashion. This, too, is not caused in a mechanical sense. It is not included in "mechanical doings." I would describe the influence of magic as causality by analogy.

Part of the method of the natural scientist is the abstract comprehension of objects and facts and their causal connection. This causal connection, called causal inference, is the content of logical and mathematical thought. Animated, polar, meaningful connections are of no importance for this way of thinking; its objective is the discovery of causal relationships which, whenever possible, are expressible in mathematical terms. Thereby understanding, as is achieved by an inquiry into the essence of things, is not accomplished; only knowledge which serves the establishment of abstract concepts and the construction of laws is gathered. For the natural scientist the world will, in the end, disintegrate into many different areas. A necessary result of this abstract thinking is the distinction between living and dead things, in contrast to the classifications of natural philosophy.

The objective of the natural scientist is "understanding", the control of nature and of vital processes. But the ultimate objective of the observing natural philosopher is the respectful admiration of the secrets of the world,

---

[6] H. Naegeli-Osjord, "Depressive Verstimmung der Lebensmitte" ["Depressive Mood of Mid-life"], *Praxis* (1956/5).

experiencing their meaning, and contemplating them.

C.G. Jung and his collaborators went this way, which the great biologist and philosopher Adolf Portman, at the 25th anniversary celebration of the "Eranos-Conventions" in 1957, defined with the following words: *"To absorb the secret of the spirit with reverence, to speak about the visible and to be aware of the presence of the indescribable — this is the spirit in which the work of Eranos stands."*

Reverence is not a part of the thinking of natural science. It belongs in the area of the qualitative, not the quantitative. A *secret* cannot remain a secret for the rationalist; it requires enlightening, analyzing research. But should this succeed, the spiritual arousal concomitant with the reverential attitude toward supra-personal events not yet defined by the human mind, would be destroyed. We all know Goethe's expression, *"to shudder is humanity's best quality,"* which he obviously wrote in the opinion that "shuddering" prevents humans from self-adulation and hubris. But humanity suffers from this danger, for if there is nothing else except mechanical causality, theoretically everything can be accomplished by humans. Higher guidance and direction then is no longer needed.

In the following, the theories of life according to Blasius are tabulated: Blasius emphasizes that *both* schools of thoughts are *scientific.*

Theories of Life according to Blasius

Natural Philosophy = Research into form and essences	Natural Science = Research into causes
Subject: Appearances, Forms, Archetypal pictures = essences = souls	Things = Abstractions of pictures
Pictures (visual-, auditory-, tactile pictures)	Facts, causes, forces
Synopsis of entirety of essences	Units, elements
Qualities	Quantities
Attributes = Appearances of phenomena	Numbers
Method: Awareness — awareness of essences [intuitive open-minded (N.)]	Abstract comprehension and explanation of things
Analogous inferences	Causal inferences
Symbolic thought	Logical (mathematical) thought
Result: Order according to archetypal pictures	Explanation according to causes
Connections [spiritual (N.)]	Relationships [within material occurrences (N.)]
Polarities	Systems of concepts

18

Cognition	Knowledge
Animated cosmos [ethereal animation of organic and inorganic matter (N.)]	Separation of dead and living matter
Objective: Interpreting the meaning of life	Establishment of natural laws
Vision of world and secret of world	Domination of the world
Concepts of the world	Use of the concepts [use of nature (N.)]
Limitations: Closed system of thought	Open, unlimited system of thought
Closed circle of meaningful connections and pictures	Dependence on natural laws (parameters, constants of nature)
Dangers = Transgressions of limits:	Treatment of spiritual phenomena [only with physical and chemical methods (N.)]
Categorization of objects and facts by analogy and polarity	
Attempt to explain phenomena which are not perceptible (unexpressed life)	[Ignoring or negating of all transcendental (N.)]
Combination of vision of world with findings from natural sciences	Overpowering and domination of the world. Disintegration of picture of the world
Examples: Bio-centric thought	Logo-centric thought
Metaphysics [magic influences (N.)]	Physics
Greek natural philosophy	
Pre-sophists: Heraclitus, Protagoras	Plato, Aristotle
Romantic natural philosophy: Goethe, Schelling, Oken, Carus	Enlightenment and Rationalism: Descartes, Newton, Kant
	Natural scientific physiology: R. Maier, H. von Helmholtz
Vitalism	Mechanism
Science of appearances	Causal-analytical natural science
Holistic approach	Singular sciences
Teachings of natural healing/behavior/ expression/categorization by type	Teachings of reflexes
Rhythm (N.)	Rules (N.)
Search for meaning	Search for purpose

(N.) = added by author

4. GOOD AND EVIL

Spiritual Characteristics of Ethical Polarity

Spiritual characteristics are implied in the expression "good and evil," since as opposites they are rooted in the archetypal (C.G. Jung). Archetypes, as unalterable creative principles, are an immanent part of the cosmos necessary for the existence of the universe. Good and evil constitute the central problem of mankind, which is expressed in the life of each individual and in world literature. *"Man was chosen by the creator to become aware of this polarity, so that the problem could become real,"* Schelling[1] said.

The spiritual, and therefore also good and evil, as part of the archetypal, acts as *"primary* agent," i.e. a force acting from within itself on the material world and human beings. No physical chain of causality is necessary; in fact, meaningful mentation leads to material manifestation and therefore to the embodiment of consciousness, as Klages would express it. In the Indian "cosmogony," the spiritual, the "mental plane," as an ethereal sphere, is superior to the material reality which is perceptible to the physical eye.

Parapsychology has been able to prove that the power of the human mind through concentrated imagination influences matter, and also influences the human being, and even creates matter. The first can be observed in magical powers, particularly in non-intellectual tribes. The last appears in phenomena of materialization, and also in its counterpart, de-materialization (*Logurgie,*[2] *Sai Baba*[3]). Results in the form of psychokinesis (a physically inexplicable change in location of material objects) and psychodeformation, the deformation of material objects, are produced. Bending of spoons through pure force of the mind — as we see with Uri Geller and many others — is learned in the United States particularly by children.[4] Children, especially, are emotionally excitable, and they do not constantly question their ability. Since mental forces, i.e., thoughts, ideas, and intentions, in the form of ethereal energy, may influence our visible world, the effect on our material environment through manifestations of ghosts and, of course, on our bodies as well (through ethereal spirits in the case of possession), approaches the realm of possibility. A direct effect on our personal spirituality or an influence on the cell chemistry of the brain appears conceivable.

---

[1] Friedrich Schelling (1775-1854): German romantic philosopher.

[2] H. Naegeli-Osjord, *Die Logurgie in den Philippinen* ["Psychic surgery in the Philippines"] (Remagen: Otto Reichl Verlag).

[3] Howard Murphet, *Sai Baba, Man of Miracles* (London: Frederick Muller Ltd., 1971). See also: Erlendur Haraldsson, *Miracles Are My Visiting Cards,* An investigative report on the psychic phenomena associated witn Sathya Sai Baba (London: Rider Book, 1987), and Erlendur Haraldsson, *Modern Miracles* (New York: Ballantine, 1988).

[4] *Esotera* (Freiburg: Hermann Bauer Verlag, 10/79).

Good and Evil in Philosophy

Philosophers are occupied particularly with the polarities of ethics and morality. Schelling emphasizes that the most important concern for them is the question of the essence of this polar concept. To him, evil is not simply a *privatio boni* (omission or negation of the Good), but an independent "positive" *power*. But evil as such exists as *conditio sine qua non* (unalterable presupposition) of human freedom. Within this framework, man is free to do good or evil. God, by creating evil, divided Himself into this polarity. After the first separation of God, namely into spirit and matter, I consider this, especially for the human being, the second decisive creative act. Symbolically, this is represented by the Fall of Angels and the Expulsion from Paradise in the Old Testament. After the separation into "Good and Evil," Schelling says, in addition to the "Divine universal will," which contains the loving principle of God, there is always an alternative which is *also* at the disposal of man: the so-called "private will," which can result in egocentric behavior. However, it is certain that the Loving, the Good, is always stronger then the egocentric Evil. As an experienced psychologist I support this view. It is also of critical importance for the process of human healing, and the practice of exorcism is based on this assumption.

Since neither for the first nor for the second act of separation of the Divine can — nor should — *physical* causality be assumed, and since the second separation into good and evil is qualitative, this is a problem which can only be resolved philosophically or within the context of natural philosophy.

Good and Evil in Natural Science

The fact that natural sciences as well as psychology and psychiatry, oriented toward the concept of physical causality which emanates from natural science, do not deal with this basic problem is because of the way these disciplines formulate their questions. Thus the question of good and evil, and therefore also the demonic, remains excluded. In psychology and psychiatry, based on natural sciences, Good and Evil do not count as archetypal, primary forces ("powers," according to Schelling), but, as with all other mental functioning of the human being, they are considered emanations of brain chemistry without which these ethical polarities could not exist at all. In this respect, the boundary, the transition from the physical into the spiritual, is still excluded from the possibility of experimental investigation. Within the realms of this assumption, Good and Evil possess no individual character, but change according to the spirit of the age or the culture. After the physical death of the individual, his mental energy and the dynamic of life, as expressed in polarities, expires. In contrast to this, one of the most fundamental principles in physics should be noted — the principle of conservation and indestructibility of mass and energy. It means that matter only changes form, but the energy potential remains constant. This basic principle is not applied to the spiritual, because the spiritual cannot be measured, although it undoubtedly represents an expression of energy. That problem is not discussed.

The premise in natural science is that all mental functioning is extinguished after physical death, and this rules out the possibility of the phenomenon of possession. Possession by autonomous intelligent spirit beings is connected to the polarity of Good and Evil. But if we, as emphasized in chapter 2, learn from parapsychological phenomenology that the mental power of imagination deforms matter, and, in fact, makes matter disappear within three dimensional space, we have evidence for the primacy of spiritual energy. In other words: the spiritual is primary, matter is merely one of its outward manifestations.[5]

---

[5] Hans Naegeli-Osjord, "Materialisation, Dematerialisation, Psychoplastik," *Grenzgebiete der Wissenschaft* (June 28, 1979).

5. THE DEMONIC (EVIL)

The Demonic as Qualitative Reality

If "Good and Evil," as an abstract concept of polarity, are seen primarily as a problem of philosophy, the demonic, in contrast, intervenes in real events. The demonic and its effects could be described as applied evil and therefore must be considered as a problem of natural philosophy. Philosophy is concerned with the definition of abstract concepts and their relationships. Natural philosophy seeks to understand the influencing forces within natural events which cannot be explained in physical terms.

It is necessary to contrast the two systems of perceiving the world, in order to demonstrate how they deal with different intrinsic areas and thus cannot be used interchangeably. Both stand, as aforementioned, on *scientific* foundations. Let it be noted once more that, corresponding with the *res extensae* — everything measurable — of Descartes, natural scientific thinking is determinative. Wherever the question of the qualitative — to which the demonic belongs — is raised, natural philosophy must take precedence.

As early as Goethe's time the quantitative aroused the greater, almost exclusive fascination. Natural sciences, by seeking exactitude and objectivity as much as possible, denied the necessary attention to the qualitative, which cannot be precisely measured. This caused Goethe to write the following ironic verses:

> Ah, there the learned man I recognize!
> What you touch not, in furthest distance lies,
> What you grasp not, must simply be untrue,
> What you count not, you fancy is unreal,
> What you weigh not, lacks any weight for you,
> What you coin not, will never pass, you feel.[1]

In Goethe's drama of redemption, Wagner admires the accomplishments of natural science; but the mature and spiritually more sophisticated Faust turns toward natural philosophy. Through it, he gains access to the magical, which provides extraordinary experiential content. Only the knowledge gained within these and other personal experiences gains Faust redemption. The close alliance with Mephistopheles, the prince of the demons, provides insight into the ethical polarity of creation, without which recognition of the Divine Being and therefore redemption would be denied us. Dante, too, first went through hell. Thus ultimate knowledge is gained only through a complete vision. Judging only part of a phenomenon and part of reality, i.e. only the material

---

[1] von Goethe, trans. by Passage, *op. cit.,* p. 176. Used by permission.

aspect, inevitably results in only a partial description.

Therefore, a true seeker cannot ignore the demonic or even go so far as to deny it. Jesus Christ was far removed from such an attitude. Opposite the positive Divine stands the demonic as an archaic power. Both together constitute the Divine whole.

The Demonic in the Ancient World View

Neither Western antiquity nor the spiritual world of the East viewed demons only as malicious beings. The Greek word *Daimon* means an insubstantial, transcendental power. In earliest times Daimon was a designation for god himself, later for his companions — as the Satyrs of Dionysus — then for in-between beings, half-god, half-human (natural spirits), and finally for a spirit being appertaining to man, which was not only negative but also positive in character. We know of the *agathodaimon* of Socrates, who experienced him as a protecting spirit and promoter of the good in himself. For Aeschylus and Euripides, demons were also spirits of the deceased. An interesting point of reference is that the word *daemon,* which is closely related to the Greek word *daimon,* means knowing or learned.

In Christian antiquity, a great number of pagan gods were redefined as evil demons. That is why, in Christian civilization, the concept of the demonic today contains practically nothing more than negative destructive forces. Demonic possession means the taking possession of a person by a malevolent spiritual being.

The Ethereal Embodiment of Demons

Evidence for the manifestation and perception of demonic beings in Indian and Tibetan cultures is associated with the practice of meditation. There demons possess positive and negative values. Personal characteristics are attributed to these beings, as was postulated by the Swedish seer, Emanuel Swedenborg (1688-1772), a successful and recognized natural scientist. According to his visions and personal opinion, these transcendental beings possessed an ethereal body specific to their nature, essence and spirituality.[2] Such an ethereal body, seen by the inner (spiritual) eye of the meditating person, or the envisioning seer, i.e. in the Tibetan *Thangka,*[3] is graphically expressed with physical attributes characteristic of its essence. This is true for the positive as well as the negative transcendental spirit beings. Swedenborg wrote: *"There are no abstract spirit beings, but everything spiritual — even God — resembles a person and is corporeal [ethereal (N.)]."* We should not imagine that such Thangkas were painted in full consciousness; rather, the sketching of the image, perceived through visions, took place in a state of unconscious experiencing.

---

[2] Woldemar Kiefer, "Swedenborgs Zeit und Leben," in: *Allg. Zeitschrift für Parapsychologie,* 5. Jg., Heft 1, S. 9.

[3] Tibetan *Thangka:* Devotional pictures painted or embroidered on cloth rolls.

According to my current view, in contrast to Emanuel Swedenborg, I assume that neither God nor the Devil have a personal character. They are archetypes which surpass our horizons, at least at the present state of our spiritual development. I believe angels are sub-categories of archetypes, such as humility, love, and kindness, and demons, such archetypal sub-categories as avarice, vindictiveness, and jealousy.

The Tantra Veda considers the "purely divine Being" (Purusha) to be non-matter and its emanations to be ethereal — particularly the mental sphere (Bhuddi). Angels and demons are part of this. Ethereal matter can be seen by mediums, whereby its content is transformed into visual forms.

The Demonic in Theology

The concept of a hierarchy of semi-autonomous spirit beings operating in the transcendental sphere comes down to us from old ecclesiastical tradition and also from experiences of Christian believers. There we encounter hierarchies of *choirs of angels* (cherubim, seraphim, archangels, etc.) as an expression of the transcendent good. In contrast, the "fallen" angels from these same choirs form choirs of "angel demons" with the same rank order, and thereby constitute the opposite principle. These spirit beings come from all nine devils' choirs, and are considered dangerous in varying degrees. We become aware of them in the exorcism rituals of the Christian (Catholic) church as well as in other religions. The harmless form of possession and especially of harassment (see Chapter 16) is explained by the concept of "poor souls," i.e. discordant souls, of deceased persons still spiritually bound to this world. Peculiarly, however, the Catholic *Rituale Romanum* does not refer to them anywhere. Possession can thus be viewed as the influence of demonic beings which belong to the transcendental world, and also by the spirits of deceased persons.

Corresponding to the "poor souls" in Christian thinking are the "suffering souls" in Zen Buddhism. According to Motoyama,[4] they not only require a categorical order to leave the person who is besieged by them, but also a loving explanation. Dr. Carl A. Wickland and Dr. Titus Bull also observe this rule in their methods of medical exorcism.[5]

Modern Catholic theology, especially in German-speaking areas, reacts uneasily to possession, especially since the lawsuit against the exorcists of Anneliese Michel, in which medical aspects were virtually the only decisive factor. At the German bishops' conference at which this lawsuit was referred to, it was decided not to use exorcism without simultaneously seeking medical consultation. Because almost all physicians are oriented toward philosophical materialism, they rarely resort to exorcism. According to attitudes held by many, even Jesus would not be allowed to exorcise today!

Protestant theology abandoned exorcism a long time ago. Rationalist currents of Protestant thought attribute to myth the healing of the possessed by Jesus Christ.

---

[4] Hiroshi Motoyama, in: *IARP Newsletter* (Tokyo, Nov., 1979).
[5] See the chapter on C. A. Wickland.

Natural religions employ countless customs and rites to ward off hostile spirits (demonic angels) as well as spirits of the deceased. Even today, primitive man possesses "imaging" abilities with regard to ethereal forces and beings of the transcendental world, because he still lives in a sphere which has not yet gone through the process of intellectualization.

Western Man's View of the Demonic

Educated man, in contrast, through new religious movements and intellectual thinking, succeeded in suppressing conscious awareness of transcendental influences. However, nothing was eliminated thereby, as we will see later. To the person with average education, the demonic is no longer the dynamic negative power of a transcendent sphere, but a verbal terminology for the hostile and destructive psychic make-up of the individual — or simply pure superstition.

Most of today's mental health professionals do not take seriously the possibility of cosmic influences on the *psyche,* or the influence on it by autonomous ethereal beings. Since the concept of a soul existing after death does not conform with their dogma, it is seldom mentioned, even in a negative way, nor does their training expose them to the empirical evidence of psychic research.

In the rival views of what best explains the nature of life, it must be stated that neither side can prove — in a "scientific" sense — its case. Naturally, scientific proof of the extinction of the spirit and soul *after* physical death has never been demonstrated — the negative can never be proven. This caused Max Thürkauf to argue that *"Since the natural sciences demand proof for all their postulates, they have become unscientific themselves with regard to this question."* Continuation of life after death is negated, because rational materialistic thinking is oriented exclusively toward matter, which is comprehensible in only *three* dimensions. But modern physics and many of its most prominent representatives (Pauli, Bohr, Jordan, Heisenberg, Heitler) were able to expand the horizon. The physicist Burkhard Heim, through the use of mathematics, succeeded in demonstrating a six-dimensional space,[6] in which the world of four dimensions, too, would constitute a subspace. Therefore, it may be expected that the multiple-dimensional space of the parapsychologists can be integrated into the natural scientific perspective of the world and that eventually, the disciplines of parapsychology and natural sciences will no longer remain incompatible opposites, but will become complementary to each other.

New *technical* possibilities are also helpful in this regard. For example, filming and taping allow for the impartial recording of "walking on fire," the resistance of human tissue and fabric to fire.[7] At the turn of the century, this phenomenon was ridiculed as collective hypnosis, since it was considered

---

[6] Burkhard Heim, "Der kosmische Erlebnisraum des Menschen" ["The Cosmic Sphere of Experience of Humans"], in *Imago Mundi,* Vol. 5, p. 28.

[7] H. Naegeli-Osjord, "Feuerschreiten und Feuerlaufen" ["Fire Walking and Fire Running"], in *Parapsychology Review,* 1970.

incompatible with the known laws of nature. Unfortunately, the modern academic — already overstressed in his specific field — can only peripherally take cognizance of results in parapsychological research. This slows down a change in thinking, but it cannot stop the course of development.

Manifestations of the Demonic

The demonic, often caused by ethereal beings, should not be ignored just because it is rooted in multi-dimensional space. These dimensions — as stated before — are coming increasingly into the focus of natural science, although the qualitative aspects of the phenomenon of possession belong to the domain of natural philosophy. The demonic, in philosophical and psychological understanding, represents a reality as an archetypical principle and thus must manifest itself in a world of activities which can be experienced. In a certain sense, it may be understood as a part of the plane where the ethereal and material world meet. Manifestations of the demonic are revealed not only in the psychic, but materially in structures and patterns of behavior which can be found throughout the world among all peoples. Phenomena of poltergeists and ghosts bound to a specific locality are often viewed as expressions of demonic effects, but relatively few people have actually experienced ghosts because not only must there be a desire to manifest, but also, in most instances, a mediumistic individual. It seems to me that personal experience is indispensible in order to contemplate the possibility of possession as the alternative explanation for tension within the psyche.

A further field in which the demonic manifests itself is in *black magic*. Magic, black or white, presents insurmountable difficulties to rational understanding. Magic can be defined as the effect on matter by intentions materialized through the most concentrated form of mental imagery, as contrasted with stage illusion. The German magazine *Esotera* reports the case of Black magicians in Ghana (Gold Coast) who fill a round container with water and stare fixedly at its surface. When on it, through concentrated imagination, the picture of the victim reaches sufficient intensity, the sorcerer stabs into it. On exactly that part of the body, the victim, who may be at any distance, will experience a visible stab wound.[8]

A phenomenon parallel to this can be observed in the Philippines: There a (white magic) healer imparts so-called "spiritual injections." The healer imagines holding a syringe in his hand and executes the gesture of injecting, at varying distances from the body. This results in a sensation of pain, and often also in actual bleeding. Not only have I seen this phenomenon many times, but I have also experienced it several times.[9]

The circumstances in both cases were magic; for the psychic surgeon of the Philippines it took religious preparation and at least a partial trance on the part of the healer.

---

[8] Reported in *Esotera,* German New Age publication.

[9] H. Naegeli-Osjord, *Die Logurgie in den Philippinen* (2nd ed., 1982).

In Eastern thinking, mental powers, such as thoughts, imagination and emotions, are parts of ethereal *matter*. By means of focused concentration of imagination, material — i.e. touchable and visual manifestations — can develop.[10] This knowledge and experience, achieved by great yogis through deep states of meditation, makes the activating force of magic comprehensible. In similar ways, haunting by poltergeists and other paranormal phenomena in the environment of possessed people could be explained with an animistic (psychological) as well as a spiritualistic (survival) hypothesis.

Expanded Thinking Needed

In the Western civilized world, the majority of educated as well as uneducated people deny the existence of an ethereal world, since it supposedly contradicts modern "knowledge." However, this so-called "knowledge" is — to emphasize it again — a belief, which corresponds with dogmas of scientific authorities, accepted unconditionally. How differently C. G. Jung expressed himself! He used to say: *"I do not believe in God [i.e. an immaterial form of being in the cosmos, (N.)], I know that He is."* Jung arrived at his knowledge not only through mediumistic inner experiences, but also through an extraordinary knowledge of many areas of the liberal arts. He was thoroughly familiar with alchemy, astrology, the spiritual world of the East and antiquity, as well as books by Paracelsus. He also possessed excellent natural scientific and psychological understanding. The diversity of his own experiences, coupled with the processed knowledge of countless cultural levels, enabled him to reformulate the way in which we can look at our world.

Let us examine the thinking of many psychologists and psychiatrists in relation to Jung's way of looking at the world. As an experienced practitioner, I can not help but judge the results of many psychological-analytical as well as psychiatric-chemotherapeutic methods of treatment as unsatisfactory, although I do not doubt they are sincere attempts to relieve the lot of the psychically ill person. However, they had to align themselves with the demands for exclusive rationalistic-materialistic thinking, which will never do justice to the complexity of the human soul. Nevertheless it is this thinking which is predominant in almost all university psychiatric clinics. It is known that successful scientists who have "arrived" and are recognized in their own time, frequently reject new and pioneering impulses. Pioneering work almost always comes from academic outsiders. Not only do Freud, Jung, and Szondy come to mind, but also chiropractors and acupuncturists, whose early work was rejected by prominent scientists. Younger scientists striving for academic achievement usually learn to adjust to opinions of teachers and colleagues if they don't want to be sidetracked as a nuisance. This inhibits the ambition of the researcher and does not provide room for him to spread his mental wings, leading to conscious and unconscious adjustment to the predominant views of the times.

---

[10] O. M. Hinze, *Tantra Vidya* (Zürich: Theseus Verlag), p. 204 ff.

The Religious Aspect of the Human Soul

The religious aspect of the human soul is usually neglected within contemporary clinical-psychiatric and psychological treatment orientations, i.e. unless they take the Jungian approach. Paul Tournier[11] received some attention from the literate population at the time, but not from the university clinics and even less from within the departments of psychology at universities. Tournier's motto: "j'accepte," (I recognize without contradiction the condition of my present situation and its causes,) would force the patient to act in the present and to take on independent responsibility for further changes, but the majority of psychologists encourage the sufferer to believe that genetic and environmental factors, parents, and educators are the causes of his misery. As a result, the patient's own responsibility is minimized and his personality downgraded to a mere "object." I always ask the patient: "Are you a nobody?" i.e., "Are you not an acting and planning individual?" Since neither the past nor the parents can be changed, all that is left is resentment and protest. This is loudly acted out by the patient, but it does not relieve the psyche nor does it result in external improvement. Hatred which poisons the soul is not likely to be removed by bringing repressed experiences (Freud) back to consciousness nor by screaming catharsis, "primal scream," (Janos) — a precept which would be challenged by many of today's therapists. Removal of hatred only happens when a kind psychotherapist attempts to evoke a loving understanding for the often only allegedly guilty persons. **Hate can only be removed through love!**

Tournier also emphasizes the effectiveness of joint prayer. From my own experience, and also my contact with possessed and besieged people, I have to agree with him. *"Anima naturaliter christiana;"* (more neutrally expressed: *"Anima naturaliter religiosa")* contains the inherently natural connection of the soul with transcendental realities. I see the human soul as a condensation of spiritually transcendent archetypal principles — always in individual mold. But rationalistic-naturalistic psychotherapy, deprives the soul of its relationship with the universal, disconnects it from its origins, thereby making it insecure. Only prayer — which could be called a small *"unio mystica"* — tears it from the meaningless chance events of today's typical concept of the world. Reconnecting with the divine links the soul with the positive archetypes, which, as mentioned before, are more powerful than the demonic. We will see later that it was the simple, devout prayer which the Protestant exorcist, Johann Christoph Blumhardt, used effectively for the possessed Gottliebin Dittus. Following a simple undogmatic worship, which places many of those who need healing and others who are present in the chapel into a state of semi-trance, the Philippine psychic surgeon David Oligane heals the possessed and bewitched.[12] He lives — like Blumhardt — the life of Christian charity, of which I became convinced during a long period together with him.

---

[11] Dr. Paul Tournier, *Médicine de la Personne* (Neuchâtel et Paris: Delachaux et Niestlé SA, 1941).

[12] H. Naegeli-Osjord, *Die Logurgie in den Philippinen* (Remagen: Otto Reichl Verlag).

Demonic possession reveals an illness of the soul. I consider the genetic and external causes diagnosed by psychologists merely to be an opportunity for transcendental destructive forces to enter. Generally, this leads only to less spectacular *neuroses,* but these, too, can only be definitively healed when the psyche is reconnected — *religio* — to its cosmic and religious origins.

The statement by C. G. Jung may be appropriate here: *"The ideas of moral laws and deity are a constant in the human soul which can not be exterminated. Therefore, every psychologist who is not dazzled by narrow-minded, arrogant interpretations, must deal with these facts."*[13]

---

[13] C. G. Jung, *Gesamtausgabe* ["Complete (German) edition"], 8: 528).

6. POSSESSION

General Observations Concerning Possession

The hypothesis of a physicochemical misregulation of the brain and body fluids in the case of schizophrenia, under which possession is frequently subsumed, remains current. Claims of proof that such a misregulation causes schizophrenia continue to haunt the field of medical literature, even though never definitively confirmed. A scientifically valid distinction between schizophrenia and possession, based only on chemical and physical evidence, is not possible.

Genetic factors and morbid personality developments are rightly considered factors in *dementia praecox,* but all psychological attempts at explanation remain unprovable in the strictly natural scientific sense. On the other hand, a natural-philosophic manner of observation — research into the spiritual nature of things — is capable of comparing and evaluating the phenomenological data in both schizophrenia and possession according to their characteristics. In doing so, the main issue is to decide, by means of illuminating the basic contrasts, whether what is involved in the case of a delusional patient is merely an inner psychic event misregulated solely by the patient (schizophrenia) or an alien influence, a regulation occurring through an ethereal being (possession).

Not only are cases of possession seldom reported, professionals view the issue with so much skepticism that serious consideration is rarely found. Because this phenomenon is difficult to understand, I suggest that the reader first study the cases of possession involving Gottliebin Dittus (Chapter 11) and the boys of Illfurt (Chapter 13), and then return to the following explanations.

What would be the clinical-psychological definition of such states of possession? They would be termed "affective psychosis" in cases where the patient is subject to attacks of domination by a very negative part of his personality, in psychological parlance, usually called a split personality.

Demonic possession is expressed in word and deed, and occasionally in paranormal events: in the form of words, through blaspheming and obscene insults of persons present; in deeds, through destructive fury toward sacred objects and all kinds of utensils, and often through self-destructive acts. The possessed person beats his head against the wall, for example, and frequently inflicts painful cuts on himself. Paranormal events include poltergeist phenomena of all kinds. In addition, there are smells of putrefaction and the stench of sulphur. In drastic cases, we encounter the occurrence of materializations from the body. Feathers, iron fragments, smelly fluids emerge from the surfaces of the body or are vomited. The attack can occur spontaneously, it can be announced, or it can be provoked by priests and exorcists. During periods when the possessed person is free of attacks, his behavior is normal, aside from certain strangely capricious behaviors which are not very consistent with his general character.

An almost symptom-free condition during a period when the possessed person is free from attacks offers one of the best characteristics distinguishing possession from dementia praecox. The schizophrenic can behave very normally in everyday matters, in bathing, eating, even in games of chess or bowling; but when spoken to about personal matters, he always reacts the same for months and years, and at all times of the day, in terms of his delusions, fears, and aggressions. The possessed person, however, is not subject to any abnormal delusion during attack-free periods, which can last for days or weeks — and has an almost balanced psyche.

Only during an attack does the possessed person manifest curious resemblances to the schizophrenic. In an excellent work entitled "Depressive, schizophrene, schizoaffektive Erkrankungen (Repetitorium der Syndrome und Differentialdiagnose)" ["Depressive, Schizophrenic, and Schizo-affective Diseases (Summary of the Syndromes and Differential Diagnosis)"],[1] Dr. Ch. Scharfetter, a professor in Zurich, describes the symptomatology of schizophrenia as follows:

> *Disturbances of the ego-experience are at the core of the schizophrenic syndrome: What is involved is that the patient, particularly in severe, acute cases, no longer really registers experiences correctly (a disturbance of ego-vitality); that he perceives his thinking, acting, his feeling, everything that is afferent and efferent, to be* directed by someone else *(activity-disturbance of the ego); that* even in a physical sense he no longer has the feeling of a unified being; *that he feels himself torn, splintered, disintegrated, dissolved (consistency-disturbance of the ego);* that in the realm of his private self he is no longer able to delimit himself from the external realm *(disturbance of ego- boundaries); that ultimately he is no longer certain of his identity, at times not even in the physiognomic and morphological sense.*
>
> *In the schizophrenic syndrome the so-called disturbances in thinking are characteristic: the* thoughts are registered, interrupted, fragmented, lost, or become diffuse without any initiative on the part of the patient, or even against his will. *In severe cases the thinking can then become muddled, erratic, and paralogical. Of the various kinds of hallucinations that occur, hearing of voices is particularly characteristic: the voices speak directly to the patient. Very often the voices are* not really heard, but are registered by the body as a kind of inner knowledge. *Profuse misperceptions within the body, occasionally quite abstruse and painful, can be extremely torturous. Other hallucinations diminish in frequency; in particular,* vivid optical hallucinations are not characteristic of the schizophrenic syndrome. *If vivid optical hallucinations do occur, great care is necessary in the differential diagnosis.*

[1] *Praxis (Schweiz. Rundschau für Medizin),* Vol. 6, (Bern: Feb. 3, 1981).

Delusion almost always occurs at some stage within the schizophrenic syndrome. In the majority of cases, it is the delusion of being controlled, persecuted, destroyed. *As students in this field will recall from their studies, however, numerous other topics of delusion occur, including the delusions of megalomania and omnipotence, which will not be dealt with in detail here.*

In the schizophrenic syndrome, affectivity assumes many different forms and is by no means consistent. Many schizophrenics seem to be quite natural, even sensitive and warmhearted, while many are mistrustful, remote, irritated, or tense. Others are primarily anxious and insecure. Many, however, are simply depressed, tortured by hallucinations — particularly hallucinations of the body — and tortured by their isolation, loneliness, and alienation. In difficult situations and when their ego experience is threatened, many are inclined to conceal their distress in a hebephrenic manner. Many react parathymically: the affect that is expressed does not accord with the doctor's feeling for what the patient describes as the content of the experience.

Characteristics of the catatonic form of schizophrenia are primarily motor manifestations, peculiarities of movements, of mimicry and gesture, and lapses into stupor, possibly interrupted by massive outbreaks of excitation.

In reading this definition attentively, it becomes clear that the syndrome of schizophrenia is largely characterized by the feeling of being under the control of a being other than oneself. The fact that this alien being is projected by academic psychiatrists onto a part of the patient's own unconscious personality, is the result of the prevailing mode of thinking. On the basis of scientific methodology, however, this projection can neither be proved nor disproved. The question is up for discussion. In terms of belief — and natural science is also an expression of belief — it is subject to the predominant attitudes of our era. Should these, as was once typical during the highly civilized periods of antiquity as well as the Middle Ages (and still is in the contemporary Christian church), conceive of a world of spirits in addition to the material reality, the possibility of an influence on the human psyche by non-material beings comes in for consideration again. In my opinion, our present era is headed in this direction.

The conceptual distinction between schizophrenia and possession is extremely difficult. Possibly there are no basic differences, or at best those of a gradual kind or those expressed in terms of varying nuances of characteristics.

There may be a possibility here of distinguishing between these manifestations, however. The typical schizophrenic lives in the world of his unconscious contents, although, of course, we never know whether the contents were induced (suggested) by spirit beings. These contents that flood his consciousness invalidate the real data of the external world. As a consequence, the patient is thrown back onto himself and becomes socially isolated. On his own, he rarely seeks help from his associates, and is referred for treatment by his relatives.

But in popular parlance, the person considered to be possessed struggles for liberation during the periods when he has few symptoms and is free of attacks. If religiously oriented he turns more readily to persons in the priesthood, feeling that the problem has psychic aspects, rather than being a medical problem. He is not a social isolate, and even during the manifest phase of possession, i.e., the attack, emphatically interacts with others.

This distinguishes him in fact from the hysteric who, although extremely autosuggestible, rarely interacts with others because of his own egocentricity. The hysteric also retains a clear recollection of his attacks, whereas the possessed person is usually subject to total amnesia.

Epilepsy, as the third clinically evasive explanation for possession (see the case of Anneliese Michel), resembles possession only in the fact that seizures are characteristic of both illnesses. *The epileptic seizure, however, is entirely different from that of possession, as it is preceded by an aura and the crisis is of much shorter duration. In such seizures, we observe cramping muscular contractions which hurl the patient to the floor, but which, unlike the seizure of possession, are never accompanied by planful activities with coordinated movements. The actual diagnostic confirmation of epilepsy is based on the specific pattern obtained from an electroencephalogram, which is lacking in the possessed non- epileptic.*

The differential diagnosis usually is simple, unless an epileptic or a schizophrenic, in the clinical sense, is *also* possessed by a spirit being, which is naturally within the realm of possibility. When differentiating between *possessio* and schizophrenia, the whole "script" must be considered. If a person has shown abnormal symptoms and strange behavior such as autism (willfulness and very little contact with parents and peers), such a person would likely be clinically diagnosed as schizophrenic. Impoverishment of the outer personality leads to inflation of the inner personality, resulting in inconsistency of behavior and lack of control of will and the emotions.

If a person who has always shown normal living habits and behavior becomes overtly extroverted and demonstrative to everyone, the possibility of *possessio* or harassment is very strong.

Cases of possession become obvious in a *crisis,* a state of excitation during which the victim's ability to make decisions remains blocked, and the possessing entities have complete control. Based on my observation, the crisis usually, but not always, ends in a kind of exhaustion that can extend even to loss of consciousness (see the case of Mrs. C.). Following this phase of exhaustion, the victim usually again behaves in a normal manner and often is not disturbed for an extended period of time. It is impossible to judge whether during this interval the possessing entities have withdrawn or whether they, remaining in the body and in the being of the victim, have merely lost a part of their energy. In my view, "devils" are also subject to energetic processes and can temporarily succumb to exhaustion. On the other hand, statements of victims in which the "demons" speak of returning on certain dates, support the idea of the temporary absence of the possessing spirits. The opinion of Delacours,[2] maintaining that the victim is uninterruptedly caught in the claws of the demons, is thereby called into question.

---

[2] Jean Baptiste Delacours, *Apage Satana!* (Geneva: Ariston Verlag, 1975).

The Forms of Possession

The concept of possession is rarely used in traditional psychology, although there are cases of ego-possession (over- rating one's own personality); manic states; Jung's concept of *animus* and *anima;* etc., which certainly could be viewed as bordering on possession.

It is conceivable that spirit beings of the opposite sex control the victim. Jung considered the cause of such states to be unconscious processes, but here, too, how the events occur is hypothetical, which is not to say that Jung's theory is false. It is simply a matter of one opinion versus another.

Regarding spirit possession, since the end of the eighteenth century the church has distinguished between three different types of manifestation of possession: *infestatio, circumcessio,* and *possessio.* The last-mentioned is actual possession; the first two variations of possession will be dealt with in later chapters.

The Causes of Possession

The most probable cause — and the one most plausible for our contemporary psychological understanding — is represented by the identification with demonic contents that are classified as "evil." In terms of inclination, that is, through genetic endowment, there is a wide range in the human being's propensity toward good and evil, positive and negative. As already explained in the chapter entitled "Good and Evil," the factor of evil is necessary for the perception of the universal divine. Whether the differing endowment is determined by karma,[3] that is, through former incarnations, seems conceivable, but is perhaps too speculative. However, if a person is burdened to an exceptional extent with negative characteristics, an entryway is formed for demonic spirit beings which simply find an appropriate home in him or her. There is great diversity among these possessing spirits, whose constant role Goethe perceived to be negation but in obedience to a divine purpose. We are confronted with sly tacticians — for instance, destructive politicians — and blustering primitives. Perhaps the latter could be considered the prototypical, extreme manifestations of possession.

In the chapters concerning Gottliebin Dittus and Anneliese Michel, we will deal with almost incomprehensible cases of possession in persons who seem extremely positive. Kierkegaard's comments concerning the strange lack of freedom of evil, in connection with its constellation by good, should be kept in mind. Representational (expiatory) suffering, an imitation of the passion of Jesus Christ, resembles the martyrdom of many saints. Such instances, occurring in the form of a voluntary possession permitted by God, constitute a confrontation with evil and an expiatory suffering for the redemption of groups of people who have gone astray. In former times, possession was generally viewed differently than today, when even highly placed persons

---

[3] Karma: The concept of Karma is not new. In Hinduism and Buddhism it has long been accepted as a part of life — the concept of actions seen as bringing upon oneself inevitable results, good or bad, either in this life or any previous lifetime. Others view it as the cosmic principle of cause and effect or rewards and punishment. [Publisher's comment]

within the church hierarchy lack understanding for the incidents concerning Anneliese Michel. Her own priests not only left her to her fate, but even believed they should accommodate to the scientific attitudes of the era.

Susceptibility to possession can involve an unusually positive as well as an exceptionally negative state, a situation which appears paradoxical only to the inexperienced.

Curses are closely related to enchantment, even though they do not inherently have the same emotional intensity unless based on personal, unconquerable hatred. Everyone who is familiar with the material (J. Ch. Blumhardt, Pater Rodewyk, *Rituale Romanum)* refers to the curses to which an infant is exposed, particularly by close relatives. The natural scientist will rightly claim that an offspring of such inadequate, even inhuman parents must naturally manifest negative characteristics as a result of the genetic process. But keep in mind the efficacy of the letter and the spoken word as transmitter of the essence of Being — a process that is less causally and much more magically conditioned, and as often emphasized, belongs to the world of correspondence. As I have learned from the descriptions of Philippine exorcists, when a curse is performed on behalf of a third person, it gives rise to more or less intense organic disorders, but almost never to compulsive attacks of rage. Nonetheless, persons in the Philippines whose organs are affected are considered possessed and are exorcised.

Pastor Kurt Koch describes very vividly that, particularly among the black population of Africa, contacts within demonic sects, or so-called "churches of Satan," lead to actual *possessio* through demonic beings. The local population believes that frequently possession by the devil himself is achieved. From the magical point of view, this is also not astonishing. To what extent anything comparable is possible in Europe is not known to me. I know of no Satanic cults within Zürich and its surroundings, which does not mean, however, that there might not be such.

Psychic Prerequisites

We know that mediumistic sensitivity plays an important role in cases of invasion by spirit beings. This is particularly familiar for those who know about Dr. Carl Wickland's extensive work and writings. The medium is "open to the four winds." This means that his perceptive faculty of sensation, among the four functions of perception defined by C. G. Jung (intellect, sensation, feeling and intuition), is accorded a decisive role. The term "medium" means intercession between beings of the outer and inner world. The medium has acute intuitive insight in time (prophecy, retrospection) and space (telepathy, clairvoyance).

Wickland noticed in his treatments that mediumistic activity creates particularly intense bioelectrical radiation around the head, similar to a halo, that irresistibly attracts spirit beings. Since an ability as a medium is more frequently expressed among women and primitive peoples, instances of possession are far more frequent in those cases. Among males and intellectualized peoples, the perceptual function is suppressed by critical thinking. Hence, women and children are far more in danger of possession.

Melancholic and phlegmatic temperaments, as passive natures, are most frequently affected. They are more inclined toward weakness of the ego and suggestibility. However, choleric temperaments are also endangered. States of psychic and physical exhaustion likewise facilitate spirit seizure.

The Nature of Possession

Possession can be considered the most spectacular expression of the polarity between good and evil. It is the framework for the encounter of demonic-destructive powers with the elemental human being — who, as reported in the wisdom of the Old Testament, was formed in the image of God, imprinted by the divine, and destined to development and perfection. This encounter is not an offense against the divine; rather, it serves as a material and spiritual illustration of the principle of polarity. But even in possession, as Goethe expressed in the foreword to "Faust," the demonic can only "appear free." The demonic can be active only to the extent permitted by the divine, as illustrated clearly in the drama of Job. Nowhere do we experience more impressively than in exorcism that the demonic must yield if the positive divine forces desire it. This accords with the experience of every practicing exorcist, and in J. Ch. Blumhardt's battle with Gottliebin, becomes a jubilant affirmation of God.

There is no more sublime occasion for showing the faithful the strength and mercy of God and the victory of good over evil than a successful exorcism in the church. Naturally, I do not consider the grace of God as the functioning of a loving Father; rather, it is the grace shown to mankind to develop and to achieve the highest levels of knowledge.

I consider it a serious error on the part of the ecclesiastical authorities that the Protestant church has already lost this opportunity and that the Catholic church is also in the process of losing it. The situation will change, however, as the world becomes less inclined to believe that the tenets of natural science provide the best answer to all human experience.

Of basic importance, too, in the ethereal realm, is the superimposition of a person's ethereal oscillation potential by that of a spirit being of demonic character, regardless of whether by means of angel demons or a departed and still disharmonious soul.

From the preceding, it should be clear that to a large extent possession is a religious problem and, because of the rationalistic world-view of many psychiatrists and counselors, cannot be as readily understood by them.

The Characteristics (Signa) of Possession

The *Rituale Romanum,* issued by Pope Paul V in 1640, summarized the experiences of the church throughout the centuries with possessed people, for the purpose of recognizing a genuine case of *possessio.* The following are considered unmistakable signa:

1) The comprehension and speaking of foreign languages that are unfamiliar to the possessed (Xenoglossy).

This primary *signum* clearly supports the concept that a spirit being is involved, because there is no other way that speaking Latin, for example, which the patient never learned, could be drawn from the possessed person's unconscious. It has never been possible, even under deep hypnosis, to communicate in a language unknown to the hypnotized person except in cases where the reincarnation hypothesis is taken into account.[4] It is also impossible to attribute such a language to the exorcist's unconscious because the unconscious, at best, stores words but not content from a foreign language for intelligible future conversation.

2) Knowledge about secret matters which the possessed is incapable of knowing and about which he knows nothing after the attack.

In this context, clairvoyance, retrocognition, and precognition (prophecy) could occur when the subject is in an exceptional psychic state. But if we examine the numerous details available to us, these correspond to a clairvoyance not frequently observed. Rarely does such clairvoyance refer so spontaneously and directly to persons present or elsewhere. However, unconscious paranormal capabilities from one's own psyche cannot be excluded here.

3) Physical strength that exceeds comprehension.

We know that physical strength can increase enormously under the influence of emotions and danger. But we know of numerous reports according to which, in addition to levitations, an abnormal diminution of weight even to the point of floating and also an abnormal heaviness of individual limbs can occur. This phenomenon, the opposite of levitation, occurred in the case of the possessed person in Löwenberg.[5] The report states that one of the possessed person's legs became so heavy that several men were unable to lift one of her feet from the floor. Exceptional muscular strength could not have been the cause in this instance, so this must be viewed as a paranormal phenomenon.

4) Aversion against anything having to do with the Divine.

The possessed person is unable to enter a church, to carry a Bible, or to pray on his own. Even the smallest quantities of consecrated wafers or holy water that have been mixed into the food and drink of the possessed person without his knowledge are detected and vigorously rejected by him. Such an aversion can also be noted in animals.[6]

---

[4] Erica Fromm, in a fascinating case study, has cited a man of Japanese (Nisei) background who spoke fluent Japanese at age four when age regressed. He denied ever knowing the language, but his parents confirmed that in a California World War II detention camp he was fluent in the language and later forgot even having learned the language. His case suggests that age regression does not always provide foolproof evidence for reincarnation.

[5] See Chapter 13.

[6] See Chapter 13, The Possessed Cat.

5) Paranormal occurrences within and outside the body, particularly during exorcism.

Such occurrences are not specific; they also occur in poltergeist phenomena, without indications of possession in the person affected. What could be involved, however, is *circumcessio* in the person affected by the poltergeist, with special symptoms.

In addition to these five main characteristics, symptoms are indicated in the *Rituale Romanum* which justify a suspicion of possession. These include troubled sleep, constant restlessness, the uttering of animal sounds, and bestial behavior.

7. Positive Possession

Considering the polarity of all events, it would be astonishing if there were not a positive, or angelic, counterpart to the phenomenon where the human spirit, soul, and body are taken over by demonic elements. Among the persons taken over by angelic *spiritual powers* — not by spirit beings — I would include all great charismatics, chiefly the great prophets Moses, Buddha, and Christ, who seem characterized by archetypes of the good that foster the development of the mind and soul. Gabriel, the angel of prophecy (called "man of God" in Hebrew), can be considered the archetypical force determining the life of Jesus. The critic may raise an objection to my interpretation, but I think it should be kept in mind that no event can be attributed to our un-philosophical concept of "coincidence," which is alien to reality. Rather, what occurs constitutes in its ultimate meaning a magical connection to origins. That is always the case with names which hold more than a coincidental significance. The evangelist's choice of Gabriel as the angel of prophecy is based on an intuitive recognition of spiritual relationships.

The spiritually powerful charismatic, saint, or beatified person seems so permeated and consumed by positive elemental principles that spirit, soul, and body all become actively effective. I refer to the collection of pronouncements concerning candidates for sainthood and beatification *(Heilig-und Seligsprechungsprozesse)* issued by W. Schamoni.[1] All are persons seized by the archetypal good, as in ancient Greek thought, where melancholy is conceived as the consequence of being in the grips of Saturn. Being seized resembles being possessed, but this is perhaps more in a quantitative than qualitative sense.

The question can be debated as to whether such sublime, angelic instances of possession are the opposite of actual possession by the "devil." Since the demonic always strives for a spiritual regression of the human being, its manifestations constantly remain in the material sector and attached to the personality. But the fact that worldwide effects are also possible is evidenced in the negative figures of history who were probably demonically possessed (Nero, Napoleon, Hitler, atheistic and imperialistic dictators, etc.). But as we know, they too soon cause a counter-movement. Consequently, despite everything, we can recognize the predominance of the creative will toward organization.

Those blessed by charisma who are at work in the large sphere obey archetypical powers. In addition, however, some are destined to be effective in

---

[1] W. Schamoni, *Parallelen zum Neuen Testament* ["Parallels to the New Testament"] (Abendsberg: Verlag Joseph Kral, 1971).

the small sphere. Let us first recall the concept of "Boddhisattva" in Indian thought — a human soul that has achieved such perfection that it is capable of entering a state of "nirvana." Out of love for mankind, it chooses rebirth in order to serve as a teacher (guru) and to show the seeker the correct way. Comparable to them would be "avatars" (the divine reborn) such as those I met in India (Sai Baba, in Bangalore; Sri Ganapathy Sachchidananda, in Mysore). Their capabilities and feats far exceed those usual in the Western world.

Evidently, though, there are also some who died without having reached the extreme perfection of the blessed, but whose lives were positive and spiritually far advanced, who would like to transfer the blessed achievements of their lifetime to a still-living person who seems to them suited for the task. Such persons do not immediately reincarnate, but continue to be active from a sphere close to the earth. The person chosen by them also appears at times to be possessed. At times his individuality is extinguished and replaced by the personality of the deceased.

A good example of this kind of phenomenon is George Chapman, an Englishman who is still alive and active today. Chapman, born in 1921, feels himself chosen to continue the medical practice of the prominent successful English ophthalmologist Dr. William Lang (1852-1937). Thousands of persons have attested to healings or cures received from Chapman (Lang) in England and the European continent (and some in the U.S.) over a period of more than thirty years. When in trance, Chapman actually speaks quite differently than when in his waking state and his face is transformed. Surviving relatives of Dr. Lang, who practiced at Middlesex Hospital, London, have given Chapman much of Lang's medical equipment and office furnishings, to indicate their interest in, and support of, this impressive phenomenon.

Together with my deceased companion Katharina Nager, I had the opportunity of witnessing Chapman (Dr. Lang) in 1974. Shortly before that time, Mrs. Nager had developed glaucoma in her left eye. For two-and-a-half weeks the eye doctors were unsuccessful in diminishing the excessive pressure in the eye. Despite this unfavorable factor, the operation, with removal of the lens, was successful. Because of the long time that excessive pressure had been on the optic nerve, the surgeons expected a recovery of vision of only approximately 35%.

We consulted Chapman in Lausanne, and found him to be the perfect English gentleman and "doctor." Without having been told the details of the case, he seemed thoroughly informed about the eye disease and the appropriate terminology. Yet, Chapman had no prior knowledge of the patient and had no medical training. With sympathetic gestures mimicking a real intervention, he performed an operation a few centimeters above the eye. The operation was of the kind which evidently was customary at the time of Dr. Lang, and in Chapman's hands touched the *ethereal* substrate of the eye. He promised almost normal vision, possibly the materialization of a new lens in six months. The latter did not occur, perhaps because a contact lens had previously been used. Nonetheless, the patient's vision was restored to 90% of normal, which is very unusual.

The present president of the Swiss Parapsychological Society of Zurich, the physicist and engineer Professor Alex Schneider, described his visit with George Chapman and how Chapman is taken over by the spirit of Dr. W. Lang, in the May 1974 issue of *Paraps:*

> *"While in a trance, Chapman related that the doctor was saddened, following his burial, about no longer being able to make his abilities available to his patients. Subsequently, the doctor found himself in the company of other doctors in the Hereafter. There he learned how to cure the "spirit body" suffering from infirmity, the corpus subtile of "deceased persons," by means of operations similar to ours; it was supposed to be possible, to a large extent, to heal the physical body of the incarnate person by such "operations" on his corpus subtile. He sought a suitable person, George Chapman, who offered himself as a medium. He assisted in the training until the medium functioned perfectly. For speaking and operating, he uses the physical body and organs of his medium. In addition, he is assisted by his son Basil, once a respected surgeon, and by other spirit doctors and spirit nurses, as well as his earthly friend Hunt, who serves as secretary in 'summoning into memory' the particular case histories. These assistants, of which there are reportedly now nine, invisibly act from the spirit sphere on behalf of the patient.*
>
> *"When 'Dr. Lang' performs surgery he sees very many patients per day, who are introduced directly to Dr. Lang. As in a normal medical practice, each patient is usually allotted a quarter of an hour. Chapman has no recollections of the day's work. He dreams as if in normal sleep. He has no contact with the visitors and prefers not to be provided in advance with any written details about the complaints to be treated. His son Michael receives the patients, answers inquiries, and does the administrative chores."*

We also learn from Alex Schneider that

> *"elderly patients whom Dr. Lang had treated during his lifetime, and former colleagues still alive, confirm that when Chapman is in a trance, in sharp contrast to his waking state, he behaves exactly like William Lang. The treatment room still contains the same furniture, pictures, and equipment he used during his lifetime."*

And in conclusion:

> *"Anyone who has met Chapman and seen his documents, particularly those relating to successful cures, rejects the hypothesis of deception as nonsense. On the contrary, in this instance the researcher has the opportunity of investigating a well-developed, deep trance. Entrance and exit occur in unerring precision, and the medium shows no unfavorable after-effects at all after being in a deep trance for eight to ten hours. The takeover is so strong that the discussion with Dr. Lang*

flows as with an awake person, except that one gets the impression of a lifeless facial expression. The room is slightly darkened, but there is sufficient light so that one has no difficulty recognizing the equipment and in reading. When Chapman is in trance he does not seem to be sensitive to any external disturbances."

In the Chapman case, Dr. Lang's taking over clearly manifests itself and has been verified by his former colleagues. Chapman[2] never knew Lang, who died 16 years after Chapman was born.

The case of the still-legendary psychic surgeon Zê Arigò (1922-1971) of Brazil has been less successfully explained. He felt himself led by the spirit of a German physician, Dr. Adolpho Fritz, who died during World War I. It was never possible, however, to find out anything about the real Dr. Fritz. While in a trance, Arigò spoke his native language with a strong German accent, using isolated German words, although there were few people of German origin in his homeland in Northern Brazil. Arigò, with an exceptionally positive ethical nature, was almost illiterate. However, a Brazilian colleague was able to show me three prescriptions written in his presence by Arigò while in a trance. The handwriting was that of a typical doctor, and the prescriptions were pharmacologically faultless. I witnessed the same thing during a visit in Rio de Janeiro with De Freitas, another Brazilian healer.

Arigò performed operations while in a trance, mostly using primitive kitchen knives and frequently operating on the eye. This is documented in a filmstrip in my possession. Occasionally, however, he merely used his hands on the body of the patient in the manner of the Philippine psychic surgeons, as described by Andrija Puharich, M.D., LLD. and John G. Fuller in the United States.[3]

To interpret these incidents as the unconscious split-off medical personality of Arigò, as if that were the only possibility available to parapsychological animists, is pure nonsense. In my judgment, positive temporary possession through a disincarnate spirit being is the much more plausible explanation!

Now, in the 1980's, Dr. Edson Quieroz, a Brazilian physician, also goes into trance and performs "psychic surgery" in the same manner as "Dr. Fritz" used to do through Arigò and de Freitas. Dr. Quieroz has demonstrated his ability before large audiences in Europe as well as in Brazil and has treated many patients with all kinds of afflictions.

The situation is different among the psychic surgeons of the Philippines. Very few psychic surgeons there receive a direct assignment via a "divine being" during a suddenly occurring trance state. Juanito Flores is something

---

[2] George Chapman, *Extraordinary Encounters* (Lang Publishing Co., Ltd, with Faith Press, Ltd).

George Chapman, *Surgeon from Another World* (London: W. H. Allen, 1978).

J. Bernard Hutton, *Healing Hands* (London: W. H. Allen, 1967).

Spirit Surgeon (VHS Videotape), (New York: Trignon Communications [P.O. Box 1713, Ansonia Station, New York, NY 10023]).

[3] John G. Fuller, *ARIGO: Surgeon of the Rusty Knife* (New York: Thomas Y. Crowell Publishing Co., 1974).

of an exception since he claims he receives his help through the archangel Michael, while working in the field. But this is not comparable to being taken over via possession. Through many years of practice, these psychic surgeons awaken their delicate nerve centers (Chakras) to avail themselves of Prana, a universal life force, which they transfer to the patient via the meridians of acupuncture. The phenomenon of psychic surgery, however, is of course more complex.

Wherever cures take place among non-intellectual peoples, the healing event is attributed to the aid of a numen (a deity believed to reside locally or to inhabit an object) and not to the individual person — in other words, the explanation is based on the idea that the healer is permeated by a numen which has overlaid the person's ego. All such healers are positively possessed and are facilitators of a constructive event.

The deceased Austrian physician and university lecturer, Dr. Karl Nowotny,[4] had a very positive spiritual relationship with his co-worker Grete Schröder during his lifetime. After his death, Mrs. Schröder still felt in extremely close contact with him. Messages received and healings that occurred are described in five volumes. Analogous to George Chapman, a positive possession via the spiritual being of Nowotny cannot be excluded in the case of Mrs. Schröder, regardless of how animistic parapsychologists try to make Mrs. Schröder's unconscious responsible for her achievements. But naturally, this interpretation can only be an hypothesis.

Other cases could be mentioned here, but Emanuel Swedenborg, an eminent natural scientist, is a primary example. He remained lucid in every respect throughout his life. He experienced clairvoyance and visions and wrote about his conversations with angels and about wrestling with evil spirits. "I recount the things I have seen," he wrote, ". . . a plain statement of journeys and conversations in the spiritual world which have made the greater part of my daily history for many years . . . I have proceeded by observation and induction as strict as that of any man of science . . . It has been given me to enjoy an experience reaching into two worlds — that of spirit as well as that of matter."

---

[4] Dr. Karl Nowotny, *Mediale Schriften — Mitteilungen eines Arztes aus dem Jenseits* ["Writings through a Medium — Communications of a Doctor from the Beyond"] (Remagen: Otto Reichl Verlag).

8. THE EXORCISM

The word exorcism is derived from the Greek, *horkizo* "to swear an oath, to conjure" and *exorkizo,* "to conjure, to cast out, to drive away."

Exorcism was known to all ancient and high eastern cultures, just as it is known to all peoples oriented toward magic. Hippocrates (460 - 377 B.C.), a well-known critical thinker, was able to distinguish very clearly between possession and mental illness, expressed in his suggestions for treatment. Jesus Christ, too, knew the difference, and he sent out his disciples not only to heal but also to exorcise. At all times and among all cultures we find exorcistic practices.

In Christianity, we find allusions to an institutionalized benediction for exorcists dating back to the third century. At that time, when the organized church was attempting to consolidate its power, it strove to monopolize treatment of the phenomenon of possession. Previous to that, at the time of Tertullian, every baptized Christian had the right to exorcise, and to some extent this is still the case today. However, though it is not expressly stated, women do not generally perform these rites. Within the Catholic church the so-called "Major Exorcism" is reserved for the priest who is authorized by the bishop, and it is only permitted in the church. Major and minor exorcism will be described in the chapter "Forms of Exorcism."

Even today, the guidelines determining the ritual of the Catholic Church are based on the instructions published by Pope Paul V in the *Rituale Romanum* of 1614. Pope Pius XII in 1954, adjusting to the "Codex Juris Canonici," published certain changes which are still valid.

Leo XIII, around the turn of the century, created guidelines for the new "Minor Exorcism," which are applicable to a compelling need today. For the present situation, it seems significant to me that the German Bishops' Conference in April 1978, in reaction to the exorcist trial in Aschaffenburg regarding Anneliese Michel — at least for Germany — set new guidelines for exorcistic rituals which take place in churches. According to these, exorcism should only take place if simultaneously, medical — or as the case may be — psychotherapeutic treatment of the "possessed" has been assured. Since physicians categorize the phenomenon of possession as a psychosomatic event, instead of as a spiritual conflict between good and evil, this demand cannot be expected to produce reasonable and liberating results.

Modern psychology and psychiatry place any exorcistic effort into the categories of persuasion, i.e. conveyance of a (counter-) opinion to convince the patient; suggestion, direct influence of the emotions and imagination of the patient; and auto-suggestion, a change of opinion and perception accepted by an essential part of the personality.

The dogma of natural science traces everything spiritual and mental back to the chemistry of the brain; psychic reactions are assumed to be caused by external stimuli, which through the senses and neural pathways are led back to the brain where they cause a chemical reaction. Efferent nerve impulses (coming from the brain) lead to mental reflections, to emotional expressions, or to muscular actions. It is too seldom noticed that even the nature of transmission of impulses out of the brain via synapses (junctions between brain substance and neural pathways) remains unexplained.

To the natural philosopher, the relationship between mental and physical appears as synchronous (simultaneous) correspondence. Klages defines the circumstances as a "sense for the appearance of the sense," as was explained in the chapter "Natural Science and Natural Philosophy." According to this, a chemical reaction in the brain may accompany the transmission of impulses from the mind to the material or may occur parallel to this, but for the purely mental, i.e. the world which our senses can not grasp, it is not a condition. For the person versed in these esoteric matters, the mind possesses primacy over matter and does not necessarily need the brain. *Mental energies can therefore influence ethereal beings which do not have a human brain.* Contact takes place by means of an ethereal stream of energy. We are reminded of the energy influences in the meridians of acupuncture and its effect — also during laying on of hands — on the energy potential of the partner. This understanding is decisive for the effectiveness of exorcistic possibilities. For ancient High religions, and also those of the modern Eastern cultures, the described circumstances are valued long-established experiences. They also are familiar with the effect of the *Word* as a primary mental energy and ethereal stream of energy. Each number contains archetypal essence. The number one, for example, contains totality, number two contains polarity, three the harmonic. Archetypes are force fields par excellence and causal agents, although not in the sense of classical physics, but within magical causality by analogy. This fact explains the effectiveness of number magic. As we know from the Cabala, a number has to be assigned to every letter (Aleph = 1, Beth = 2, Gimmel = 3, etc.). This does not only apply to the Hebrew letters. In the Tagálog of the Philippines, this connection was discovered independently of the Hebrew alphabet *(Rizal)*, but to a certain extent it occurs in every language. Specific forces of influence, which are capable of transmission to the human psyche as well as to matter, belong not just to the archaic-mental character of the letter, but in the form of analogy, to each word and each sentence. The transmission to matter also demonstrates the mental component. For this reason, the spoken word during the exorcism, in connection with other components of energy, is effective. It also conceals *contents of essence,* which counter those of demonic possession. These contents of essence are imprinted in association with the *good:* in the name of the Trinity or Jesus Christ.

It is primarily the *mind* which must help the psyche, onto which the negative is superimposed, in order to free it from evil. Mental phenomena are closer to the archetypal than psychic phenomena, which correspond to the more superficial emotional phenomena. Emotions are even found in the world of animals, but the mind reigns only in humans. Academics have asked me many times to differentiate between and define mind and soul. This differentiation is difficult even for the educated person. The soul, of course, can be understood as the sum of all emotional energies, but individual emotions are simultaneously phenomena of a particular archetype; for example, compassion, or the drive to destroy, which have always been attributed to gods or demonic beings. The expression mind-soul is a way out of the dilemma.

But "The Spirit blows whence it will." Does not this phrase already point out that the spirit is nothing static, but contains something which is energetic? According to the Scriptures the spirit of God had already blown over the waters when *life* was not yet created. In humans, the spirit reached its highest development of intensity and differentiation.

Since we must recognize in every human a part — although very small — of the created universe, humans then are also a thought — a part of God — and thus filled with His spirit. Spirit is the *primum movens* (a basic condition of all movement and appearance). As a primal archetype, it is not subject to emotional limitations and is superior to emotional values.

The spirit represents the archaic, par excellence. "In the beginning was the Word" Luther translated. Logos[1] does not have anything to do with a spoken word (the body of the word), but signifies meaning and spirit, both primeval categories, which contain the primary energy. Although the spoken word always contains spiritual primary energy, the body of the word affects the world of the senses and the emotional side of human beings. Ever since natural science used the measurability of matter and the repeatability of the measurements as the sole criterion of existence, the *spiritual* was left to theology and philosophy. Psychology and psychiatry (the theory of the manifestations of the ill psyche) joined natural sciences, as we already know, and today completely overlook the primary effect of the spirit. All psychic events are understood as an influence of the senses on the emotional world of humans and animals.

It appears to me to be of essential significance that during exorcistic confrontation and influence, it is not just a psychological influence from psyche to psyche that occurs, but one within the basic categories of good and evil. During an attack of possession, the psyche of the possessed (as well as individual tendencies) loses its freedom and is superposed by a foreign demonic (negative) frequency potential — a foreign power. When the superposing power is a "poor soul" which is seeking certain goals of individual development, it can be counselled and enlightened — as Wickland did. But when "angel demons" are involved, it is primarily a power struggle within polar opposites. Only a transmission of energy with positive contents can weaken the negative power potential to the point that necessitates its leaving.

Intense positive thoughts and wishes during the exorcistic ritual affect demonic spirits and their intentions directly and not through the brain chemistry of the possessed. We are reminded of the fact that in the Indian-tantric theory of cognition — especially the theory of five bodies — thought and concept are considered to be "Prakriti" (matter). We recognize that an

---

[1] *Logos,* the rational principle that governs and develops the universe.

emotionally-enriched thinking effort influences any spirit and every spiritual realty which, though consisting of ethereal matter, are also a part of Prakriti. Within the ethereal plane — here the category of good and evil — ethereal psychoplastic takes effect. (Psychoplastic is the deformation or transformation of matter via mental effort). I am thinking in this situation of angel demons. These probably possess, in contrast to deceased entities, a less clearly expressed individuality, but represent a hierarchically-ordered partial component of the cosmic category of evil.

The exorcistic thought forces the demonic into transformation through this ethereal psychoplastic, whereby the demonic is threatened with the loss of its specific identity, in order to finally sink to a level of less dense matter within the mental or even causal sphere. Heaven and hell are viewed as the extreme categories of good and evil, an archetypal situation of the least material, probably the causal sphere (Sanskrit: Avyakta), a spiritual sphere of the mere possibilities of still-undeveloped matter. In the theory of five bodies, the Avyakta is placed between Buddhi, the mental sphere, and Purusha, the pure godlike existence.

I consider it interesting that Paracelsus[2] also speaks of the death of ethereal beings. According to him, there are "spirits suspended from the stars, who are born and who must also die." By this, however, he does not mean beings belonging to the cycle of reincarnation.

Demons, hurled into the "abyss," into hell, have presumably lost their power of influence in the world of higher material density. It is possible that only from there, in an extremely ethereal, and for us unearthly world, the last chance for salvation — the unification of opposites — is made possible. This event, too, could be imagined as a psychoplastic trans- forming and re-forming into pure godlike existence (Purusha, Nirvana, Pleroma).

After working out these speculative ideas I had the opportunity to discuss them with Oskar Marcel Hinze, an expert on the science of Tantra and author of the book *Tantra Vidya*. Hinze asks one to keep in mind that the Avyakta-Prakriti, as matter of Purusha which is not yet developed, is adjacent to the highest godlike existence and thus has to be considered the highest sphere of ethereal matter. In his opinion, demons — though ethereal — belonging to a lower and earthbound sphere, cannot accomplish an ascent.

To speak of "destruction" — as in the vision of Gottliebin — is out of the question in any case, since, in the case of the demons, we are dealing with beings full of energy. Energies can never be destroyed, they can only be transformed. Rather a banning, a fixation into an inactive condition which would thereby be a fall from activity into inactivity, seems possible to me.

In the understanding of persons versed in these esoteric matters, *this* can not be the final condition either, since everything which has evolved in matter — and here we must include ethereal matter — must again return to godly existence. This would correspond to the principal law of a cosmic pulsation, and in the religious sense, of redemption by grace.

---

[2] Paracelsus, *Sämtliche Werke* ["Complete Works"] (Jena, 1932), Vol. 4, p. 471.

In general, the theory of banning is not completely satisfying. An emotional event concerns the Manas-level (astral level) of the tantric theory of five bodies. Is it at all permissible, within this, to speak of higher and lower levels? Using anthropomorphic concepts here, would the creator spirit, which intentionally enters matter as duality, want to go down to lower levels? Does the separation of good and evil begin only with the Manas-level (emotionality)? Isn't it programmed at the beginning of creation and a necessary condition for cognition? Must not evil, which we, through a subjective valuation, categorize as lower, have its "primal roots," here as archetypes such as love, hate, preservation (Vishnu), or destruction (Shiva), in the "Buddhi" of the mental level? But then they must already — to use an appropriate expression by Jakob Böhme — have their origins in the Avyakta, the level of un- evolved matter, the primeval condition.

From these viewpoints, at least a temporary ban of the demons to a polar negative force field of the Avyakta would be conceivable. All five levels of materialization of the theory of five bodies contain, in my opinion, both an evolutionary and a destructive reality. Even the aspect of Shiva existed with the beginning of the world and this necessarily also in the Avyakta.

I am aware that my thoughts are speculative and hypothetical. Let us be reminded of the apocryphal notion that even Jesus had to descend to hell in order to reach his final perfection. Even if, according to our present understanding, this idea is merely the intuitive view of the apocryphal author, it has to be emphasized that only intuitive, and never intellectual, cognition projects into the core of the cosmic. Magnificently described in the apocryphal books, too, is the lively conception that Jesus supposedly embraced the devil while in hell in order to reconcile him with God and thus redeem him. This is the actual union of opposites, the *mystericum conjunctionis,* necessary for the attainment of eternal godliness, the Indian nirvana and the Christian heaven.

Familiarity with the Gottliebin case has made it possible for me to better comprehend the exorcistic efforts of Johann Christoph Blumhardt, an exceptional charismatic. He was said to have healed about 80,000 sick people by laying on of hands. In countless cases of exorcism the unusual forces involved rarely manifested to such an extreme extent as in the Gottliebin case.

During exorcism, as will be shown later, we encounter a variety of approaches. But a psychoplastic event, influencing first the *corpus subtile,* then the body, is always present. This is true of every psychoplastic. In this situation, it is the demonic spirit which first of all, in a certain sense, distorts the ethereal substance of the possessed, which then transfers to the psyche and then to the material body. Welts, which I saw develop on the arms and thighs on one of my possessed clients during exorcism, appeared from one moment to the next, at a speed which is not physiologically possible. They also disappeared at a physiologically impossible speed.

I am convinced that psychic healing, especially within the realm of psychic surgery in the Philippines, first functions as psychoplastic on the mental-astral level via ethereal energetic events and confrontations. Subsequently, a condensing at the level of the representative physical body (etheric body) takes place, then it transfers into the *soma,* the material body. The latter step may require some time. For example, during psychic surgery for the treatment of kidney or gallstone complaints, an immediate freedom from pain or a subjective healing often occurs. A short time afterwards the stones can still be seen on X-rays, but will have dissolved two to three months later. This is the event at the somatic level.

In the area of minerals, the thought and conception of the "spoon bender" Uri Geller, and many others, first psychoplastically affect the "ether or representative physical body" — the only ethereal body of "dead" matter — in order to transfer from there to the metal.

In exorcism, we find that the positive (divine) proves to be stronger then the demonic — reinforcing religious thought. The positive exorcistic thought forces the demonic to undergo transformation, as I have already described. I venture the thought that every conclusive event of spiritual redemption represents a psychoplastic return of the earthly world of polarities to divine unity — Purusha, Pleroma, Nirvana — i.e., into purely divine existence.

The fact that materializations and psychoplastics carry over into the material realm, is part of the many events which occur during exorcism. Thus, smoke and stench occur at times as the materialization of spiritual demonic intentions. In addition, a wide variety of objects are materialized out of the body; and uncontrolled muscle movement, such as vomiting against the priest and the Host, as well as the development of unusual strength, are observed. These are not only demonic responses to provocation by exorcism, which become visible to the human on the material level; the same thing often happens in the case of possession without the provocation of exorcistic rituals, simply to impress and intimidate the human and priestly opponent.

We are often asked why exorcistic rituals only take place in exceptional situations today. It appears that spectacular cases of possession have become rare, or it may be that only sensational cases are reported. Since the unfortunate trial against the parents and priests in the case of Anneliese Michel, there is not much open talk about exorcism in German-speaking Catholic areas. Just as exorcism is not officially performed in the Protestant church, in spite of Blumhardt's report (which, even during his lifetime, got little support from the church), we also encounter more and more restraint in the Catholic faith. In the monasteries nearest the city of Zürich, exorcism is performed when demanded, but hardly ever in the form of the major exorcism. The minor exorcisms, after private agreement, are executed by a priest familiar with the procedure, but rarely prove to be — as far as my experience goes — successful. The cases which I have known from my own practice were not spectacular and, in my opinion, belonged more to the realm of "magic," which still exists,[3] where discarnate humans, and not demons, are the primary actors. Understandably, the priest, then, is not sure whether a case involves possession or a psychosomatic illness. He wants to help, but is insecure. In that case, a minor exorcism seldom helps. With the predominant thinking of the natural sciences in our times, the modern Catholic priest does not feel as secure in his faith as was formerly the case. Younger priests call on Jesus Christ or the archangels without the conviction of earlier generations.

---

[3] see Theodor Locher, SVPP, 36th "Orientierungsblatt" ["Information Sheet"], Jan. 1981.

Scientific thinking has had its impact on the church, while in the world of the layman, a contrary movement is noticeable. Otherwise, the book published by Dr. Peter Gehring, *Eugenie von der Leyen: Meine Gespräche mit armen Seelen* ["My Conversations with Poor Souls"],[4] would not have sold 20,000 copies within one year.

For reasons of discretion and consideration of the possessed person, the congregation is no longer invited to such rituals, and thus an essential source of power has been excluded. I am convinced that without the presence of parishioners who were experienced, convinced and gifted as mediums — especially female parishioners — the miracle of San Gennaro in Naples, for example, could not have happened. They are the actual sources of power which cause the *blood* miracles, because it is especially the strongly-believing emotional *state* which moves and causes the miracle. Professor Hans Bender, who investigated this paranormal event and described it extensively, did not fully recognize these connections, although he acknowledged the phenomenon as such.

Possessions of minor scale are, in my opinion, still quite numerous, but are clinically categorized as schizophrenia, especially paranoia. Each era has its own form of expression. The *grande hysterie* of the turn of the century is no longer found in any psychiatric clinic today, although in the thirties of this century, I still observed some cases. The demonic seems to express itself differently today. There appear to be enough opportunities in politics and business for "invading entities" to find expression.

The struggle against evil can be fought only with spiritual power. The legal domain is not adequate to the task, since by definition its activities must necessarily be preventive. Efforts to exert an influence through the news- and mass media are minimally successful in decisive places, since they are all too dependent on economic forces and today's predominant academic and theological views. The church has, to a high degree, lost its influence over the economically powerful and governments (especially dictatorships). It must influence the individual person, and when a majority can be approached and reached as was the case in Poland, it will be a special blessing.

Nothing stimulates the cognitive functions: emotions, sensations, intuition and intellect of the participants and observers, as much as witnessing the improvement or cure of a possessed person who has been stamped as mentally ill. Both the church and humanity would benefit if there were greater recognition that man is also a spiritual being and not limited to material existence. The concept that life is spiritual in origin can only increase respect for life in all its forms — human, animal and plant. Albert Schweitzer's life exemplified the awareness that all life is more than physical, and fortunately there are signs that this healthy awareness is growing.

Contemporary life rests on the belief that we are more "enlightened" and more intelligent than our preceding generations. In my opinion, this is not the case. The intelligence of mankind has not changed significantly for centuries;

---

[4] Dr. Peter Gehring, *Eugenie von der Leyen: Meine Gespräche mit armen Seelen* (Stein am Rhein: Christiana Verlag, 1979).

at most its intellectualization has changed, which has nothing to do with intelligence. In fact we may be more biased than ever before, considering the hubris of the natural scientist caught up more than ever in dogmatic theories. The present tendency of many of the news media to deny parapsychological phenomena illustrates this point.

Major Exorcism

The Church had always issued guidelines for exorcistic rituals or procedures. At first, they were summarized in the *Sacerdotal*. As already mentioned, Pope Paul V published the *Rituale Romanum* in 1614, in which all of the then-existing experiences were taken into consideration. In 1954, Pius XII adapted it to contemporary understanding. As direction for the performance of the exorcist, the *Rituale Romanum* lays down 21 rules; among which are: the test for whether a case really constitutes possession or not; also, that the exorcist, as much as possible, shall use the words of the Holy Scripture instead of his own; should ask the number and names of the possessing spirits; and other reasonable rules of conduct.

The actual text for the exorcistic ritual contains a succession of invocations of God and his servants; worship, prayers, psalms and readings from the gospel; insults toward the possessing demon; his exorcism and the order to leave. The use of the sign of the cross in accordance with the individual words is also precisely regulated.

As an example of the prescribed texts, this short excerpt may suffice:

> *"I command thee, whosoever though art, unclean spirit, and all of thy companions, who oppress this servant of God: by the mysteries of the incarnation, the crucifixion, the resurrection and ascension of our Lord Jesus Christ, by the mission of the Holy Ghost and through the return of him our Lord on the Judgment Day, tell us thy name, the day and hour of thy departure, with some kind of sign: And thou shalt obey me, God's unworthy servant, throughout all; nor shalt thou harm this creature or those present or their messengers in any way."*

The Major Exorcism, which lasts a minimum of four hours, but can last considerably longer — especially when the possessed, under the influence of the possessing spirits, shows resistance — may only be conducted with permission of the responsible bishop, by an especially chosen priest, and must only be performed in a church. Unfortunately it is celebrated publicly only in rare cases. Nothing would be more impressive for modern man than to witness such a cure, of a person considered mentally ill within the framework of contemporary thinking.

It should not surprise us that the ritual of exorcism greatly resembles the rites of primitive peoples, and especially the cults of shamans, since it actually demonstrates the connection between human and deity.

Minor Exorcism

Minor exorcism was introduced by Pope Leo XIII at the turn of this century in response to a need. It can be conducted anywhere, even by a person other than a priest, just as was the case in early Christianity. This "Leontine Exorcism" is considerably shorter but must be introduced by a prayer; for example, the Lord's prayer. It not only resembles the baptismal exorcism, but also the one which I conduct, except that it does not treat the possessing spirits kindly. From the point of view of someone versed in these esoteric matters, I consider this a detriment.

Exorcism Within the Protestant Church

Zwingli and Calvin, as intellectual theologians, did not give consideration to exorcism. Luther, much more down to earth, practiced it himself. In the Lutheran faith, exorcisms — at least until the 17th Century — were performed in the churches, but began to be more and more suppressed because the Protestant religion became more susceptible to increasing tendencies toward "enlightenment." In the Lutheran sense, the word of God was more highly regarded. By the 18th century, exorcism appears more and more banned from public view and used only by charismatic ministers (Blumhardt) in private. Prayers, fasting, laying on of hands, and ethical integrity, however, proved to be just as effective weapons as the ritual of exorcism. Today, as noted earlier, exorcism within the Protestant church is virtually unknown.

9. TYPES OF EXORCISM

By Martin Luther

Magister Sebastian Fröschel in Wittenberg reported on the exorcism that Martin Luther conducted for an 8-year-old possessed girl in the area of Meissen (Bodini II, p. 84). The girl supposedly was tormented and "torn" in many ways. Luther ordered her to recite her confession of faith but when she came to "I believe in Jesus Christ," she could not continue and the demon tortured her terribly. Then Luther said: "I know you well, you devil. You would like us to create much ado about you and honor you, but you will not get this from me."

The girl then was brought into the sacristy of the church for the sermon. Luther reminded the worshippers who were present to consider the devil as a haughty spirit who could not endure prayer and contempt, and that the proceedings to follow were therefore the best armor against him. He laid his right hand on the child's head and told the worshippers to do the same. Then he prayed and called on God for help. Afterward he derided the devil. The girl from then on was cured.

Compared with the *Rituale Romanum,* this is a very simple procedure and represents the spirit of Protestant thought. Based on reports handed down, the exorcisms performed in the spirit of the *Rituale Romanum,* with all its display of activity, were also successful.

After thorough examination of many exorcistic efforts, I am of the opinion that the main ingredients are the integrity and radiance of the exorcist.

Exorcism in The Christian Philippines[1]

Some of the exorcisms in the Philippines with which I am familiar occur in connection with the phenomenon of "psychic surgery." They take place within the context of suspected witchcraft. These cases are not of raving, possessed persons but of those who are organically ill. Witchcraft is a common phenomenon in the Philippines and it would be foolhardy to treat it as superstition. Non-intellectual peoples, such as the rural populations of the Philippines, are, in my opinion, better observers than many Western investigators because they have had the personal experiences and know how they feel before and after treatment. Witchcraft, which has been observed there for generations, is recognized as a reality.

It should be mentioned that most healings by "psychic surgeons" do *not* involve witchcraft but are paranormal or paraconceptual techniques which are incomprehensible to most Westerners and are therefore often dismissed as

---

[1] see H. Naegeli-Osjord: *Die Logurgie in den Philippinen* (Reichl Verlag). (Not yet translated into English).

sleight-of-hand. It should be added that with the influx of thousands of sick persons from Europe and the United States, desperately seeking help, usually after conventional medicine has declared their cases are hopeless, pressures have mounted among some of the healers to resort to trickery when their "powers" were weak, causing skeptics to dismiss the entire phenomenon.

The healers view themselves as channels of invisible force, usually in a religious context, that can produce healings. They feel that positive forces, guides or spirit helpers are working through them. It is only in cases when they sense a bewitchment that they treat the patient with exorcistic rituals and at times produce or extract (materialize) foreign objects from the body that give the person a feeling of relief. I have witnessed Alex Orbito, one of the healers, remove ("materialize") a large handful of hair that seemed to come from the abdomen. Just as Blumhardt believed that the objects which worked their way out of the body in the case of Gottliebin (discussed in Chapter 11), so I assume that the materialized hair had been brought into the body ethereally through the practice of "witchcraft" or "magic." It caused discomfort, and during the healing was materialized and extirpated.

The conquest of the possessor takes place within a religious setting through the vital forces of the healer or exorcist. These forces, in the case of healer David Olegane, radiate especially from the middle finger, and his breath. The place of transmission is the middle finger of the bewitched person, who suffers pain thereby, screams and asks to be spared.

Although there are psychic surgeons in Brazil and Mexico, as well as in the Philippines, this phenomenon is most prevalent in Luzon, the largest island in the Philippines. Both Spiritism and Catholicism have influenced the beliefs of the people in that region. *Eleuterio Terte,* born in 1905, is generally considered to have been the first psychic surgeon in this century, starting his ministrations in the late 1920's and continuing until his death in 1979, with the exception of the World War II years.

Tony Agpaoa, who reportedly discovered at age 9 that he could heal when he was able to stop the flow of bleeding of a playmate, became the best known internationally and thus also the most controversial. Many phenomenal reports of successful treatments by him have been filmed and reported in Europe and the United States. Tony Agpaoa died from a stroke while still in the prime of life.

The number of "psychic surgeons" in Luzon province is usually estimated between thirty and forty and there are an estimated two hundred who do "magnetic healing." Two currently better known and respected healers are *Alex Orbito* and *Josephina Sison*. Western investigators who have visited the Philippines generally agree that the phenomenon cannot be understood within the context of modern medicine. Leaving out the cases where sleight-of-hand is used to produce simulated effects, there remain many cases where genuine paranormal phenomena occur which can only be understood as cases of "materialization" and "de-materialization." Many of the spectacular bloody scenes which show clots and tissues and tumors appearing are surface phenomena. Those who have witnessed thousands of cases estimate that deep body openings occur in about 3 to 5 percent of those treated.

David Olegane

Eleuterio Terte

Dr. Naegeli and Tony Agpaoa

Alex Orbito

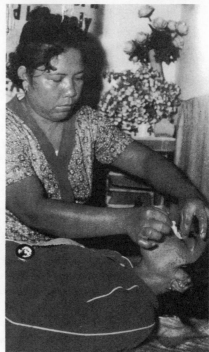
Josephina Sison

Gert Chesi, an Austrian writer and free-lance journalist, wrote a detailed account of his visits to the Philippines in a book[2] published in 1981. He included numerous photos in color and black and white, as well as interviews with healers and his own observations and tentative conclusions. He concluded that there were genuine paranormal phenomena and also sleight-of-hand when pressures to "produce" were too great. Chesi characterizes David Olegane as a "witch-hunter and exorcist" because he specializes in treating people who often are thought to be possessed.

In an interview I gave Chesi while he was preparing his book, I summarized my impressions about this controversial phenomena:

> ". . . I gave to the Institute of Forensic Medicine in Zürich (blood samples which) were all subjected to the 'Uchtoloni-Analysis' which examines the precipitation lines. Each animal species has its own albumin precipitation lines. Human precipitation lines are not always identical which means that their interpretation depends on the scientist examining them, so errors are naturally possible. The 'Uchtoloni-Analysis' revealed that some of them were human, others animal in origin. Dr. Lachsche in Paris informed me that the sample he had taken in my presence during one of Josephina Sison's operations was sheep's

---

[2] Gert Chesi, *Faith Healers in the Philippines* (Woergl, Austria: Perlinger Verlag, 1981).

blood. This, however, is impossible as sheep cannot live in a tropical climate. The blood would have to be brought down from the mountains which are several hundred miles away. Results like this naturally nurture skepticism. . . .

". . . Dr. Motoyama, a well-known Japanese physician, uses another method, the 'Absorption-Inhibition-Analysis'. In most cases he has proved that the blood which is produced during these operations is identical with that of the patient. I regard this method as more exact than our 'Uchtoloni- Analysis'. I discussed this with Professor Schiebeler in Ravensburg and we decided that in most cases the blood materializations are probably not produced from inside the patient's body, but from underneath the healer's hands in accordance with his ideas. The key question is whether the intense ideas of a healer in trance can be materialized. There is much to be said in favor of this theory. . . .

". . . So, materializations do exist! This is an indubitable fact, even if the phenomenon does not fit into our Western pattern of thinking. There is another thing one must bear in mind also: As argued by Oskar Marcel Hienze, the Indian mind does not differentiate clearly between matter and soul. Every thought, every fantasy is incorporated into the mental sphere, it is matter in an extremely diluted form. In a continual process of condensation, the mental sphere merges into the astral sphere, the realm of sensations, then into the ethereal sphere, the realm of incorporeal forms, and then finally, into the sphere of matter. The process is one of continual condensation ranging from thought to matter. This means that the Indian mind regards thought as matter and therefore finds it natural for thoughts, which are matter in contrast to the Purusha, the purely divine soul, to be materialized. If one takes this into consideration, at the same time endeavoring to think in other categories of logic, one realizes that the phenomena in the Philippines are logical and perfectly comprehensible. . . .

". . . I do not know to what extent sleight-of-hand is common today. I only know that in most cases the operations no longer involve penetration into the body. The blood is materialized under the healer's hand. This kind of materialization involves coagulated blood. According to Motoyama, the healer's middle finger emanates the greatest power, and this is where one of the meridians end. Mrs. Seutemann, who worked for Agpaoa for a couple of months, informed me that the coagulated blood always appears somewhere near the middle finger. Now, if the blood was a trick it would either be completely coagulated or not coagulated at all. Normal blood coagulates within two or three minutes. The healers would have to be very clever indeed to have blood in this condition at their disposal for all operations. I regard it as impossible. Too many people have watched them too closely for that. Unless you have spent months in the Philippines and seen thousands of operations, you have no way of judging it. . . .

". . . Western man believes there is only one science. He does not know that there are many different forms of perception. As. C.G. Jung *put it, there are at least four primary functions of the mind predomi-nant: thinking, feeling, sensation and intuition. Scientists continue to ignore this. The 'Westerner' just cannot work in other categories of thought. He recognizes one medical science only, and completely ignores the fact that there are other possibilities, such as acupuncture, for example, which is a much older practice than our medical science. . . . The opposition to these methods is a consequence of people's lethargy when it comes to finding out anything about them. People do not want to change their scientific beliefs. They have grown up with them and intend to die with them. A change of attitude would deprive them of their confidence."*

Baptismal Exorcism

Baptismal exorcism can be traced back to the original baptism of heathen adults, whereby their earlier religious practices were treated as idolatry and the work of the devil. At first, any contact with such cults on the part of the candidate to be baptized had to be renounced *(abrenuntiatio diaboli),* but then, connected with the exorcism of demons performed by Jesus Christ, the exorcism of the devil by the baptizer was added.

In the 4th century, child baptism was performed, too, whereby the priest first breathed the unclean spirit out of the infant to be baptized *(exsufflatio),* in order to then breathe the Holy Spirit symbolically into it *(insufflatio).* Thereby the following formula was spoken: "Leave, thou unclean spirit, make way for the Holy Ghost," or "I adjure thee, in the name of the Father, the Son and the Holy Ghost, that thou yield and leave this servant of Jesus Christ." The exorcism of infants is naturally connected to St. Paul's teaching of original sin.

Baptismal exorcism was always valid in Catholicism. Among Lutherans it fell out of use during the 18th century, only to regain ecclesiastical acceptance during the 19th century. Swiss reformers rejected the baptismal exorcism, which also had an influence on the exorcism of adults.

Non-Christian Exorcisms

A comprehensive description of the various non-Christian exorcisms already has filled a number of books. Thus, I will restrict myself to one example from Chr. Scharfetter, M.D., Professor of psychiatry at the University of Zürich.
He reports:[3]

> *"The demonologic theory of diseases and demonic exorcistic therapy is still widespread in Ceylon (Sri Lanka). There, such attitudes of faith are basically independent of the religious affiliation but are more or less differentiated in their therapeutic methods, depending on religious orientation. This is how a Christian exorcism in Ceylon (Sri Lanka) takes place: The patient, a person believed to be possessed by the devil,*

---

[3] *Psychiatrische und paramedizinische Beobachtungen in Ceylon* ["Psychiatric and Paramedical Observations in Ceylon"], *Praxis* 1977/32, p. 1012.

is tied to a cross and whipped one night long by the priest. Buddhism has quite different methods, recorded in old textbooks.

Depending on the person's maladies and complaints, pulse rate, and the behavior of two drops of oil put in a glass of urine, diagnosis and prognosis are determined. If the drops of oil sink, the prognosis is bad and no therapy will be attempted. In such cases, the native therapist recommends the Western medical treatment at a hospital, which in his opinion is a refined type of his demonologic method. After the finding, it is "determined" which demon afflicts the patient and holds him possessed. This in turn determines the form, extent and length of the ceremony of exorcism.

"In a simple ritual, the "exorcism" of the demon takes place as follows: A Yantra, which is a magic square with diagonals, is laid out on the floor using rice kernels. At each of the four corners and the intersection of the diagonals, a coconut, flowers, sticks of incense, frankincense and a small oil lamp are placed. In a censer alongside, glowing charcoal is kept and repeatedly strewn with frankincense. Next to it, the patient sits or lies while the therapist speaks and sings in front of him. Then the therapist, reciting, sits down in front of the Yantra square, draws blood from his own hand with the prick of a needle, and places one drop on each end of a warmed chicken egg. This is then also smoked with incense.

"After a longer period of singing, the therapist lies down on a mat. Two cross-bars are shoved under the mat. He is then lifted up by his helpers and turned once around his axis. Then the therapist lying stretched out on the floor, holds the egg between the first and second toes of his right foot. Now he intentionally goes into an extraordinary state: he pants, he hyperventilates interspersed with breathing pauses, grinds his teeth, foams at the mouth, clenches his fists, groans, and repeatedly inhales the smoke of frankincense (without coughing). His eyes are tightly closed. His head jerks to and fro at times, almost like the beginning of an epileptic seizure. Then his head is pushed backwards and his whole body turns rigid and stiff. Now his limbs can neither be bent by the therapist nor by the persons surrounding him, even with the greatest exertion. His pupils are moderately dilated, and react normally to light. His tendon reflexes are inoperative, the reflexes of the soles of his feet function minimally. His abdominal wall is soft.

"The therapist remains in this state of stiffness for about one-half hour. To remain in it longer than 45 minutes would be dangerous for him. He is unable to come out of the stiffened state by himself.

"After the predetermined time, his helper puts some drops of a potion mixed with strong-smelling essences onto his face and on his tongue. Breathing becomes more regular. Arms and legs continue to be completely stiff. And now four strong men go to work. After much trouble and effort, they succeed in bending the therapist's elbows and knees. With that, the spell is broken, the therapist has regained power over his own motor functions, and he sits up, obviously exhausted. He drinks the rest of the potion and takes the egg which he had been *holding with his right foot until now, into his hand. Through the energy of the therapist, the demon now is in this egg. In this exceptional psychic state, through exorcising, singing, and incense burning, the therapist was able to tear the demon from the patient and banish it into the coconut (which was lying on the intersection of the diagonals); from there, through touching, incense smoke, and further exorcistic formulations, it was transferred into the egg. At a pathway branching in three directions, the therapist now throws the egg backwards over his head and it breaks. At this point the demon can escape.*

"This is a simple ritual, which lasts about 3 to 5 hours, including all preparations. In cases where the demon is difficult to exorcise, such a ritual can last for several days. In addition to the patient, the family, the villagers, and the helpers of the therapist take part."

I would like to comment regarding this report: Possession in Sri Lanka apparently is treated separately from other psychic illnesses (neuroses, depression) and is intuitively recognized. As in the Christian churches, angel demons and spirits of ancestors (poor souls) are accused.

The necessary ritual is supported by assistants and many intensively participating persons. Their mental-spiritual potential is urgently needed. Diagnosis and prognosis with the two drops of oil, which behave in different ways in the glass filled with urine, will not be taken seriously by Westerners. But at the beginning of this ceremony, the therapist has already entered a light state of trance in which his clairvoyant and prophetic gifts can act. This influences, by the process of psychokineses, the drops of oil, depending on the mediumistically-received insight. That the healer has to release enormous psychic energy during the state of trance and rigidity is clear as indicated by the danger of transgressing the time limit. These enormous energies force the spirit first into the coconut, which as a refuge symbolizes the womb — though it promises only a false security — and then it is projected into the egg, the symbol of growth and development.

From there it is thrown backward (into the unconscious? into the past?) along the pathway branching in three directions, where according to Ceylonese opinion, it will probably not easily find its way. To place it into another being, as demons often demand during Christian exorcism, would be a dangerous undertaking.

Again, in Christian Scharfetter's words: "There are therapeutic experiences which cannot be achieved by the abilities of Western mediums [because they represent another mental level! (N)], and which often cannot be explained."

10. MEDICAL EXORCISM

Medical Exorcism in Brazil

There are many millions of members and supporters of the Kardec Espiritista persuasion who have established their own clinics and hospitals, in some of which regular physicians are allowed to practice. I visited parapsychological clinics (parapsicologia clinica) in both São Paulo and in Salvador (Bahia). These centers resemble psychological ambulatory counselling centers, but in addition to psychological counselling with which we are familiar, they also use hypnosis as part of their therapy and find that often the personalities of deceased persons, with their specific voices and characteristics, come through.

Hypnosis plays an important role during clinical exorcism.[1] The procedure used strongly reminds one of Dr. Carl Wickland's methods. In a room especially designed for this purpose and painted light blue as is common in institutional rooms, the patient who is considered to be possessed is asked to lie on the floor with his head in the middle of the room. On all three free sides, three healthy persons, gifted as mediums, lie down in the same way, head-to-head, forming a cross. One person, especially, is placed in trance with hypnosis and serves the same functions as Mrs. Wickland did. The two other helpers usually become entranced, too. It is the particular role of the hypnotized person, however, to answer questions by the physician and to react to commands and admonitions in place of the possessed person, whose possessing spirit has transferred into her. Afterward, the possessed person feels calmer and relieved. With regard to definitive success in healing, I have no direct experience, but since this therapy has been used for decades, it can be considered effective. Nevertheless, I doubt whether a comparable procedure could be conducted in middle Europe. Salvador, especially, is a "black" city. The population, with ties to Afro-Brazilian cults, is much more open to the described procedures, and less resistant, also, to possessing spirits.

From a theoretical point of view, this phenomenon is remarkable. The *personalidade intrusa* (intruding personality) is considered a reality and not the fiction of an ancient superstition. A Brazilian physician and head of the clinic, who for a long time previously had been active as a surgeon, is just as accurate and acute an observer and thinker as is his European colleague, except that he is not as dependent on the dogma of philosophical materialism. Eliezer C. Mendes, M.D. is the publisher of three books about clinical parapsychology: *Personalidade intrusa, Personalidade hiperconsciente,* and *Personalidade subconsciente,* which are of great relevance for the subject under consideration here.

---

[1] Eliezer C. Mendes, M.D., *Personalidade intrusa,* p. 68.

Each continent has its own actualities and realities. They form a spectrum corresponding to the totality of the world only when they are viewed together — mindful that viewing concepts of other cultures as biased and primitive often reveals a limitation imposed on one's own beliefs.

The Author's Method

Exorcism can be performed in medical practice only under certain preconditions. The first condition is to learn as much as possible of the anamnesis (prior history) of the actual disturbance as well as the personality structure of the individual to be exorcised. The patient must possess critical judgment and self-discipline. Consent and preparedness for the exorcism is important.

For younger persons, the consent of at least one parent, and for married persons, the consent of the partner is required. If at all possible, the mother or partner should be present during the exorcism. Close friends and/or relatives of unmarried patients are also welcome, since the mediumistic potential of third persons is helpful.

The nature of possession as well as exorcism has to be explained thoroughly to the person suspected of being possessed, harassed or infested. It is best to counteract remnants of rationalistic attitudes, but this is often unnecessary because the person who believes him/herself to be possessed or bewitched has already, at least partially, cast philosophical rationalism aside.

The physician should point out the importance of a regulated and meaningful life, and concentration on individual positive spiritual values and their enhancement, even if this requires sacrifices. The person to be exorcised must fight against hatred toward imagined or actual adversaries and forgive and pray for them, which is often especially difficult.

An honorarium should be accepted by the physician only in the case of prolonged concomitant psychotherapy and then only in the form of modest charges. In special cases, i.e. with distrustful persons who suspect the therapist of greediness, it is best to waive all fees.

The physician should not conduct more than two, or at the most three exorcisms per day. Ten within one week are too many. Exorcism not only requires extreme concentration, but also demands a considerable expenditure of ethereal energy. For every exorcism, the necessary amount of time has to be provided. It must not be impaired by the pressure of waiting patients. Although I am a non-Catholic, I use holy water which I know has been blessed by a responsible priest, and this also applies to the lighted candle which I use. An icon of archangel Michael, which was given me by an ethical, respected woman, is placed in view of the person to be exorcised. Archangel Michael, the dragon slayer, is the archetype of good *par excellence,* upsetting to the demonic.

The person to be exorcised should be seated comfortably in an easy chair to compose him/herself for a few moments. He/she should then join in saying the Lord's prayer, especially the concluding: "For thine is the kingdom and the power and the glory, forever and ever. Amen," which must be spoken with special devotion. Genuinely possessed persons find this especially difficult.

I then hold my hands over the patient's head and move them around toward the sides, always at a distance of a few centimeters. The radiation of warmth is thereby clearly felt. Then I point the left middle finger at the seventh chakra (Sahasrara Chakra) in the area of the former fontanel, and at the same time the right middle finger at the sixth chakra (Ajna Chakra), slightly above the base of the nose. I do this for about half a minute. At this point, the person to be exorcised, if he/she has mediumistic abilities, will often see colors. The biomagnetic radiation emanates most strongly from the tips of the middle fingers.

The actual exorcistic adjuration then takes place, not by using a rigid formula, but slightly varied in accordance with each psychological situation:

"In the name of the Father, the Son, and the Holy Ghost, I give thee a protective mantle against all harmful powers and forces which act internally and externally, and I give thee the energy to be thyself again so that thou canst reach and accomplish the goals given thee by God. And I ask thee, Archangel Michael, to come with thy godly assembly and thou, too, personal guardian spirit, I ask thee to take over this sphere [the spiritual sphere of the head] fully and completely so that thou harmful forces and powers must yield — whoever and of which kind thou may be. If thou art deceased, and have not become aware of thy transition from the material to the non-corporeal world, know this: according to the understanding valid here, thou art dead and do not possess a material body. Thou art clinging to a spirit still dwelling in a body and are disturbing this person. Thou must evolve into a new but only spiritual sphere. Let one of the angels of Michael guide thee to where thou wilt receive instruction and salvation. If thou art of demonic nature, know this: thou too art a creation of the Almighty. When the purpose given thee has been fulfilled, namely to teach to human beings the difference between Good and Evil, by His grace thou too wilt return into the harmony whence thou camest. But thou must obey his orders. Let him show thee the place to where thou must go." [Similar soothing words are also used during exorcistic rites in Zen Buddhism, since otherwise, according to Dr. Hiroshi Motoyama (a Shinto priest in Japan), the spirits will immediately look for a new victim]. *"Do not lose time, thou hast no business here any longer because this human being belongs to the good — belongs to Jesus Christ"* [which women, especially, want to hear (N.)].

Then the actual exorcism follows, using determined and strong words: *"Now I command thee, disappear, yield, leave, in the name of the Father, the Son and the Holy Ghost."* The right hand performs the sign of the cross three times over the head of the person being exorcised. The hands are held over and around his head for a short time longer, and at the end, a gesture of a flowing out of the head in all directions is performed.

As during biomagnetic treatments by a healer, the exorcist should shake his hands, in order to get rid of bad alien fluid forces. I shake my hands toward the flame of the blessed candle.

A short prayer of thanks, especially with religious persons, may end the exorcism. Often we are told that the exorcised person feels much calmer afterwards. As with the exorcism in church, the medical exorcism may also have to be repeated many times.

Where it is not clear that we are dealing with beings of the transcendental world, or just an unhealthy psychic development as in schizophrenia, I request the positive spirits of St. Michael and his angels who have been called upon, as well as the guardian angel of this sick person, to help me by using the following:

> *"Help me increase the radiation of this person's aura. May it shine in harmonic colors and radiate through the whole body. May the aura increase its absorption of all positive forces and be impermeable to everything bad. May this occur in the name of the Father, the Son and the Holy Ghost."*

Dr. Carl Wickland's Method

The research by the American psychiatrist Carl A. Wickland, M.D. and his mediumistic wife Anna,[2] made a significant contribution to the understanding of possession. Wickland succeeded in clearly identifying possessing spirits as deceased persons, and it was possible through his method to transfer such entities, for a short time, into the body and mind of Anna Wickland. The author expressly emphasized that he had received permission for this procedure by positive transcendent spirits who expressed the wish to work with him.

Wickland's method demonstrates convincingly that many deceased entities are not aware of their death. This is the case when, due to their rationalistic belief, they had not believed in a life after death, especially when they had died a sudden death. When, in addition, these deceased persons, due to intense interest in their earthly activities or having been in various affective states, such as hate, jealousy, avarice and other passions, are tied to particular persons or a particular place, they remain in a sphere near the earth and wander around restlessly as "poor souls."

Such spirits, according to their own statements through Mrs. Wickland, would feel particularly attracted by the bright biomagnetic aura of a human, of whom they — often in large numbers — would take possession.

Mediumistically-gifted persons, according to Wickland, possess an intensely bright aura and are especially vulnerable. However, it is possible — in fact, it seems probable — that mediums with strong egos are less vulnerable. [N.]

Wickland, who worked as a physician in a psychiatric clinic, was given the information through his clairvoyant wife that an electric apparatus using direct current with its soft electric shocks, would not cause damage to the patient but would feel extremely unpleasant to the spirits and would facilitate

---

[2] Carl Wickland, *Thirty Years Among the Dead; Dreißig Jahre unter Toten* (Remagen: Otto Reichl Verlag). (Originally published in English in 1924. Reprinted by Spiritualist Press, London, 1978. Also a shortened version by Amherst Press, Amherst, Wisconsin).

their temporary transference into Mrs. Wickland. The question arises here whether, when other therapies are unsuccessful, electroshock treatment (which still is employed by some practitioners) may be successful at times because the possessing spirit is thereby driven out. For the patient, electroshock treatment using a strong current is dangerous, because it may lead to later disturbances of memory; and moreover, since the spirit does not receive an explanation during the treatment, it is likely to attack (i.e. possess) another suitable person. From the viewpoint of someone versed in esoteric matters, such treatment is unacceptable.

With the apparatus recommended by spirits (an electrostatic generator) Wickland's method made possible the transfer of possessing spirits from the patient into the body and psyche of the physician's wife for a short time, and permitted a contact with them via the vocal apparatus of Mrs. Wickland. The dialogues between physician and the spirits are very revealing; the book is definitely worth reading. It is also worth noting that these exorcistic efforts, unlike the Christian exorcisms which use imperative language, consist of friendly counselling. I have used similar counselling in my own clinical practice. Dr. Wickland did not always achieve success, but he was able to heal a considerable percentage of his patients. It was surprising to me that Carl Wickland never spoke about angel demons. He recognized malevolent possessing spirits, but many were merely described as *ignorant or beings burdened with the usual human imperfections.* Primitive deceased entities, in Wickland's opinion, cannot free themselves of illness and pain, and they burden the possessed host-souls with physical suffering. Suicidal persons are often seized by spirits of persons who previously committed suicide and have not yet realized that their attempt succeeded. It has to be added here, however, that spirits usually superpose the psyche of a human who has a similar character structure. The melancholic character of a person seized in such way can then be pushed to suicide attempts which were not entirely self-chosen.

Wickland experienced, just as did Van Dusen (see next section) — and this seems to be a sign of primitive deceased people — their senseless repetition of sentences, which we can observe in catatonic mentally ill people as "perseveration." *It appears to be most difficult, however, to produce insight in religious fanatics. Even in the world beyond, according to Swedenborg's experience as a medium, they exist in constant dispute with those of different beliefs.*

Independent of Wickland, and probably without knowledge of his activities, the psychiatrist Titus Bull[3] had the same experiences at about the same time. Bull also worked with excellent mediums who transmitted to him messages from deceased people he knew.

The observations of Wickland and Bull — though shared by only a few researchers — deserve serious attention. They provide a real insight into some areas of life after death. As genuine and conscientious researchers, Wickland, Titus Bull and Van Dusen profess to insights which are rejected by most

---

[3] Titus Bull, psychiatrist, born 1871. Graduated from Belleview Hospital Medical College, New York City. Wrote a monograph "Analysis of Unusual Experiences in Healing Relative to Diseased Minds and Results of Materialism Foreshadowed."

contemporary thinkers. In the not-too-distant future they may well be recognized as pioneers.

Observations by Wilson Van Dusen, PhD[4]

After many years of working as a psychotherapist in a supervisory capacity at a State Mental Hospital in California, Wilson Van Dusen discovered that it was possible to speak with spirits "hallucinated" by patients. This was only possible, however, when the patient was capable of differentiating between his own thoughts and the ones heard and seen in his "hallucinatory" environment. Various obstacles, easily understandable, impaired such a conversation, and — according to Van Dusen — often, not only the patients but also the spirits manifesting themselves needed explanations and comfort.

The patient was asked to report, word for word, what the voices, namely the spirits, were responding to Van Dusen's questions. For him, these voices became objective reality, and he ended up in long conversations the content and meaning of which the patients themselves often did not understand. The response often concerned highly symbolic expressions on the part of the voices, in which Van Dusen believed he recognized a "higher order" and a positive nature. The patients, too, had the opinion that they had had contact with another order of beings, which they experienced as "living entities." Most of these patients were suddenly overcome by these entities (voices), which then tenaciously maintained their occupancy.

Van Dusen also recognized spirits of a "lower order" which always tried to produce destructive effects. They would torture their victims with filthy, often sexual rudeness, and would give ridiculous orders, like "lift your right arm high in the air and remain that way!" [Who would not be reminded of the catatonic positions of patients categorized as schizophrenic which show no signs of fatigue in rigid postures. (N.)] The range of vocabulary and imagination of these spirits is reported to be very restricted and primitive. They would lie [deceitful spirits (N.)], but had no identity, although they would take on a name and a personality, which the patient would give them. They were either without religion or opposed to it. Mostly they would appear to the disturbed patients as rather ordinary humans, but in one case they had described themselves as "demons from hell."

Van Dusen reports further:

> "voices of the 'higher order' represent only a fifth of my experiences. In a certain case, such a voice replaced the one of a 'lower order.' Such beings (the voices representing a 'higher order'), respected the freedom of the seized patient; they used symbols, were encouraging and corresponded to Jung's archetypes [as we can observe within the so-called 'great dreams' of depth analysis (N.)]. The ones of the 'lower order' approximated the level of the 'Id' of Freud's theories. The 'higher order' itself indicated that the purpose of the 'lower order' was

---

[4] Wilson van Dusen, author of *The Depths of Man* (1972) and *The Presence of Other Worlds* (1974), both published by Harper & Row, New York.

to bring to consciousness the weaknesses and mistakes of the seized person."

Here too, we recognize the evolution of humanity intended by the creative spirit, guaranteed only by the polarities of good and evil.

In Van Dusen's conclusions, he points to the impressive conformity of his findings with reports of possession in the bible. Even the simple mention of religion caused mockery and derision in the "lower order," while the "higher order" had to be described as sensitive, wise and religious. He was dealing with the polarities of good and evil.

What most fascinated Van Dusen, however, was the similarity of his experiences with the teachings of the great Swedish scientist and visionary Emanuel Swedenborg. Van Dusen especially mentions the following quotes by Swedenborg: "In the average person, spirits are assigned to his mind or, which is essentially the same, to the more unconscious levels of his mind of which he is not aware. They filter into his emotions, i.e., into the fertile soil of his thinking. The spirits are in the unconscious and they live there according to their needs in a way which appears to the person to be the origin of his thoughts and emotions. Under normal conditions the person does not know of their activities but attributes everything to his own thought and perception. But the spirits also have no feeling of being part of the life of a person. Parallel to the experiences of the person, they have corresponding spiritual experiences. They do not hear or see the world of the person. These spirits, placed at the disposal of the person, have inclinations similar to his.[5] "Soul, mind, or inner human being are basically the same things."[6]

Swedenborg is of the opinion, always valid for the Christian church, that God, in addition to the spiritual, created a material parallel world, whereby the first is seen as causative and primary.

With regard to the hallucinations he observed, Van Dusen sees a close connection with Swedenborg's ideas described by the headings *obsessio* (imprisoned by false ideas) and *possessio* (possession by alien spirits, which have an effect on thought, emotions and even physical activities of humans. The Swedish visionary emphasized that these spirit beings are normally separated from human awareness by a barrier. This barrier to awareness is broken when the person withdraws from the world of social usefulness into inner fantasies and arrogance, which comes fairly close to contemporary views on causes of schizophrenic illnesses. Lack of love and emotional coldness are also always part of the picture. Only then would negative spirits operate against the will of the patient, whereby they behave exceptionally verbose, persistent, aggressive, malicious and deceitful. Swedenborg points out that if voices represented only the "emerging unconscious" of a patient, it would not make sense that they express themselves either for or against religion. Nevertheless, one can count on their vehement rejection of religion.

---

[5] Swedenborg, *Erklärte Offenbarung Johannis,* ["The Revelations of St. John"].

[6] Swedenborg, *Himmlische Geheimnisse im Worte Gottes* ["Heavenly Secrets in the Word of God"].

This observation deserves attention. A person's unconscious is not necessarily connected with his conscious attitudes. Moreover, a massive conscious opposition to religion generates, according to my years of experience, a counter-reaction in the unconscious. Thus, when "voices" behave in a contrary way, this more likely indicates a possession by other entities rather than an uninhibited expression of personal inner tendencies.

Van Dusen's observations concerning spirits of a "lower order" coincide, to a large degree, with my experiences with harassed persons, who are accosted day and night by these spirits which often quarrel with each other, thus rendering unacceptable the hypothesis that this is only the theatrical representation of the personal unconscious. What is especially difficult for those of us doing contemporary research is to find a clear differentiation between *possessio* and clinical schizophrenia. Swedenborg believed that all humans are possessed by spirits, but that these are usually in conformity with the goals and inherited characteristics of the person they possess. Thus, they do not disturb the harmony of life.

Using contemporary terminology, we could describe the circumstances as follows: The negative spirit forces exist principally within the human soul in a polar opposition to the positive forces necessary for development, and which does not lead to external disharmonies. But if a person possesses only a weak ego which does not guarantee self-control, his egocentric- egoistic tendencies can lead to boundless overestimation of his personality, an ego-inflation. This leads to the suspension of all appropriate references to reality. The harmonious interaction between the polarities is lost. It would be conceivable that in persons gifted as mediums, the spirits of deceased persons may have been attracted beforehand (Wickland), or angel demons even superposed the personal mental frequency potential because of a weak ego. This would correspond to the symptomatology of the contemporary concept of schizophrenia. There would then be no fundamental difference between schizophrenia and possession. On the other hand, there are gradual differences in the form and extent of the phenomenon. It should be emphasized that the term "hallucinations," as used in psychiatry and also by Van Dusen, is not an accurate characterization in these cases. "Hallucination" describes the perception of events by a mentally ill person. They have no realistic foundation, but at most are immaterial and unreal mental perceptions. In contrast, I would like to point out that, just as for the phenomenon of "voices," which are not perceived in the anatomical but rather the ethereal center of hearing, something similar operates in the recognition of the aura of another person by those gifted as mediums. The aura is not experienced through the anatomical center of vision but through a perception of ethereal realities by the medium. This is no more a hallucination than is the hearing of voices. The recognition of the *corpus subtile* (Paracelsus) as a reality is naturally the prerequisite which is indispensible for the interpretation of many parapsychological factors.

The congruency of Swedenborg's opinions, as well as Van Dusen's observations, with contemporary attempts to explain schizophrenic personality development, is striking. Only the philosophical background is different. Ethereal beings, and even ethereal representations of the anatomy of the human body, are unfamiliar to the natural scientist since they only can be experienced and not proven. They were not unfamiliar to Paracelsus or the great natural philosophers Goethe, Carus, Driesch, Klages, and many others, and in my opinion their views will have a more important role in the years to come.

II. The Case History of Gottliebin Dittus in Moettlingen

(Reported by Pastor Blumhardt, Zürich, S. Höhr, 1882)

The Course of Events

One of the most informative cases of possession described by the minister J. C. Blumhardt (1805-1880) is the case history of Gottliebin Dittus (1815-1873).[1]

Nowhere else have deep seated human guilt, magic, the appearance of spooks, the demonic and possession melded into a whole as impressive as in Blumhardt's report. In that report, it becomes evident that the phenomenon of possession is not only a problem of inner mental activities of the individual, but it is also connected to the influences of transcendental entities (beings). Likewise, the phenomenology of the manifestations points towards something more than four-dimensional events, since materializations and apport[2] phenomena — the latter only understandable as de- and re-materialization of objects — cannot be explained causally according to *classical* physics. They belong to the realm of the occult, which is subject to causality by analogy.

Only the essentials of this case of possession will be described here. Gottliebin Dittus, born in 1815 in the Swabian locality of Möttlingen, had already experienced spook-like phenomena in early childhood, which, according to Blumhardt, can be explained by *magical influences*. Pastor Blumhardt believed them to be "magic" by transcendental beings which had injected themselves into the mother-child relationship.

Following the early death of her mother, the girl was cared for by a cousin who was described as evil and suspected of sorcery. The cousin had expressed her intention to introduce her foster child into the art of magic at age 10, but died before that time.

Dittus grew to be a loyal, dependable and honorable maid, until the year 1840, when she and her three siblings moved into a shabby first floor apartment. Two years before, a woman in bad repute, who had previously unburdened herself through a partial confession to Pastor Blumhardt, had died in this place. Shortly after her move in 1840, Gottliebin and her siblings heard nightly shuffling and knocking. Dittus also saw the figure of the woman who had died two years before, carrying a dead child in her arms, and who would often repeat the words: "I want to have peace" or "give me a paper and I won't come back." I would interpret the latter wish by noting that an object of the still- innocent Gottliebin would have provided the unhappy spirit

---

[1] Blumhardt's role in this case is discussed in *The Gift is Already Yours,* by Erwin Prange (Plainfield, New Jersey: Logus International, 1973), pp. 88-95.

[2] *apport* — various objects materialized in the presence of a medium.

being with positive magical powers.[3] According to Blumhardt's report, the deceased sought all means in order to avoid "satanic" entanglement.

Once Blumhardt asked a friend to sleep overnight at the home of Gottliebin. She also noticed apparitions. Led by a shimmer of light, other witnesses discovered under the threshold of the door to the room, a sooty piece of paper, covered with illegible writing, suspected of being a recipe of a secret art. Next to it they found a number of different coins.

Another time, Pastor Blumhardt was present himself when several persons of unimpeachable reputation followed the noise and searched the floor boards which were the target of the mysterious knocking. While touching them, all persons present saw the flare-up of a small flame.[4] There they found, again wrapped in paper, a small amount of powder, a little sack of money and a pot containing bones which, on examination, turned out to be bones of birds, presumably ravens. Such bones were often used, in those times, for certain magical effects. Despite the removal of all these objects which, as one was inclined to assume, were causing the haunting, all phenomena increased in intensity and were also, in addition to other apparitions, observed by a physician who stayed overnight in this house for two days. Several council members arrived at the same conclusion. They noticed that the knocking resembled invisible blows, the furniture shook and the glass panes rattled.

Gottliebin was then moved to other quarters. Yet, in spite of it, the knocking was heard until the year 1844, and continued in the new dwelling. She herself began suffering from severe convulsions. Pastor Blumhardt, who clearly recognized the demonic influences on the events, then began pastoral counselling. Through fervent prayer and laying on of hands, Blumhardt tried to dispel the possessing entities, which only produced resistance. At the invocation of the name of Jesus, a rude voice announced from the mouth of the possessed: "I can't stand that name." The same voice admitted not being able to find rest, because of the murder of two little children buried in a field. He accused himself of sorcery and being in the grip of the "most wicked of all," namely, the devil. The entity possessing the girl vanished temporarily, but always returned.

One night Gottliebin suddenly was grabbed by a burning hand, which left burns on her body. In hypnotic experiments "burn blisters" can be caused to appear under the skin, which can be explained as a reaction of hysteria. But burning and charring of the top layer of the skin never take place in such instances, and collections of lymph under the skin produced by hypnotic experiments disappear rapidly. At a later time in the history of the suffering of Gottliebin, her throat was burned from the inside, and was painful for a

---

[3] We find similar themes in Peter Gehring's book *Eugenie von der Leyen: Meine Gespräche mit Armen Seelen* ["My Conversations With Poor Souls"], p. 58: "Adelgunde, The Child Murderer." Eugenie asks the spirit of the child murderer: "How can I help you?" The spirit: "Give me your hand!"

[4] Compare Haraldur Nielsson (Full Professor of Theology in Rejkjavik): *Eigene Erlebnisse auf dem okkulten Gebiet* ["Own Experiences in the Realm of the Occult"] (Leipzig: Oswald Mutze, 1922), p. 16: "The light phenomena began as tongues of light with bluish-red coloration." (During mediumistic sessions with Indridi Indridason, spirits had materialized and declared themselves through voices, luminosity and many other para-phenomena).

long time thereafter. As a paranormal parallel, the phenomenon of bibles and cloths branded by demonic hands should be considered.[5]

The entities expressed themselves through the mouth of Gottliebin — as in other cases of possession — in many different languages, including some which none of those present could understand. Voices belonging to a "higher region" (Blumhardt), with quotes from the Old Testament (Habakkuk and Jeremiah), also made themselves heard through Gottliebin while she was in a state of trance. This must be evaluated as an indication of a bipolar ethical event. Van Dusen has reported the occurrence of rare but genuine voices which are of spirit beings of a higher order (positive nature) than those of spirit beings of lower rank, manifesting in the same person.

As the case developed, the symptoms of possession shifted more and more into the body of Gottliebin. Who would not be reminded of the drama of Job, in which God's challenger, after the first unsuccessful attempt, and then later, in agreement with Jehovah, attacks Job's body? Blumhardt describes an unusual bloating of the body, after which Dittus vomited buckets of water, the origin of which the physician present could not explain. In addition, unimaginable amounts of blood flowed from body openings and gushed from a point high in the middle of her head, at a place where, in the presence of Blumhardt, a crooked nail worked its way out. In spite of the enormous amount of blood loss Dittus felt better and stronger after a relatively short time. Since the discharged blood, according to the evidence provided by the consulting physician Dr. Sp., produced a very strong odor and had a dark color, we are brought to considering the phenomenon as paranormally apported or materialized blood. The same applies to the unusual amount of vomited liquid. Otherwise, the quick recovery after the loss of blood could not be explained. Blumhardt thought of a dissolution of the atomic structures, which would explain the temporary invisibility (dematerialization of the liquids named). This would be similar to the Tantric-Indian conception of a waning density of matter within individual planes of being.

Gottliebin assumed that food influenced by black magic caused her physical changes, because once, when she threw the remainder of a meal to a chicken, it immediately began racing around and then, showing symptoms of suffocation, fell dead. In the throat of the chicken a large number of shoe nails were found. Here also, apport phenomena or direct materialization appear to be involved.

The repeated emission of crooked, rusty nails, pins, sewing needles and pieces of iron must be clearly designated as paranormal. This occurred from the tongue, jaw, base of the nose, and the eyes. They appeared to have worked their way from the inside to the outside, as if directed by a mysterious being, whereby the skin — physiologically explicable — produced considerable resistance. Blumhardt, with the help of his wife, frequently had to intervene. Once, two long pieces of wire, bent many times, were imbedded around the

---

[5] Professor Dr. Georg Siegmund: "Das Phänomen der eingebrannten Hände" ["The Phenomenon of Branding in the Shape of Hands"] *Allgemeine Zeitschrift für Parapsychologie* (Hamburg, 6. Jahrgang, Heft 3, Sept. '81).

whole body under the skin, "and I and my wife needed to work a whole hour until they were out, and more than once Gottliebin fainted. . . ." Sand,[6] pieces of glass, big shoe-buckles and broad pieces of iron were vomited, during which time the girl lay for a number of minutes as though dead. Not infrequently, knitting needles, often in large numbers, bound together with paper and feathers, pushed their way out of the pharynx. Finger length knitting needles came out of the ear. Unbroken knitting needles rotated under the scalp in a manner which could be felt and heard, worked their way into the throat and were extruded there. All these represented only a modest list of paranormal occurrences which Blumhardt experienced, always in the presence of witnesses, over a number of months.

Although persons suffering from hysteria often swallow objects, or put them into the vagina, this is not comparable to the occurrences described in the case of Gottliebin; they surpass every human capacity. There remains no other explanation than paranormal materialization or apport phenomena. Whoever has had the occasion to observe how Philippine psychic surgeons remove bloody egg shells, coins and other objects from the interior of the body, will recognize the analogy.

Although Blumhardt's report seems incredible and bizarre, it should not be automatically dismissed; photography and tape recorders had not yet been developed to record the phenomena. In recent years, similar, although not as extreme, phenomena have been recorded.

Until Christmas time in 1843, Blumhardt was involved in a struggle which seemed endless, but he relied on his unshakable faith. Once, Gottliebin, while only half conscious, attempted to make an opening in her torso for a passageway for a needle which was moving painfully and independently outward. With a knife, she frantically probed through her abdomen, hit the stomach, and food she had eaten shortly before emerged from the wound. The consulting physician confirmed this. Later the wounds tore open again, and Blumhardt was urgently called. But he prayed intensively at home and asked Gottliebin to come to his house, "which was made possible through her faith." And this wound, too, healed within a few days without complications.

The modern physician would hardly take these occurrences seriously, because under normal circumstances such injuries would have undoubtedly led to the most serious peritonitis (inflammation of the peritoneum). But Gottliebin was placed in an extraordinary spiritual condition, which affected matter and organs in a completely different way. I own a film in which Arigò, a famous psychic surgeon of Brazil (during the 1960's and early 1970's), can be seen poking around in the eye with an unsterilized kitchen knife. This is attested to by Dr. Andrija Puharich. It does not lead to an infection but to the healing of the eye. In the year 1977 I visited the Mexican healer, Pachita, who, with a kind of butcher knife, poked around in the kidney areas of a female patient, which led to extensive bleeding. Two years later, the physicist

---

[6] In the magic of Kenya, sand appears to play an important role when a person suffers a deadly spell.

Prof. Livio Vinardi (Buenos Aires), who had also attended the session, told me that the above-described intervention had healed his assistant's kidney disease. However, I can understand why a person who has never witnessed such bizarre phenomena cannot comprehend such occurrences.

In 1843, around Christmas time, a final struggle occurred, which affected the sister, Katharina Dittus, and to a lesser degree the half-blind brother and Gottliebin. In the case of the brother and of Katharina, the possession occurred for the first time. Katharina was driven into a wild rage with the urge to kill. The voice acting through her made himself known as "Angel of Satan" (angel demon).

This unexpected expansion of the area of struggle cannot be easily understood. It is possible that the uninterrupted efforts by Blumhardt may have developed a kind of protective mantle surrounding Gottliebin, which from a psychological point of view would correspond with the concept of increasing ego strength, thereby making it more and more difficult for alien beings to undermine her ego, so the Pastor could expect to triumph.

For the demonic powers a way out remains; namely, to attack and draw into satanic involvement, the siblings who had not yet been "treated" by Blumhardt. Many an exorcist would have allowed himself to be confused and would have feared that Satan's power had extended the field of battle *ad infinitum*. Not so Blumhardt; he remained unshakable and continued with his nondramatic methods of laying on of hands and prayer. Possibly the unpretentious, humble behavior provided the evil with less range for attack than a spectacular exorcism, even though this approach — as we know — can at times be very effective.

Be that as it may — Blumhardt remained victor in the name of Jesus. From the throat of Katharina came the demon's "gruesome shriek of despair," and the possessed was shaken in such a way, as though "all limbs wanted to be shaken apart from each other."

> *"Finally came the most moving moment, which would be impossible for anyone to imagine, who did not see and hear it with his own eyes and ears. At two o'clock in the morning, the girl's head and upper part of her body bent over the back of the chair, and the alleged 'angel of Satan' howled with a voice one could hardly believe to be human: 'Jesus is Victor! Jesus is Victor!' She then became increasingly calm and quiet. This was the end of two years of struggle, which had now come to its final conclusion."*

In the case of the two sisters only inconsequential relapses occurred. Gottliebin was healed from all earlier ailments — even her shorter foot — and she became an understanding and devoted helper in the ministry.

As can be read in the highly recommended book by Dr. Peter Ringgers: *Das Problem der Besessenheit*[7] ("The Problem of Possession"), Gottliebin Dittus married in 1845. She was later — according to a report from the *Apage*

---

[7] *Das Problem der Besessenheit* (Zürich: Verlag Neue Wissenschaft, 1953).

Satana[8] — occasionally bothered by devils, especially two years before her death. Whether this is correct cannot be determined, because no references were given. However, this is not inconceivable when considering the polarity of the human psyche in the realm of *good* and *evil*.

Pastor Blumhardt's Personal Opinions, Compared with Contemporary Viewpoints in Parapsychology.

Pastor Blumhardt's personal opinions are interesting. They stood in such stark contrast to the rising rationalism of those times that they were not taken seriously. From my own experience I know that even today ministers, including those with parapsychological interests, are not able to understand Blumhardt's conclusions about his experiences. If I had not had personal experiences with haunting, psychic surgery, sorcery and possession, I would have felt the same way, even though I am an interested parapsychologist. It is not book knowledge or hearsay, but experiences that shake all of our senses and mental faculties and allow us to become acquainted with the essence of objects and phenomena.

To me, it appears to be significant that Blumhardt apparently did not believe in magic or concrete manifestations by satanic powers before his experiences with Dittus. He gained his later perspective through years of experiencing, probing and thinking.

He even took seriously the ancient notion of a magic-demonic exchange of babies (the changeling phenomenon) into consideration, which at that time was already considered unscientific. Blumhardt wrote:

"G. is able to relate circumstances in her childhood, which indicate snares to weave her into a net of magic. I regret having to mention something anew which, as a rule, should belong to the realm of fairy tales and superstition. I now have no reason to reject these notions. Soon after her birth, she was in danger of being carried off. Her mother, who died 10 years ago, told her often how she had the child next to her in bed, and in her sleep suddenly became afraid for her child. She woke up, could not feel the child and cried out: 'Lord Jesus, my child!' Something fell to the floor near the door of the room, and it was the child. The same thing happened once again in a similar way. The children in whose place the so-called changelings are placed, if there is any reality to this, seem — based on conclusions from other experiences — to be destined to fall into the hands of a sorceress who will introduce them at an early age into the total field of sorcery. Such superstitious sounding ideas never had any meaning for me, and only gained meaning in this case on contemplation of my experiences with G."

---

[8] Jean Baptise Delacour, *Apage Satana* (Geneva: Ariston Verlag, 1975).

These unverifiable reports of the mother and Blumhardt's interpretation gain some meaning with respect to the satanic fight for the possessed at a later time. From the perspective of parapsychology, this is a case of levitation and telekinesis. It appears extremely improbable that the bio-energetic forces necessary for the phenomena originated from the unconscious bio- potential of the mother, as orthodox parapsychologists would explain it. We know nothing about any rejection of the child by the mother. To simply blame the woman's unconscious would be an unprovable and scientifically unacceptable hypothesis.

In my opinion, Gottliebin possessed an unusually high degree of mediumistic ability. Such an ability is innate. An event which supplies proof for this, was reported by Friedrich Zündel.[9] I found this in Peter Ringger's booklet "Das Problem der Besessenheit" ("The Problem of Possession"). It states therein:

> *"In the summer of 1844, when Blumhardt returned from a missionary festival on his way home to Möttlingen, he remembered the well-known song 'Jesus victorious hero of all . . . .' As he, together with another minister and two Möttlinger residents, began singing this song to the melody of 'Holy God, we praise thy name. . . ,'* [10] *it suddenly seemed to us as though hundreds of voices from the nearby woods so powerfully rejoiced with us that the two Möttlingers were so moved, they became silent. But Blumhardt continued to sing vigorously. When he returned home, while greeting his own family, Gottliebin, who also appeared quite moved, told him the verse he had just made up and sung."*

We could interpret in the same way the girl's astral excursions to Far Eastern countries, which were described exquisitely by the uneducated Gottliebin. During one such trip, she became the witness of a demonic-cataclysmic event, the eruption of a volcano, combined with earth- and sea-quakes. Blumhardt was surprised beyond measure when, a short time afterwards, the event perceived by Gottliebin was described identically in the newspapers. We must classify this vision as clairvoyance. According to this description, the hypothesis that clairvoyance may be associated with astral excursions increases in probability.

During her astral excursions Gottliebin also claims to have experienced the damnation, "the plunge into the abyss," of about 1000 demons, among which she recognized many of those which had tortured her before. Subsequent to this vision, Gottliebin did not see any more demons, which she had previously seen before her mental eye, surrounding Pastor Blumhardt during religious service. She interpreted this as their certain destruction.

Because of this clairvoyant experience of Gottliebin, Pastor Blumhardt arrived at the conclusion that his own battle with the demons corresponded

---

[9] F. Zündel, *J. C. Blumhardt,* (Gießen: Brunnen Verlag, 1928).

[10] "Großer Gott wir loben Dich," *Katholisches Gesangbuch,* attr. to Ignaz Franz, 1719-1790, transl. into English by Clarence Walworth, 1820-1900.

with events on a cosmic dimension and in the world in general. He felt encouraged in his opinion by statements made by demons through the mouth of Dittus, who claimed to be responsible for the many city fires during those years. One of the devils identified himself as responsible for the city fire of Hamburg in 1842 and, when asked, claimed to have done it out of lewdness. In those days it was not known that many arsonists act while driven by sexual intentions and thereby experience sensual pleasure. Blumhardt naturally assumed that such a demon was able to force his will on a living person. Also weather catastrophes, the drought in the year 1842, and the wet period in 1843, appeared to Blumhardt to be parallel events to his own battle. In my opinion, this should not be interpreted as ego-inflation. Blumhardt was merely aware that transcendent spiritual impulses produce parallels in the events of the world. Here we again encounter the concept of causality by analogy. The minister describes his opinion further:

> *"It was frightful to listen to the threats of the demons to set the whole place, and particularly my house, on fire. Often they grinned at me with horrible faces: 'Blood or Fire!' It was really striking that in one of the more difficult nights of battle the flock of sheep was attacked by an unknown dog. The shepherd was unable to overpower the dog, which brought fear and confusion to the flock, and the next morning two of the biggest sheep lay ripped apart in front of my window. I only mention this because it was once said: 'Blood, even if only a sheep.' "*

This unusual and singular incident should, indeed, not be ignored. It not only reminds us of the pre-scientific belief in the existence of the werewolf, but also of the experiences of the magic scene in Africa, where demonized fellow humans are able to turn themselves into vicious lions. We designate this phenomenon, described by Ernesto Bozzano, as *Lycanthropy*. Although these are living humans rather than spirits, they too, as the tribal members believe, are possessed by evil powers and are in alliance with them.

Today, parapsychologists recognize that the old dispute between animism and spiritualism is no longer valid, since it is a matter of the expression of bioenergetic forces, and not the physical forces of classical physics. Blumhardt arrived at the strong conviction that all the objects: nails, shoe buckles, pieces of glass, etc., were transferred into Dittus by witchcraft. "Some of it must have been in her for 2 years." Most had to be pulled out of her; among other things, also one living, oversized frog. Grasshoppers and bats flew out of her mouth by themselves, but Blumhardt was only witness to the exiting of a snake, which was clearly visible to Gottliebin. Blumhardt, however, was only able to perceive a beam of light, which, when it came out of the mouth of the possessed, took its route across her bed.

Blumhardt assumed these were deceased people as well as demons, who, with the object, entered the possessed, and which they guarded as a symbol of themselves, until, through Blumhardt's presence and also his prayers in the parsonage, they were compelled to exit. I explain these exiting animals as personified demons. I see support for my explanation in the essay by Andreas

Bänziger[11] about the practice of magic in Kenya. In this essay, Kabwere, a magical healer, reports Genies (spirits) which can take the form of birds.

"The bats, which are hanging from the trees in Kabwere's large court yard, are Genies, and none of the many children would dare to touch any of the bats. Spirits may also appear in the form of cows, sheep and large snakes."

In Europe we must regard bats as useful animals, but we know from personal experience how many sensitive women fear them. As sinister creatures of the night, which silently reach our sphere, their characteristics as well as their form compels us to think of demonic events. The depiction of the devil with bat wings, which appears discordant compared to the wings of birds and butterflies or insects, is widespread. In the teachings of philosophy regarding forms and essences, particular characteristics are attributed to all ethereal and material forms. Personally, I happen to like bats and do not see demons in them, but I could imagine that they are suitable for being seized by demonic spirits. Possibly, negative spiritual beings materialize themselves ethereally in the shape of an animal and are then recognized by the clairvoyant, or they condense themselves to the point where they become visible to everybody. These would be two hypotheses not yet proven by natural science. The possibility of the materialization of spiritual contents is certain — a process which I personally had occasion to experience in India and in the Philippines.

Blumhardt's assumption, that some individual objects which were placed into Gottliebin by witchcraft had remained there a long time, is only comprehensible when we consider that they could only be put into the body in the form of an ethereal substance and remained in this condition for a time. I may be permitted here to describe an event with a psychic surgeon in the Philippines, which I experienced with the parapsychologist Katharina Nager as witness. A young man complained to the healer Rosita del Rosario about terrible pain in his throat. The throat of the ill man was not swollen nor bulging. The healer placed him on a cot and reached for the right side of his throat. She pulled an enormous number of rice hairs out of the intact skin, whereby each hair slightly bulged the skin, just as if it were pulled out against a small resistance. Finally the psychic surgeon held a lump of rice hair, the size of a fist, in her hand. No sign remained visible on the skin. The patient reported that he was freed of pain. Rosita explained to us that the man had not suffered from an infection of the throat, but from "witchwork." Later I was instructed by the reliable psychic surgeon and exorcist, David Olegane, about analogous magic, through which a great variety of objects are transferred into the body of the diseased as ethereal substances, where they remain and cause illness. Only in the moment of exorcism or psychosurgical treatment do they return to material reality.

I would assume that the spiritually powerful clergyman (Blumhardt), through his presence, his caring, and his urgent praying, returned to material

---

[11] *Tages-Anzeiger* (Zürich, Sept. 22, 1981), p.47.

reality the objects — both ethereal and those constellated for the purpose of demonic challenge — which had been brought into the possessed. As we read in Blumhardt's report:

"Since, furthermore, a demon was always, so to speak, a guardian of objects, it so happened that the magic often was only aroused into action by my presence and especially when I felt compelled to pray while I was absent from G. Usually, before or after the removal, a demon emerged."

And at another place, Blumhardt writes:

"Whenever I visited her during this time, called or not called, something moved and after some time a magical piece worked its way out of some part of the body. The pain in each case was so dreadful that she often lost consciousness."

The bitter fight between good (Blumhardt) and evil (the demons) is clearly expressed. The parallel to the psychic surgery of the Philippines, especially the healer performing exorcism, is obvious. On the one hand, we find the patient into whose body, by a magic spell, objects were ethereally placed, and on the other hand, we experience the healer — working with sacred objects, bibles, banners, and an absolute conviction in a positive numen, i.e. in Christ, archangels and apostles — who is chosen to be their instrument. The psychosurgical exorcists, too, emphasize that the magicians complete their works by calling on demonic powers, while as an exorcist, one must fight and overcome only the demonic. They do not pay much attention to the magician, who is merely assured of their pity.[12] Blumhardt observes the connection as follows:

"According to the foregoing, a deceased person and a living person function together to carry out witchcraft. Through the idolatry described earlier, it can of course happen, and unfortunately does happen to a frightful degree, that a human, unknowing and unnoticing, becomes bound by the spirit of Satan in such a way — to be sure, a philosophical riddle — that the spirit can be absent from the body [leaving it together with the astral body (N.)], although the soul — it appears — remains present in the body. Through his spirit he can again be brought to meet and relate with other humans bound in similar fashion, as well as with the deceased who had also more or less bound themselves during their lifetimes [i.e. he can have an effect from a lower spiritual plane close to earth. One thinks of ghosts or of the spirit beings driven out by Wickland (N.)]. The latter are really the ones which practice magic or sorcery, while the former are used for the retrieval of materials. The living must be bound to Satan against their will and serve him with their

---

[12] S. Kap. David Olegane in: *Die Logurgie auf den Philippinen;* also Gert Chesi, *op. cit.*

spirit; they are bound by their inclinations, etc., as well as by shameless cursing, gross carnal sins, etc., as could be learned from several statements by the demons. The purpose for which they are used, however, varies according to the degree of the commission of the sins of idolatry."

From the psychic healers of the Philippines and the picture of magic in Africa and South America, we know that magic is executed with the clear intention of the magician or sorcerer, even though at least a subsequent partial trance helps decisively. Blumhardt assumes that

"the majority of so-called witches or sorcerers who are accused of all sorts of bad luck, illness, and plagues of humans and animals, are as they are, without their own knowledge. They do have a vague feeling of what they do in spirit, but cannot explain this feeling. In any case, they are extremely unhappy people."

The minister probably arrived at this conclusion because he could not imagine how someone would want to use magic intentionally in order to control this unimportant girl. It would hardly have brought any earthly gain. I, too, share this opinion. There is evidence to hypothesize that invisible entities as well as the living (possibly without conscious knowledge) can have a negative or demonic influence. Many such humans, generally considered as evil, are accused by their fellow men who have experienced something puzzling, of using magic intentionally. I know of such cases from my psychiatric practice. Usually they were patients whom I was able to counsel and observe over a long period of time. Thus, I feel entitled to make a judgment. I thereby arrived at the conviction that for all the patients seeking counsel, the effort which would be required for active magical effect would not have been worth it. As for cases of poltergeist phenomena which I personally examined, I can only deduce the existence of transcendent entities which, for their own purposes, use the mediumistic potential of living people who are frequently under tension.

In the case of Gottliebin Dittus, it is notable that living persons were not suspected by Blumhardt and therefore, in our judgment, only the mediumistic powers of the possessed should be taken into account. She, herself, consequently could be considered to be the living partner of demonic deceased persons or angel demons, in whom the fight between good and evil raged. The condition for this would be that her unconscious contained the polarities of good and evil, hints of which are found in the case history. But it must be emphasized that this polarity exists in every human being. It remains unclear, however, why it affected this unassuming girl in such a fundamental way. Possibly, as I pointed out before, the powerful, positive person — the minister himself — as a constellating force field, is responsible, particularly because he was considered the true reviver of Swabian Pietism. We could assume something similar in the case of Jesus, when he saw the devil fall from the sky in a bolt of lightning. Undoubtedly, every prophet and every charismatic person presents a challenge to evil. Additionally, there was the unusual mediumistic ability in the case of Gottliebin, without which — I have learned from many years of experience — it is very difficult for spiritual entities of any kind to manifest themselves in this world.

Whether Blumhardt — combatant in the name of God and challenger of the demonic — or Gottliebin, with her great ability as a medium, played the primary role, cannot be determined. Perhaps both were essential.

Gottliebin already met spirits, such as the child murderer, before Blumhardt's direct involvement. That her kidney and stomach diseases, as well as a physical deformity, should be attributed to the influence of witchcraft, should not be doubted, in view of the fact that this evil disappeared after the final liberation. The actual possession was first observed after the appearance of the child murderer's spirit, when Gottliebin, while saying grace, fell unconscious to the ground in a sudden attack. Before this, the girl appears to have been merely harassed. Before Blumhardt began to intervene actively, she also saw in her imagination not only the child murderer, but also other persons.

Later, spirits encroached upon her in ever-increasing numbers, some even supposedly coming from as far away as America. It is interesting to note how spirits actually took possession of Gottliebin. Blumhardt writes:

"The stories of G. were revealing, describing how at night in her imagination she saw persons of all types and stations come to her bed; while she was lying motionless, they put bread into her mouth and/or touched various other parts of her body. Soon she noticed changes in herself, which corresponded with the objects which later emerged from her. The particular nail and the smaller nail, from which the profuse bleeding had resulted, she believed were placed into her head through special manipulation one evening, by someone in a vestment waiting in the middle of the street, but only seemingly so (i.e. in spirit). She was unable to resist in the least and soon the bleeding began. One night, in this same way (as spirits), three men stood before her holding a poisonous essence. Again she was unable to move. One opened her mouth, the other held her head, and the third wanted to pour in the essence. A little of it went in, and her jaws were now pressed together in order to suffocate her; but the fumes of it went out through her nose and she, able to sigh, was thus saved. When the men noticed that they had not accomplished anything, they emptied the glass over her head and left. In the morning her nightcap was eaten away by a yellowish, ugly-smelling substance and was easily crumbled."

Understandably, a description such as the one above would not be given serious consideration by the person oriented to natural science. The same applies to reports of 1840 when, either by magic or demonic influence, materializations and also de-materializations, in the form of coins and flour occurred. Gottliebin, living in poverty, ate the flour, "whereby she eased the way for demonic events to happen in her body," Blumhardt believes. Today, when we have observed materialization and de- materialization, and witnessed resistance to fire (fire-walking, etc.), on film, such reports can no longer be so easily dismissed as fantasy or hysteria.

Blumhardt considered demonic and divine influences to exist in close connection and reference to one another. This is particularly obvious from the descriptions of one of Gottliebin's suicide attempts, which were always made during a trance.

"After many months of drought, it was in the evening of the day when the first thunder clouds appeared in the sky; I will never forget the day. While the patient walked past the front door of her cousin's house at six p.m., she was attacked, as she described it, by the forms, and began to bleed profusely. In order to change, she hurried back to her own home, and there, while sitting on a chair, it seemed to her that she unceasingly had to swallow something, which in a few moments completely upset her. She raced through both of the rooms and passionately demanded a knife, which her frightened siblings denied her. Then she quickly went to the loft, jumped onto the window sill and was already hanging out into free space, only one hand holding on inside, when the first bolt of lightning of the approaching thunderstorm struck, which startled and woke her. She came to her senses and cried, 'for God's sake, I do not want this!' The moment of clarity vanished, and in the returning delirium she grabbed a rope (from whence it came she cannot explain to this very day) and tied it skillfully around the beams of the loft with a loop which could easily tighten. She had already managed to stick her head almost completely through the loop when a second lightning bolt seen through the window struck her eyes and again brought her back to consciousness. The next morning, tears streamed from her eyes when she saw the rope on the beam, which, even during moments of clearest awareness, she would not have been able to tie together so skillfully. She now remained slightly aware and crept, exhausted from the bleeding described earlier, the short way to her cousin's house. To mount the stairs to her loft room was all she could muster. Once in her bed she sank into unconsciousness. I was called, after the thunderstorm had already begun, at about eight in the evening. I found her flooded with blood, which was seeping through the garments of her upper body. The first comforting word which I called out to her resulted in her waking up a little and crying: 'Oh, the forms!'."

Regarding this report, C. G. Jung would probably think of synchronism. However, the event contains strict causality in a theological sense, the intervention of the good after provocation by the demonic. This made the advocate of God aware that he not only was called to a dualistic confrontation, but that he was drawn into a much wider — a cosmic — dimension.

There are parallels to events like the lightning bolts, which decisively intervened in Gottliebin's attempts at suicide and can be viewed as transcendental effect on the material world. From the New Testament, we know of the thunderstorm at the death of Jesus, as well as of the fundamental release of psychoplastic phenomena in the temple, when stones burst and the veil of the temple was torn.

A significant phenomenon took place after the death of C. G. Jung.[13] A short time after his death, a localized thunderstorm gathered. A lightning bolt struck the great psychologist's beloved tree, but did not destroy it. Only one strong branch was severed from the trunk and fell exactly onto the table at which Jung loved to work when outside. It would require much courage to consider all this a game of the proverbial Chance.

Blumhardt's testimony makes clear how much his concept of and attitude toward the world changed during his struggle with the possessed. He experienced this conflict; we, living today, can only accept his story, as a description of events which very few of us can connect with parallels in our own lives. Thus we meet with incomprehension, doubt and disbelief, which is very understandable. Whatever appears for the first time in our world of perception appears strange and unreal. Only the person who has experienced something similar and who has thoroughly familiarized himself with the literature about possession will be able to follow Blumhardt's final spiritual conclusions. He will be confronted with a concept of the world which someone who thinks in terms of natural science cannot share. This becomes evident in the following section.

The Case History of Gottliebin Dittus from the Viewpoint of Contemporary Psychiatry

Ever since natural scientific thinking has attempted to explain all forms of expression of the human soul within a framework of cause and effect in the sense of Newtonian physics, psychologists and psychiatrists have also ignored the primary influences on the human being within a framework of magical causality. Subjective experiences (i.e. experiences which cannot be objectified), hallucinations or illogical opinions are considered misregulations of the intra-cranial brain chemistry or an affective misinterpretation and wrong processing of experiences, especially those of childhood.

Today, from the impression obtained from the paranormal voices phenomena (which in my opinion can be thought of as electromagnetic psychoplastic phenomena by transcendent beings) it can not be assumed *a priori* that each auditory perception which cannot be objectified has the characteristics of a delusion. The possibility of a true perception in the *ethereal* body should not be excluded because detecting instruments are lacking. Although the *corpus subtile* cannot be integrated into our predominate concept of space and time (nor can the existence of transcendental ethereal spirits be integrated into that system), real influence on the *ethereal* auditory center should at least be discussed. Since this would be equivalent to an extensive critique of the concepts of modern psychiatry, adaptation and change of the interpretative system within the academic branches of psychiatry probably will not take place for decades.

---

[13] Personal ocumentation from Jung's son, the architect Franz Jung.

Benedetti's Observations

Twenty years ago this perspective would have been impossible; however, in 1960, the well-known psychiatrist Prof. Gaetano Benedetti, Basel, Switzerland, wrote an excellent paper on the case history of Gottliebin Dittus, as described by Blumhardt. The paper stands out not only in a formal sense but also reflects a profound humanitarian commitment and candid opinions. According to currently valid psychiatric theories, his paper represents a psychological masterpiece. It is also clear that the author is neither an atheist nor does he reject all transcendence.

We need to consider the following clarification by Benedetti:

> *"This paper is not written with the intention of investigating Blumhardt's well-known case history from the viewpoint of modern clinical-diagnostic methods, in order to capture the medical character of the illness. Rather, its intention is to clarify the therapeutic and existential structure of phases through which this case history moved and by which healing was accomplished. It investigates the relationship which connected these two persons, Blumhardt and his patient, for about two years; and its intention is to explain the nature of the process of healing with this relationship as its background."*

Nevertheless, Benedetti is unable to avoid diagnostic formulations of academic psychiatry. These are also essential for the comparison of academic psychiatry and parapsychology so that they must be referred to in the following elaboration.

Benedetti at least suspects a magical causality, and in this way he proves to be a thoroughly independent thinker. He writes:

> *"Therefore, the history of Gottliebin's illness at times takes on symbolic aspects of an event which not only affects Gottliebin but also, to a degree, the world: earthquakes and conflagrations are brought into relationship with the illness and explained as influenced by those demons (forces) which Blumhardt encountered through Gottliebin. A rationalistic mentality would find cause to smile about the unrealistic naivete of such parallels, and believe that one sees here clearly, how faith distorts reality. But if we recognize in supranatural events, the contemporary pictures of an experience of deepest spiritual participation, then our eyes will open to the psychotherapeutic reality which is brought about, and which deeply appeals to us in spite of its mythological raiment. The case history of Gottliebin, for Blumhardt, is like the history of mankind, which, like the deterioration of the diseased, is threatened by destruction, but liberated and renewed through faith in God. Such a story has cosmic dimensions; it concerns the world, because it concerns the totality of the soul. Today we understand events within us only in lonely self-discovery; but at the beginning of the scientific era, man often still projected internal experiences of his soul onto nature and world events. Nature, earthquakes and conflagrations reflected the internal tremors —*

the lighter and darker aspects of the soul. The concept of the world was not yet scientific."

With regard to the projection onto nature and world events, Benedetti neglects to see the reality of the synchronistic event. The lightning, for example, which struck at a critical moment when the girl, in a state of trance, tried to commit suicide, and which brought her back to consciousness, was part of a thunderstorm most memorable for all Möttlingers. There is no reason to interpret it as an intra-psychic hallucinatory event, but for a system of thought based on natural science, there is no other choice. For him, the same explanation would apply for the poltergeist phenomena, which caused the severe psychic disturbances of the girl. With obviously insufficient knowledge of these parapsychological phenomena, the psychiatrist believes a clouded consciousness and disturbances of the senses can be assumed. That completely strange and critical visitors at different times perceived identical phenomena — including Blumhardt himself — is not taken seriously.

> *"Induced insanity today only occurs in small groups, whose members are closely dependent on one another. But in former times, the sociological prerequisites for induced collective phenomena existed on a much broader scale than today. Within this framework, we cannot deal with such problems, and we will restrict ourselves to the most important characteristics of the illness of Gottliebin Dittus."*

The latter may be accepted as quite legitimate, but interpretations within the usual psychiatric terminology should then not be attempted. To the parapsychologist, particularly, this ghostly background is significant. This and the latter utterances of the spirit (the child murderer) from the mouth of the possessed is described in very realistic terms by Blumhardt, and makes me think of a transcendental event, in which the girl serves as a tool for a soul which is struggling for salvation. That later the whole collection of demons becomes involved in the struggle is, within parapsychological literature, rather remarkable in its dimension, but not without parallel. I previously indicated the role of the positive spiritually powerful clergyman in constellating and provoking the demonic. Most academically trained persons would have difficulty in accepting such an interpretation. Not only would such a person be misunderstood by his colleagues, he would also be ridiculed as an odd person adhering to medieval opinions; thus, he is forced to describe the complex and colorful palette of the phenomena of possession as "severely aggressive outbreaks, impulses of self-destruction and tactile hallucinations of a most severe chronic psychotic hysteria."

While Blumhardt recognizes the demons as "Powers," Benedetti sees intrapsychic events in their expressions. Thus he appraises the physical fainting spells, which Gottliebin experienced during the prayer of the clergyman, as psychic shock, while the person familiar with the phenomenon of possession thinks instead of a resistance by the "demon," just as Blumhardt does. Both opinions are based on their respective concepts of the world, and often also contain a common denominator. Benedetti quite accurately recognizes the simultaneous shock of the therapist, which led to an identification with the patient. Common distress had bonded the two, and through the devotion and endurance of the clergyman, had led to therapeutic success. The liberation — according to Benedetti —

> *"happens, because Blumhardt, in a spiritual way, takes on aspects of the patient which in a certain sense are demonic, are suffering psychic bondage, and are seeking liberation, and therefore longingly turn toward him. He cares for them within himself, without falling victim to them."*

It does not really matter whether unconscious demonic aspects and drives of the patient or the influence of transcendental entities is assumed. The words which were quoted above are as valid for the psychotherapist with a modern education as for the exorcist. In Benedetti's words:

> *"Blumhardt appears to have acquired some sense that demonic forces — in contrast to the predominant theological interpretation of his time, and quite in accord with our modern psychological knowledge — can produce characteristics of human beings. Some human endeavors, caught in a state of isolation, temporarily lose their demonic character-istics when they receive appropriate human interaction. When, in Blumhardt's sense, they are redeemed."*

In reference to this it must be said that it is not appropriate to regard our modern psychological views as "knowledge" in an absolute way. Although to a considerable degree, they rest on experiences which we have collected within our contemporary Western intellectual world, they do not necessarily corre-spond with those of Eastern cultures, or cultures not yet intellectualized. In the areas in which the Cartesian separation into spirit and matter has found no response, another type of experience, predominantly gained through intuition, prevails.

How much our so-called knowledge misleads us into giving different meaning to events becomes obvious in Benedetti's attempt to establish the experience, described by the mother Dittus several times, as only psychologi-cal. Contrary to the clearly-worded description by Blumhardt, Benedetti reports: "The mother woke up with the feeling of having dropped the child to the floor." From this, he concludes the existence of a disturbance in the mother-child relationship and a resulting inability of the mother to provide security for her child. This is most likely not a conscious distortion by Benedetti, but an affective inability to recognize magical events.

He encounters similar difficulties in commenting on other black magical occurrences. In a "sleeve of a man's shirt filled with flour next to a six pound loaf of bread," which Gottliebin found on the table in her tightly-locked living room, the psychiatrist sees hallucinations resulting from poverty and repressed sexuality. To the unorthodox parapsychologist, and also for Blumhardt, this revealed a connection with ghosts at the beginning of the girl's possession. Apport phenomena, telekinesis, materializations and psycho-plastic phenomena are associated with both positive and negative invisible entities, as well as the living.

Most astounding in Benedetti's work, however, appears to be the complete omission of all those unusual (also for us) paranormal events which occurred in the body of the possessed. Even a hysteric is not capable of wrapping a wire around his body inlaid under his skin, of swallowing knitting needles tied together with feathers or of having crooked nails travel within a very short time from the inside to the outside of the body. Since Benedetti found all this utterly incomprehensible — which is understandable — he apparently does not consider it worth mentioning. But even if Gottliebin had been a case of hysteria, one should have paid attention and searched for further diagnostic alternatives.

As far as I can judge on the basis of uncorroborated reports, I cannot share the opinion that the case of Gottliebin could have been a "severe psychotic hysteria." Such an illness can only develop when the innate character structure contains basic elements of it. This cannot be found in the available anamnesis. Gottliebin was described as a dependable and loyal servant, who was remembered well, and who in school and bible classes had proved to be willing and able to learn. Nor are there clues in the after-effects of the illness. Blumhardt describes in his epilogue that Gottliebin, as no other female person known to him, was capable of caring with so much insight, love, and patience for children, and particularly the mentally ill. For the latter, she was indispensible to him. The accomplishment of such chores would have been impossible for a human being with hysterical characteristics, since such characteristics express themselves especially in excessive egocentric-ity and lack of control over one's feelings.

It appeared important to me to use a concrete example to compare parapsychological and academic psychological thinking and contrast them with each other in this chapter. Except for Benedetti, as far as I know, no academic and no psychiatrist oriented toward natural science ever undertook to evaluate this extremely impressive case history. In spite of his background in natural science, but based on a principled, unusual openmindedness, Benedetti was able to say about Blumhardt:

> *"His report is a unique combination of religiosity and psychotherapy. A truth seems to be expressed by the word of prayer interwoven with the whole history of the case. Fasting and prayer in this case are expressions of the existential relationship of the therapist with the patient as well as with the transcendence which sustains them both. Prayer, as an expression of this relationship, functions from a distance, like love, which influences in invisible ways; it reaches further than therapeutic behavior reduced to a mere technique."*

12. OTHER CASES OF POSSESSION[1]

The Possession of Mrs. P. 1952

Peter Ringger published, in his paper "Das Problem der Besessenheit,"[2] the report by the Swiss minister T. about the possessed P. in the year 1952. It is interesting that an unusual number of parallels to the case of Gottliebin Dittus are apparent. Since Ringger's publication is very difficult to obtain, a summarized description is given here.

The possessed's past history is vague. Her allegations that her grandmother was already in alliance with the devil and that her mother had pledged her to Satan with blood while she was still unborn, have, to my knowledge, not been substantiated. Mrs. P., aside from having an hysterical disposition, apparently also was endowed with a tendency to unbridled fantasy. It is noteworthy, however, that in the *Rituale Romanum* such behavior is cited as pathognomonic (significant and characteristic) in cases of possession. At the age of 37, Mrs. P. had already had a troubled past. According to her statements, she at times had already vomited small iron nails before she came to stay with the Protestant minister T., but had kept it a secret.

The abundance of manifestations first became apparent during the confrontation with Pastor T., in a way similar to the case of Gottliebin Dittus. Ringger refers to Sören Kierkegaard[3], who expressed it thus:

"The demonic exists in a dependent relationship to the Good. Therefore it becomes all the more evident when it is touched by the Good. For this reason it is noteworthy that the demonic in the New Testament shows itself only when Christ comes in contact with it."

In the diary of Pastor T., we learn of the following parallels to the case history of Gottliebin: crooked, rusty nails exited from the jaw, the sides of the nostrils, above the right eye and from the lower lid of the left eye. A pair of scissors, missed by the wife of the minister, pushed its way out of the abdominal wall above the navel, accompanied by severe pain. Soon afterwards, the wound was not visible. The assertion of the possessed that one night a spirit put the above-mentioned pair of scissors into her body, deserves consideration. She attests to having seen spirits at several times, which entered her. Gottliebin reported similar events.

---

[1] It should be kept in mind that what some may consider as cases of possession, others will consider to be cases of multiple personality disorder. Allison and Crabtree agree that both phenomena can occur.

[2] "Das Problem der Besessenheit" ["The Problem of Possession"] (Oberengstringen-Zürich: Verlag Neue Wissenschaft, 1953).

[3] *Der Begriff der Angst* (Jena, 1923).

The Swabian clergyman Johann Josef Gassner, 1727-1779, was a very successful exorcist in his time. According to his experience, not only worms, frogs, snakes and mice, but also small scissors, nails, knives, hairpins, sealing-wax and glasses may exit from the mouth, the thighs, the arms, the knees, and ears, etc., of the possessed.[4] Several times Mrs. P. vomited pieces of glass, iron and a small horseshoe, then 8, 10, even 15 liters (!) of diluted blood smelling of sal ammoniac. In her case, the spirits left in great numbers mainly through her hands, which were thereby shaken vigorously. In the presence of Mrs. P., haunting (infestations) also took place. Aside from the above-mentioned phenomena, a long list of paranormal events can be found in Ringger's report.

That all of this happened in rural Protestant territory — yet another parallel to Möttlingen — leads one to recognize that the phenomenon of possession occurs, independently from religious confession, as should be expected. Presumably, the demonic manifests itself not through a specific phenomenology, but, on the contrary, it uses the possibilities which are available in the essence of objects and the laws of nature. This only appears "paranormal" because of its rare occurrence. Thus from Karl Blacher, professor for technical chemistry at the University of Riga, we learn that during mediumistic seances of the apport phenomena, medium B.X., aside from many pieces of iron exiting from the mouth, a 1.05 meter long piece of wire, bent many times, could be pulled out of the chest.

The Possessed M.M.

M.M., a delicate, pretty, and very docile girl grew up in an unpretentious neighborhood. The family belonged to the lower middle class. Her education in a private school, necessary because the girl was frequently ill, daydreaming and helpless, meant a considerable sacrifice for her parents. But the child supposedly had been happy, and only at the age of 16, the parents suspected, suffered the effects of "demonic" influences by a couple with whom they were once befriended. A peddler suggested the girl was "tormented," i.e., influenced by black magic. She began to suffer from attacks of suffocation.

M.M. decided to become a nursery school teacher, requiring her to take a course in another town 30 miles away. The departure, which was repeatedly postponed, was not only torpedoed by her attacks of suffocation, but also by paralysis of her arms and "scratches," which looked like streaked welts on her thighs, her arms and especially on her face. The way the girl looked, it would have been irresponsible to permit her departure.

Nausea and elevated temperatures without apparent reason became more and more frequent. Added to this were sudden jolts in her sleep and the subjective impression that she was pierced from within toward the outside. This happened on her wrists and from her back toward her sternum. While she was praying, the symptoms became worse.

---

[4] J.J. Gassner, *Weise und fromm zu leben, auch ruhig und gottselig sterben* ["Living wisely and piously, and dying peacefully and blessedly"] (Augsburg and Ingolstadt, 1775).

Parents and patient believed it was caused by witchcraft. Finally, the symptoms reached a climax. Almost every evening, precisely at 11 p.m., the girl began to rage, tearing apart whatever she could grab, and had to be restrained by several members of the family. At precisely 1 a.m., the horror ended and the girl woke as from a sleep, absolutely calm and without a memory of what had happened. A Catholic priest from another community, experienced in exorcism, was called in and confirmed it as a case of possession. He also recommended psychiatric treatment, and therefore the patient was referred to me. After a long conversation, the priest felt that my attitude, as well as my powers as a medium, were effective enough, and he asked me to exorcise the girl. He also gave me instructions regarding this case. For me, this represented an entrance into a new method of treatment which, when appropriate for a case, I still use. During the exorcism, the mother and aunt were present, and often also my colleague Katharina Nager. Even before the first actual session, while still in the waiting room, the fingers of the possessed cramped. Directly before the treatment, she had coughing fits, her teeth chattered, her head hit the back of the chair and welts on her face and her arms appeared. By stroking and holding of her head, she was calmed down, but the symptoms developed again during the exorcistic ritual. After treatment, a pronounced relaxation occurred.

Together with Mrs. Nager, I visited the girl two times at her home in order to be present during the nightly attacks of possession. Initially quiet and conciliatory, at precisely 11 p.m. the patient was as if transformed. Different, almost always male, voices reviled God, threatened and insulted the participants. The girl was very difficult to control when she became so physically violent. As if foretold, the pathological state was over in exactly two hours and was followed by a state of exhaustion.

During the day the possessed performed chores in the house and did knitting, which she often unravelled again. Sudden states of confusion became apparent. The girl spilled water onto the floor and into her own bed. Candles were burned in the fire, and garments torn apart. Often — according to the mother — the whole dwelling was penetrated by an unexplainable odor of decay.

The seven spirits[5] which possessed the girl were classified by the father, the mother and the younger, very normal sister, as well as by the patient herself, as follows:

No. 1 is a hairdresser and is always up to mischief.

No. 2 is good-natured, and one likes to listen to him, but he sometimes swears horribly. He forces his victim to solve crossword puzzles while always using blasphemous curses.

No. 3 is the most evil of all. Fortunately he manifests himself only for a few seconds. He destroys much by kicking.

No. 4 smokes (forces M. M. to smoke).

---

[5] This case would be characterized as "multiple personality" instead of possession by many psychotherapists and suggests that the line between the two cannot be precisely delineated.

No. 5 is, judging by the language, from the Hamburg area.

No. 6 predicts the future (prophecy).

No. 7 was initially mute, an angel demon, and superior to the others. But later he spoke, behaved nastily, hit and could not tolerate laughter.

No. 3, 4, 5, and 6 are, one suspects, former Nazis, i.e., "poor souls."

The exorcism was initially conducted two times a week in the medical office and later, depending on the patient's condition, less often. During the first year, the attacks began to occur less frequently, then a relapse took place. M.M. bit herself on her arms and hands. I discovered inexplicable red marks on her skin and a *lingua geographica,* a clearly defined pattern of red patches on her tongue, as can occasionally be found in highly nervous patients. In M.M.'s case, in addition, a jet black design was found on her tongue. During the Lord's Prayer before the exorcism, the possessed suffered spasmodic attacks of coughing, which could only be controlled by specific orders given to the individual spirits. At the end of the second year, a definite improvement could already be noticed. The spasms during the exorcism no longer appeared, and the state of motor agitation occurred less frequently and less severely. In the third and fourth year the possessing spirits appeared less frequently, ("went on vacation"), but then reappeared. The daily life began to normalize considerably. In the following two years, she went for many weeks without attacks. During the day, No. 2 especially reported his presence, cursed and asserted: "The wretch (as he used to call his victim) belongs to us" and "If the wretch would begin to work regularly, we would all come more often again." M.M. now came for exorcisms at the most every few months. In the 7th year, only three attacks took place. The third time, No. 2 still cursed about the "wretch," whom he hated, but reported that, if they (the possessing spirits) did not come again by summer, they would have to stay away for good. Nothing more happened, and at the end of the year, the girl married. She had met her partner a few months before. The marriage appears to be harmonious and the young woman has already given birth to two healthy children.

This case of possession (multiple personality) must be described as moderately severe. Important paranormal forms of appearances such as materializations and levitations were missing. Nevertheless, the girl missed seven years of normal living and a vocational education was made impossible for her. No psychotherapy of any kind took place. Depth analysis would have been impossible, because she was of only average intelligence. The patient M.M., while under the influence of spirits, refused with crude language any psychological testing by my colleague.

The parents often referred to the amiable and gentle character of their daughter M.M., while her sister demonstrated a wilder and more extroverted nature. I observed a harmonious and ethically very positive behavior in the young woman at this point. Again, the rule seems to be verified that evil is especially strongly provoked and evoked by its polar opposite.

The Possessed Mrs. C.

One of my female patients, whom I considered possessed and whose tale of woe I was able to follow in all its diversity, was a quite positively and ethically oriented middle-class woman. But she had married a demonic-amoral man, so that her psyche may well have become susceptible to the entry of negative forces.

The details of the course of the disease will be recounted here with the words of the patient herself. They impart a more colorful picture than the objective description of the observer, since the emotional state of the patient is best demonstrated in this way.

She reports:

"My present husband loved to look at me from the first moment. At that time, I was employed and 22 years old. I always felt that he was too flirtatious (courting others) and I was critical of some other behaviors of his. But two years later he got me; I was still completely inexperienced and became pregnant immediately. He would have loved to have a richer wife, and that is why he wanted the child to be aborted. He even provided me with a certificate, describing me as having a lung disease; but the gynecologist did not fall for it. He married me unwillingly, when I was already in the 7th month. Even the wedding night was very sad, because he had an evil illness. Since I have known him, I have not been happy. Things have gone very badly for me ever since. My husband wanted a divorce because of other women, and also drank too much. Nevertheless, I made an effort to be a loyal and good partner for him. Once he came home from another country and had terrible headaches so that he almost lost his mind. In order to alleviate his pain, I held his head with both my hands. But while doing this, I developed the same pain in my head, and since then I always get this type of headache from time to time. Shortly thereafter, I also heard the "evil voice in question" for the first time. That was during that night when he saw the white mice and lost his senses. Shortly before that, I had also refused to give myself to him because of a brownish discharge and a 'hideous' (disgusting) eczema, which he had brought home from vacation. When I heard the voice for the first time, I was paralyzed. It was quite scary and I was very much afraid. The voice said only evil things. It is a satanic voice which plagues me. The voice commands me to kill the children and also aunt Josy, although I really love them all so much. When I then respond: 'Oh, Jesus, I will never do such a thing,' it gets better. When I read the bible, the voice says: 'Put that book away — I can't stand it!' Often while I eat, I also see fat snakes on my plate; often only their head. Then I cannot touch a single bite. Or there is a knocking in the room and then the snake appears in the form of a silver streak. In my dreams, I am pursued and killed. It feels as though my whole body is tortured, my breast, my hand. Suddenly I lose my sense of feeling; then everything hurts very much again, and the voice says: 'That's really good for you!' Sometimes the voice comes from

without; I experience it like a grimace, right in front of my mouth. It says: 'I want to ruin you.' When I call on Jesus, it gets a little better. When the 'voice' pulls me by my hair, I can simply take off loose clumps of hair at that spot, and over time, my thick waves of hair have turned to sparse, straight strands. I sought help from a lay preacher, Mr. Z. When he prayed with me, I could pray along with him for just a short time. Then I sensed a heavy weight on me, and I lost consciousness. Mr. Z. told me afterwards that another, strange voice had spoken from my mouth, first only animal sounds, then horrible blasphemies against God and outrageous sexual remarks. When I became conscious again, I felt completely exhausted.

"Often when on my way to pray with Mr. Z., I received cuts on the soles of my feet, which caused a burning pain. The voice said: 'Don't go, don't go! — You are nothing but a hypocrite!' And on my way back it says: 'Jump in front of the train! Jump in front of the train!' The voice also explains to me how to cut off people's heads and loves to tell me things about 'whoring.' I am often plagued sexually; it is like the touch of a disgusting power, which stabs me in my genitals with a knife, and which threatens to continue torturing me if I don't submit. Beforehand, I hear dragging steps nearing my bed, and I feel a being, which then lies down next to me in my bed. But I never give in. So I am always restless. I consult doctors and go to health spas. Well-meaning people pray and even fast for me. But in vain! Even if the voice — at times — is silent, something pinches me here and there, I feel stabs in the area of my heart and in the sides. Something in me trembles. Most people say it is nerves."

I had the opportunity to participate in one of the exorcistic efforts by the lay preacher. Soon after the prayers began, we heard sounds of a growling animal from the mouth of the ailing woman which soon changed into a rough, almost male voice. Blasphemies alternated with threats against the preacher and me; then a regular dialogue developed between the dark and the light powers, of which the latter was masterfully represented by the preacher. The struggle ended in favor of the preacher, and my patient was rendered deeply unconscious, from which she recovered after about half an hour. After such exorcistic treatments, the patient feels better for some time; but even up to now, she has not been completely healed. A psychiatrist can recognize that all this constitutes occurrences of a unique kind, which do not correspond with our concepts and terminology of schizophrenic and hysterical illnesses.

From the psychological point of view, this case could be judged according to contemporarily valid theories: from the phenomenological point of view (i.e., according to the type of occurrences) it is so different from the typical schizophrenia or hysteria that one must necessarily ask whether there were not additional factors present.

13. UNUSUAL CASES OF POSSESSION

Extraordinary forms of possession do not occur often, but they provide a graphic picture of this vivid psychic form of expression which allows for a deeper insight into the connecting pathways between material and transcendental reality. Since the phenomena to be described run counter to all experiences and dogmas of natural scientific thinking, they are treated like Cinderella when referred to in literature. To reject them and deny their credibility because of this, however, demonstrates a spirit which contradicts a true scientific stance.

The Lads of Illfurt

From the report about the lads of Illfurt (in Alsace), we learn that their legs were often intertwined like supple rods. At that moment it was impossible, even with united effort, to unbraid their limbs. A *flexibilitas cerea* (a waxy flexibility) is also known to psychiatric literature and is considered a symptom of schizophrenic catalepsy and hysteria. However, we are not dealing with the same phenomenon here, since in the clinical *flexibilitas cerea,* the bending of bones does not occur. We merely observe how the ill person can maintain a posture into which he may be intentionally and planfully molded by another person, as well as an original catatonic posture, for an abnormally long period of time. Contrary to the above-mentioned schizophrenic phenomenon, the designation *"flexibilitas cerea"* deserves to be used only for the actual paraphysical flexibility of bones. This occurs seldom and only temporarily, as observed in the lads of Illfurt and elsewhere; for example, in the possessed Magdalena of Löwenberg.

This suppleness of the bones does not correspond with any known physiological laws and possibilities. The fact that bones can become waxen means a spontaneous and reversible psychoplastic deformation of organic (living) matter, which should be impossible according to the laws of Newton's physics as well as of physiology. We know of such deformations, although of inorganic matter (silver, steel, iron), from the "spoon benders" Uri Geller, Matthew Manning, Silvio and many others. I had the opportunity to learn from Uri Geller that often — although not always — a change occurs in the aggregate substance at the area where the bending takes place, i.e., the material takes on a softened condition, which leads to a deformation and often results in a separation. Since a plastic reshaping takes place, I have termed this phenomenon "psychoplastic,"[1] a term which has already been accepted by many others. The psychoplastic deformation of bones also shows

---

[1] H. Naegeli-Osjord, "Materialisation, Dematerialisation, und Psychoplastik" *Grenzgebiete der Wissenschaft* (Resch Verlag) No. 4 (June 28, 1979).

an extra-*motor* activity (EMA) which we can observe in people who are extraordinarily gifted as mediums (Uri Geller) or extraordinarily spiritually strong (Sai Baba, Sri Ganapathy Sachchidananda). Their abilities as mediums provide the entryway for transcendental occurrences. The incredible force with which the legs of the 10 and 8 year old boys stayed intertwined was also extraordinary. Here, too, an energy appeared to be functioning that far exceeded human capabilities, which suggests a transcendental causation.

From the description of the possessed lads of Illfurt, we learn:

> *"On Sept. 25, 1985, a remarkable event was observed for the first time: the two brothers, while lying on their backs, spun with incredible speed like tops around their own axis. Afterwards, with a strength unbelievable for their age, they demolished the furniture without showing any signs of fatigue. They also were jolted by spasms and convulsions until they collapsed lifelessly."*

This also far exceeds human strength and possibilities.

It is also remarkable that:

> *"Theobald, the older brother, believed himself to be followed by a hideous creature which had a duck's bill and claws and was covered all over with dirty feathers. When he saw this monster, he jumped upon it with a horrifying shout, in order to tear out its feathers. Witnesses reported these feathers to have had a horrible stench, and that when burned, they left no ashes."*

We are reminded here of Prof. Gebhard Frei's description of the possessed person on whom feathers developed on the outside surface of his hands and forearms while the minister was praying. They fell to the floor in large numbers and when burned produced an unusually bad smell. Also, during healing exorcisms by Philippine psychic surgeons, I saw feathers — in addition to many other things — come out of the body. Most healers did not permit their being taken, because the materialized objects would contain "bad vibrations."

"Often the brothers floated in the air either on chairs or without chairs only to be suddenly attacked by what seemed like invisible fists and thrown to the ground." Both boys were capable of climbing onto the weakest branches without breaking them. An extreme reduction of weight is conceivable, as has been found in contemporary mediums — for example, Nelja Kulagina[2] — but on a more modest scale (2 - 3 kg) and under quite different circumstances. Presumably, we see here the manifestation of transcendental or psycho-kinetic forces exerted on the branches and/or the bodies of the boys. This can be found in many similar observations described in literature about possession; for example, the case of the possessed Nicole Obri, who was lifted into the

---

[2] Nelja (Nina) Kulagina: The well-known Russian psychic who has demonstrated many psycho-kinetic effects.

air when facing a blessed candle, and could only be pulled down to the ground with very great effort.[3]

The theory that a change in the specific weight in the case of levitation and in "paranormal weight changes" are the same, can hardly be defended. For the levitating saints, who simply rise in space, this may still hold. The paranormally caused change of pure physical factors, i.e. the specific weight, would result only in a buoyancy on the spot, just as an air bubble rises in the water, without being controlled by mental intentions. In the case of levitating saints, however, we are dealing with states of mind and soul, which are filled with the symbolic content of the liberation from gravitational forces. This, to me, appears decisive here, and in its spiritual-material plane, belongs to the sphere of white magic.

In the description of the possession of Germana Cele,[4] we recognize an intended behavior in order to impress. At the height of 2 meters, the Kaffir girl floats above the parishioners, and laughing and triumphantly, she lets herself down in the choir behind the acolytes. In the case of possession, the consciousness of the affected person is not aware of any activities. He (she) must obey the directed "demonic" intentions, forces which enable and enact dynamic material activities. How much in these cases a directed influence of forces comes into play, is illustrated by the description of levitation of the lads of Illfurt. Against all known laws of physics, the boys were hurled to one side of the room, and the chairs on which they had sat before, to the other side. We are not encountering the reduction of specific weight of the possessed and the chairs, but a very forceful paranormal influence.

The same accounts for phenomena of paranormal weight, in the case of the girl from Löwenberg (see 3rd case discussed in this chapter). Not the heavy weight of the leg, but a paranormal downward pull against it, fixed the leg and the foot to the floor so that several strong men were unable to do anything about it.

> *"During the crisis, the boys did not speak in their own voices, but with the sound of coarse and hoarse voices of men, whereby the mouths of the possessed remained closed. The 'devils' spoke fluently in different languages — French, Spanish, Latin, and English — but they also understood several Spanish and French dialects. During the state of possession, the 'devil' talked to the exorcist predominantly in the Latin language, which the boys had neither learned nor were able to understand."*

The psychiatric theory which would describe the utterings of the possessed as the expressions of a split personality must be rejected, since both boys spoke Latin with the exorcist, understood several other languages and answered questions far beyond their mental level. It is quite obvious that a transcendental foreign being was superposed on the mental potential of the boys, and

---

[3] Jean Baptise Delacour, *Apage Satana* (Geneva: Ariston Verlag, 1975), p. 85.

[4] see *Apage Satana,* p. 137.

controlled their organs of speech. If someone speaks in a foreign tongue (German) and the content of his words corresponds with the dialogue, it is impossible to attribute the content as coming from the unconscious, which can collect but not process information. The 8 and 10 year old Illfurt boys not only talked and answered in Latin, but in addition to other languages, also spoke dialects of areas in southern France. A temporary take-over by an outside entity is the only reasonable explanation.

> *"In a sudden fit of rage, the brothers threw china against the wall, which, strange to say, did not break."*
>
> *"One day the 'devil' said that he would now go visit Father Superior Stumpf in order to plague him a little. In fact the clergyman was, at that time, lifted into the air by invisible forces, whereby all the pictures fell off the walls and the furniture tumbled about. When the room was sprinkled with holy water, the devilish haunting stopped."*

This resembles the haunting of poltergeists. The involuntary levitation of the clergyman is certainly a rare and unusual event. Orthodox parapsychologists (Bender, Ryzl) make an effort to interpret haunting as the influence of forces which spring from the unconscious of the involved personality. In which way the unconscious and the partial personality contained in it affects matter is not explained therewith.

From the description of the phenomena at Illfurt, it becomes apparent that it was not unconscious aggression on the part of the boys, who were still immature, which was at work, but the behavior of transcendental beings. This assumption is reinforced by the spreading of the haunting to the houses of the Illfurt families Kleimer, Brobeck, Burbach and Mayor Dresch.

When at one point, the lads of Illfurt were offered figs which had been secretly blessed by the priest, they screamed: "Away with the rat heads, the blackcoat has grimaced over them." Such words are not common in the vocabulary of such small boys. They lived with God-fearing parents, so this expression can more reasonably by attributed to an invading spirit.

> *"Once, the children suffered from lice. The more lice they destroyed, the more appeared. Since it was believed that this plague was the work of the devil, the boys were doused with holy water and the words: 'I order you in the name of the holy Trinity to leave this child!' were used. The remedy worked."*

Here we are dealing with a phenomenon parallel to the inexplicable appearance of feathers and kelp in the clothes of the two boys which, in spite of being shaken out or being soaked as laundry, always appeared anew and caused a severe itching. The question arises whether in this event, materialization or an apport phenomenon should be assumed.

Lyall Watson[5] experienced a magical tooth treatment that took place in a region of the Amazon, during which ants marched in orderly columns of two or three out of the mouth of the patient and disappeared in the grass. If we assume this to be materialization, it would have to be not only parthenogenesis, but a direct new creation of *a living creature*. Neither in the Illfurt case nor in the event in the Amazon do we know what happened to the lice and ants afterwards. Did they dematerialize? For that part of me inclined to think in natural scientific terms, the latter would be a more acceptable explanation than the hypothesis of an apport phenomenon, which would suggest that beings which were already created were dematerialized and then rematerialized in the mouth.

The assertion of the lads of Illfurt is also interesting. When asked for a reason for their possession, they stated they "once took an apple from a slovenly woman who had been chased out of the village because of her wretched conduct."

This would be equivalent to bewitchment or sorcery, which are listed in the *Rituale Romanum* as a cause of possession. Grimm's fairy tale "Snow White" contains the same theme. In a world still believing in magic, which corresponds with the world of fairy tales, sorcery was a much-practiced reality.

For a long time the boys reacted in a negative way toward all exorcistic endeavor, even in the monastery of Einsiedeln. Then the bishop appointed two exorcists, who, because of their irreproachable mode of life, possessed the spiritual power to drive out two angel demons "Orobas" and "Ypes" with one final exorcism for each. From then on, the boys remained healed.

The person who has experienced how even the best psychotherapists are unable to correct inappropriate behavior which is deeply rooted in the unconscious (at least not from one hour to the next) can only shake his head over the opinion of those parapsychologists who believe that the phenomena of possession are founded in unconscious interactions, i.e., the effect of partial personalities of the patients as well as their telepathic and clairvoyant abilities. The person who has experienced cases of possession himself and who is familiar with the subject in the literature, cannot be oblivious to this extraordinary phenomenon. A pattern of behavior similar throughout the world, which has remained the same through all epochs, speaks in favor of its authenticity.

It is no longer possible today to dismiss all of these reports by witnesses as fraud or misperception. Tape recordings show that the reported phenomena correspond to objective facts. Don Mario Boretti in Donato Livizzano (Tuscany) captured on tape a conversation in this manner with a possessed farm woman, who suddenly began to speak Greek. If the methods for objective evaluation of phenomena, such as film and tape recordings, had existed earlier, the phenomena of cases of possession in previous centuries would be accorded incomparably more importance. But as it is, most people arrogantly believe they may reject the reports of former times, even those by

---

[5] Lyall Watson, from a chapter in *Healers and the Healing Process,* ed. by George Meek (Wheaton, Illinois: Theosophical Publishing House, 1977), p. 243.

objective and highly respected personalities, because in their opinion, the reporting persons of those times were less endowed with the ability to observe critically. This is not at all the case. The intelligence of mankind does not change by one iota over the course of a few centuries; at most, only its intellectualism does. Considering the hubris of the natural scientist who is caught in current modes of thinking, I fear that today, we are more constrained than ever. The tendency to deny psychic phenomena, as presently exhibited by much of the mass media, illuminates this sufficiently.

Jeanne Ferry

The case of possession of the French nun, Jeanne Ferry, must be considered an extraordinary one, especially because it involved a large number of impressive materializations. But here, too, as with all materializations, the possibility that we are dealing with apport phenomena must remain open. In any case, materializations and apport phenomena are related.

Jeanne Ferry was exorcised for the first time in 1584. The exorcistic efforts lasted 19 months. As I described earlier in detail, it will simply not do to take the evidence reported by the participating priests lightly. One might as well doubt the experiences of J. C. Blumhardt with Gottliebin Dittus, when there has hardly ever been a more intelligent, impartial and irreproachable reporter.

I was fortunate to experience personally a great number of materializations with varying conditions and forms. I therefore do not doubt the evidence for the reported phenomena. Jeanne lost much blood during the exorcism of different demons, similar to Gottliebin, and accompanied by a horrible stench, worms and balls of hair emerged from mouth and nose. Even during times of the most lively hysteria at the turn of the past century, such an event, as far as I know, was never observed. At later exorcisms her mouth was found to be full of blood and decayed flesh. At another time, the floor of the room in which the exorcism had taken place was found covered with sugary confections.

In later developments, after Jeanne had experienced a relapse into childish behavior, a piece of paper appeared in her mouth on which was written that, from now on, Maria Magdalena desired that the archbishop again be concerned with matters regarding the nun. This then actually happened.[6] Here we see the rare case of an event of materialization on the part of positive divine powers — a proof for the assumption that in cases of possession, not only the demonic but the entire spectrum of good and evil can be involved.

During the last exorcism, the girl vomited a bullet and was temporarily healed. During later relapses, Ferry inflicted deep wounds on herself, which healed about a year later, on the same day as the occasion of the definitive exorcistic liberation.

---

[6] *Apage Satana, op. cit.*, p. 98.

A Possessed Girl in Löwenberg (1605)[7]

The Historic Report of Pastor Tobias Seiler and Inspector of Churches, Ph. Caesar, on What Happened to a Possessed Girl in Löwenberg, Silesia [a part of Poland since 1945].

The victim was a 12 year old girl, who, after the death of her parents, had the right to request an inheritance. Her legal guardian — probably with the intention of making the money his own — cursed her terribly, forced her to perform hard labor, beat her violently again and again, and threw her into a dark hole during the night. "She thus became very fearful, shaky, and timid."

On Sunday before the Feast of the Presentation of Jesus in the Temple, a black bird reportedly flew through the open door into her room and at first slipped onto her neck, then under her arm, where it disappeared. The girl fainted.

Today, we find it difficult to take a report like this seriously, but people of former centuries were much more able to perceive experiences in a visual manner. This would be especially true of an illiterate 12-year-old girl like Magdalena. Gifted as a medium — as are all those who experience possession — she saw the demonic attack as a black bird, similar to the more usual description of the devil with bat wings. Whether this was a pure vision caused by the girl's mind and feelings, or a materialization of evil, must be left undecided. Especially since, during the later exorcism, the demonic voice answered to questions of the priest, "the girl had drunk him, the 'Black,' in the form of gnats (larvae?)." According to our modern knowledge in parapsychology, we no longer have reason to doubt the materialization of spirit beings; however, that does not necessarily mean that it happened in this case. [The reader will note that the long quotation (17th Century) which follows (in original form) recounts a great variety of strange experiences. The slash marks apparently represent the fragmentatation of the phrases and sentences in the original.]

A few days after this experience, the girl reportedly vomited horribly and also suffered extremely loud hiccoughs comparable to the "screaming of the mill wheels." Also

> *"the devil began this game and sometimes rolled her into a globe or a ball/ her head at her knees/ no limb moving/ and, too, in oddly inexplicable ways she was tumbled about, high up; sometimes he stood her on her toes/ and suddenly he threw her backwards on her head and her face/ in such a way/ that her back remained hollow in the form of a bow; sometimes he placed her on her back/ so that her arms and legs/ were like interwoven willows/ often for one half/ often a whole hour held up high/ which no human could tear apart; sometimes he made her eyes bulge out of her head, as large as chicken eggs; sometimes he stretched her to the ceiling; sometimes she rammed the door of the*

---

[7] Joh. Bodini, *Daemonomania,* part II, p. 67.

room with her head/ to try to kill herself; sometimes she bit large chunks out of the wall with her teeth; often she mooed terribly like a cow; often she laughed so loud and scoffingly, for a whole hour/ that it was heard from afar/ and when she had a little rest/ reportedly/ she still could not stop the laughing. And she continued to experience such astonishing things."

"When I was asked to see the girl for the first time/ Satan had thrown her up into the air/ he stood her on her toes and turned her backwards over her head to make a bow/ sat her up again/ her arms contorted like willows/ her face turned sometimes towards the right/ sometimes toward the left side and toward the back/ her head was beaten to and fro/ and her tongue/ black like coal/ was pulled a long way out of her mouth. But when we heartily prayed for salvation/ to the Almighty foe of snakes and helper in need, Jesu Christo, and sang with everyone present/ Oh, God our heavenly Father, remain with us, etc./ the devil spoke from her body/ sometimes like a pile of young cats/ sometimes like young dogs/ which were biting one another/ sometimes he crowed like a rooster/ sometimes in various manners/ big and small voices all mixed up/ and an amazing rabbit chase was audible. And all of this came all the time from the open mouth/ without movement of lips or tongue."

During the exorcism, the demon demanded a hair or a toenail from Magdalena before he would leave. It was not granted him. He then begged to transfer into a pig or a hollow willow tree.

Then

"the cursed infamous devil also showed himself personally./ First he played his tricks with the girl by crowing/ chasing and slandering/ shaking the girl to and fro/ also in Praesentia Domini Medici/ tossing her up high/ banging her against a hasp/ so that the blood ran over her head./ All people present fell onto their knees/ and cried desperately for salvation from the Almighty foe of snakes, Jesu Christo: Then the devil danced like a black little mouse or a little tree frog on her tongue (she had held her mouth open) for a quarter of an hour/ often he came near the edge/ lastly he again jumped down into her body./ Many honorable male and female citizens saw this with their own eyes. Following this, her mouth was spread open/ and without any movement of the tongue/ for half an hour clear and loud he screamed out of her, and particularly because of the members of the Reformed church, expressed many horrible things: and when he was answered and contradicted: No/ they will still repent/ he insisted in his words and said/ their hearts had become obdurate/ they couldn't."

"When, coincidentally, a crucifix too was at hand/ which was shown her/ and she was thereby reminded to remember the crucified Jesus/ the devil roared terribly/ like a lion or a bear/ and raged through her against it./ The tongue was stuck out like a burning coal./ Her eyes

were twisted./ He spit at it: but called the thief on the left side his friend."

"Most remarkable was/ that when Satan sat on her tongue/ or in her ears/ and when she wanted to touch herself there/ he bit her fingers/ whereby she screamed miserably/ and the fantastic little holes many saw in amazement."

"The hellish murderous spirit also carried on unusual conversations/ strange, but over time, he could speak many languages/ among others: Indian, Persian, Arabic, Syrian, Hebrew, Greek, Chaldean, Turkish, Russian, Hungarian, Latin, Spanish, Italian, French, Polish, Bohemian, Upper- and Lower-German, and carried on a long discourse in an unknown language."

"When he was not given an answer/ he yelled with great mockery! 'Ha! Ha! Ha! It is Indian.' Although the girl did not know any letters, Satan also read the words written on the wall: (Woe betide those/ who despair in God and do not hold steadfast/ and the godless/ who waver to and fro; Woe betide the despairing/ for they do not believe/ thus they, too, will not be sheltered; Woe betide those/ who do not persevere/ for what will befall them/ when God judges them?)/ And when he was threatened with the words of Judas: Increpet te Deus Satana: God will punish you, Satan: he did answer: Quid mihi tecum" (Why should I be concerned with you?)/"*

"The scandalous Satan in his new shelter soon also began a new spectacle/ and this in front of the noble/ and in the presence of many honorable citizens after long tumults/ swung her like a huge bell high above: In the form of a big man/ spit fire at her: as at night/ like a very big bumble bee/ with only one big, brightly flickering eye on the head/ and having had two legs/ was stood up in the room/ swarmed around the light/ then sat upon the table/ and looked at her guards, of which there were four/ so seriously/ and scared them so tremendously/ that one of them became very ill./ On the following day, the Annunciation of Mary,/ opposing the words: Hodie Deus homo factus est: Today God is Become Flesh/ in the presence of many thousand persons/ he raged so horribly, it was unspeakable."

"On the Monday after Passion Sunday, we began to place her in the church in front of the high altar/ where many thousand persons/ natives and strangers, were present. Now when we pastors alternately began singing and praying/ for salvation we sincerely called on the Lord Jesum Christum/ the people sometimes standing/ sometimes kneeling/ next to us prayed most piously: then at times, Satan from the open mouth of the girl/ without movement of tongue and mouth/ as was always the case/ screamed uproariously. Violent things/ violent things/ thereafter raged and rioted terribly/ so that two men were not able to hold her; spit at the Crucifix of Christ/ and slandered it with the most defamatory insulting names." "This time for two hours singing and urgent praying was maintained/ but to no avail."

From a further description we learn:

"At home the devil sat on her tongue and made her dumb/ he threw her to and fro/ he made her hot/ that she looked like a red boiled lobster: she also grabbed for the knives of the bystanders/ and wanted to stab into their hearts."

"And this time the devil tyrannized, in the presence of many pastors and citizens to such an extent/ that through the wearisome fight and struggle I was completely exhausted/ and almost nobody/ till I gained some strength/ in fright and terror was able to pray the Lord's prayer: but obviously God gave power from above/ and Satan had to give up and yield."

"On the third day/ when all the people in the church sincerely cried out to God/ Satan with great fury squirted/ during the prayer something like toads/ creatures against the altar/ whereupon the girl became very weak/ cried/ lifted up her hands/ and helped sighing and calling for salvation/ and was carried home on someone's arms."

After a short intermission during Passion Week new tortures occurred and the girl was brought to the church again. Then the following events took place:

"Often he blew through her folded hands extremely loud like a well-tuned trumpet/ often pulled out her tongue/ contorted like a willow/ black and for a long way out of her mouth/ and hit her on one side or the other; often pressed on her toes so tightly/ as if she were nailed down/ that with no instrument could she be moved; often for a good while she/ had to sit with her mouth open wide and a terrible face/ often with her mouth/ snapping open and shut like a dog: even bit her arms pitifully; often lecherous swearing, also yelled at the large church assembly extremely loud / Whore/ Whore: And when they sang: This World's Prince May Still/ Scowl Fierce as he Will. Said he: I am the prince of this world; And when praying intensified/ the rogue he whimpered/ and said: Oh dear/ how the girl does pray in her heart/ that it does hurt me/ I had already departed/ but the one above had permitted me/ to plague her body still for a time."

At Magdalena's domicile the following reportedly happened:

"At a time at night/ a thunderstorm terrible beyond measure/ storm/ howling/ whistling and roaring was heard surrounding the girl/ that it must not have been more terrible at the time when Faust was carried off. Then the most amazing spectacles were seen above the house/ in the air a fierce raging and howling of the storm was heard: lightning could be seen within the house/ as though everything fell to the floor: the window and door in which the girl had been/ were suddenly flung open by the storm/ and inside was such howling and raging/ that the guards did not know/ which way to turn; The girl was tossed up and down/ to and fro; The guards got the feeling/ they were floating in the air/ sang hymns loudly for several hours out of the window."

> *"At last a white face supposedly came in at the door of the room/ and subsequently everything soon turned very quiet/ and the moon shone down brightly from the sky."*

In the conversations between Pastor David Brändel and the possessing spirit, it becomes clear how much the latter feels himself to be under the domination of God and actually is only "permitted to appear free." He must leave when the faithful congregation is sufficiently able to experience the power and superiority of God's word over all negative forces.

On May 14, the final exorcism succeeded, through urgent praying and hymn singing. From then on, the girl "did not lack in the least way in reason or health."

The case resembles the case of the brothers from Illfurt in its extremely drastic manifestations, but was caused by a curse and by Magdalena's extremely severe psychic and physical suffering and extreme weakness.

Materializations (tree frogs) and psychokinetic events manifesting as transformations of immaterial powers and forces into physical forms can be found in great number. The report was attested to by clergymen, physicians and high state officials, and we have no reason to believe it to be more freely invented than would be the case today. Although, for example, the conflict between the exorcist and the possessing spirit often reflects the *Zeitgeist* of that era, the notion that the case dealt only with interactions with the unconscious is not defensible. In our modern psychotherapeutic endeavors, nothing matching can be found.

The Nut-Eating Bewitched Woman Circumstantially Described by the Well-Known Evangelical Theologian Dannhaverus.[8]

In 1650 in Straßburg, a woman suspected that, while under the influence of the devil, she had given a bewitched nut to a ten year old daughter of a nobleman. After having partaken of it, the girl immediately felt nauseated, became depressed and saw devilish grimaces in humans and animals. Exhibiting extreme motor agitation, she began to dance on tables and chairs. Cracking sounds were heard in her bed and also in the ceiling of the room at night. Later, the girl rolled around like a windlass more than 40 times, she writhed like a snake, and stretched and stiffened in a way that made it impossible for a man to move her limbs.

In order to control the terrible condition, the mother of the child challenged the evil spirit with the following words:

> *"Satan, why do you torture this poor child? She is, yes, a pious child/ bought dearly with the blood of Jesu Christi/ then one could hear from her mouth/ which was stretched like the snout of a pig/ this voice and*

---

[8] Joh. Bodini, *Daemonomania,* part II, p. 64.

answer: This I know well/ and would torture her even more because of this/ would one not pray for her."

When the fight against the evil one was won, the girl reportedly "began to speak, as if the holy angel were standing in front of her." She now appeared open to positive influences and with harsh words, took up the fight against Satan herself. Later, too, she expressed religious-philosophical opinions which reached far beyond her mental horizon. Apparently this was the end of the demonic possession caused by a magic spell.

The report is notable because of its parallels to events which happened in the case of the boys from Illfurt: for example, the unusual turning of the body and the stiffening of the limbs. Furthermore, we notice the alternation of negative and positive influences by opposed entities. The witch who chose the girl, as well as the girl herself, may have been highly gifted as mediums. Without the presence of mediumistic sensitivity, neither positive nor negative spirits can express themselves.

The description is of special interest because of the offering of the bewitched nut. Symbolically, the nut appears as a present, which within its shell contains something hidden. It is surely a demonic force, which, ethereally placed in the nut, perhaps at first only opens up the victim for a later attack by devilish spirits. The witch — just as in the case of the possessed boys from Illfurt — probably had prepared the nut, or in the other case, the apple, by a magic ritual. This may happen through thinking a curse over the nut, or through a ceremony of black magic. There is no concrete basis for judging what actually happened here.

The Divinity appeared to have permitted the suffering of the innocent girl — as Jehovah in the case of Job — in order to demonstrate to the participants Its dominance over evil.

Here the advice from the scene of Brazilian magic also applies: never alone, always in the presence of third persons, and never capriciously cast a spell over someone. Because if one should meet a stronger person, open to positive forces, the curse would fall back on its originator.

Concerning Several Possessed Boys[9]

In Amsterdam, in the year 1566, 30 boys were struck by an unusual illness. They tumbled "as if mad" to the ground and suffered terrible pain. After a half hour, but most often a full hour, they got up again and believed they had slept/ because they could not remember anything. Medical treatment was unsuccessful. Remedies against magic spells also accomplished nothing. Thereupon, exorcistic measures were taken. During those, the boys vomited among other things, needles, thimbles, rags, pieces of glass and hair. The exorcistic effort did not help completely, since relapses occurred several times. The report of this case is quite short.

The medical person would be prepared to describe such an "epidemic" as St. Vitus's dance *(chorea minor)*. However, it should be taken into account

---

[9] Joh. Bodini, *op. cit.,* part II, p. 304.

that, from the viewpoint of natural science, the cause of this illness with regard to its epidemic occurrence has not been clearly explained. The phenomenology of *chorea minor* also did not resemble that of the 30 possessed boys.

That we are dealing with true possession is supported, first of all, by the considerable pain at the beginning of the attack and the total amnesia (loss of memory) of the victims after the paroxysmal event (seizure), then above all, by the large number of materializations, i.e. vomited objects. Secondary evidence for demonic possession would be the inefficacy of the customary medication and the ceremonies and counterspells undertaken by experts in magic. The exorcistic measures were at least temporarily effective.

The number of affected boys appears of interest, as well as the fact that no girls are mentioned. *Chorea minor,* moreover, usually afflicts girls. It also cannot be concluded that this was an epidemic of possession like the one in Loudun.[10] With regard to Loudun, I am not sure that one can speak of psychological contagion, because in this case the main emphasis is placed on an intrapsychic (animistic) event.

The double possession of the boys of Illfurt also may not be attributed to contagion. Three other siblings remained undisturbed, which would not be an important factor without the hypothesized presence of a magic spell, that only the brothers Theobald and Josef experienced.

Unfortunately, we are not told what kind of contact the 30 boys had with one another, so that nothing conclusive can be said about this case.

If we consider the Christian belief which has been handed down, according to which a prince of demons has numerous lower devils at his disposal, then a collective demonic activity under the supervision of a superior devil can not be excluded. Finally, we cannot even be certain whether the medically observed epidemics of St. Vitus's dance are or are not manifestations of demonic influences.

Following the description of the possession of the 30 boys in Bodini's work, a case in Delitsch near Leipzig is described in which a six year old boy was "taken into possession by the devil and was pitifully tormented." The possession became apparent when the boy expressed shocking blasphemies against God, and terribly mocked and laughed at the clergyman who was called in. Each time the clergyman approached, the boy reacted with "angry gestures." In town he truly feared all who were known to lead a God-fearing life and were especially-loved servants of God.

Several months of exorcistic efforts seem to have been necessary, after which the evil spirit made it known that he was forced to leave the shelter (the boy) because of the power of the prayer. As a replacement, he wanted to

---

[10] The Ursuline convent, established in Loudun, France, was the scene of an outbreak of diabolical possession in the year 1633. A detailed account of one of the most extraordinary obsessions of modern times was set forth in a French work published in 1839. The strange behavior of the Loudun nuns inspired a remarkable book by Aldous Huxley, *The Devils of Loudun,* published in 1952. Three renowned exorcists who took part in trials following the outbreak had cause to regret their roles. One of them experienced diabolical possession for twenty years. (From *Exorcism Through the Ages,* edited by St. Elmo Nauman, Jr. PhD (New York: Philosophical Library, 1974).

enter into the one year old brother on the following day at 12 o'clock and "treat" him in the same way. This then happened: at the announced hour, the six year old again behaved quite normally, but the one year old screamed in torment and agony, with a bloated belly.

The then famous physician, Johann Michael, treated the child with different medications. Afterwards, "blue-red and yellowish spots appeared all over the body, and at the same time, a filthy, ugly material was passed through the stool" (materialization?). At first this helped only temporarily, but finally the boy was healed.

Children at age one are not suggestible. The hypothesis that demonic possession may be transmitted through suggestive influence is only applicable for isolated cases. It appears clear that the demonic force, though in a weaker condition, sought to transfer from one person to another. In this case also, it would be absurd to attribute the blasphemies expressed by the six year old to an unconscious part of his personality.

The Possessed Youth[11]

Johannes Fernelius, a world famous physician in his time, reported about a young man from the family of a knight, who rotated either his right or his left arm, then only one finger or a thigh, at a frantic speed. When both of his thighs were affected his whole body was tossed about with such incredible speed and force that not even four servants were able to hold him. The head of the young man was, at the same time, lying steady on the floor, he talked clearly, and was in a healthy mood and clear mind. This happened up to ten times a day. Physicians believed it to be epilepsy and unsuccessfully tried different medications. Only when the young man began to speak in Latin and Greek, which were unknown to him, was the illness recognized as possession. The patient also began to mock the physicians and divulge secrets which only the individual physician could have known. Whenever his father — who wore a pendant of the archangel Michael on a chain around his neck, as was customary for this class of French knight — came near him, he began to scream loudly, and was unable to tolerate his presence.

> *"When asked, the devil made it known that he had previously dwelled in another person, and that he would find himself a new victim should he leave the young man. He supposedly moved in and out of the person through the feet."*

This case of possession greatly resembles the phenomena that occurred in connection with the *Lads of Illfurt* discussed earlier in this chapter. We see similar patterns and forms of appearances in various eras, as well as various parts of the world. Typically, a unique part of the body is used for entrance or exit which is characteristic for each individual demon.

---

[11] Joh. Bodini, *op. cit.,* part II, p. 230.

About a Possessed Girl[12]

Wierus, an author famous in the 16th Century, writes

"I myself held a daughter of about 15 years of age during an attack, and observed her carefully, when I discovered a piece of black cloth stretched over her tongue, which I grabbed with my fingers and pulled out of her mouth, together with a whole pile of junk consisting of many other strange objects which obviously had never been in her stomach. Her father told me that earlier, she had already vomited many strange and mixed-up materials. I kept them; they were: 1 black, coarse piece of cloth in which were stuck several needles and points tied together by a thread; furthermore several old iron nails. But the piece of coarse black cloth, which I had seen myself, was only wet from some saliva and did not contain juices from the stomach or leftover food. Saint Augustine has also attested that the devil uses the tongue of the person whose body he possesses. The devil also locked the mouth and hands of the girl, so that she could not open them without the sign of the holy cross or my own blessing. He also rolled her eyes and tormented her whole body. The devil insulted me in an unnaturally childish babbling voice." [Description abridged by the author].

This event reminds us of the case of Gottliebin Dittus with respect to materializations. We find similarities in contemporary cases, as described by Peter Ringger. The demonic always seems to use the same patterns.

The Possessed Nuns of the Convent of Kentorff[13]

In the 16th Century, a number of residents of the convent of Kentorff near Hamm were possessed, the circumstances remaining unclear. Before the attacks, the women suffered "convulsiones," which probably were stomach cramps, but before that "a stinking breath came out of the women's throats, which only disappeared some time after the attack was over." This plague befell them one to ten times per day, and not infrequently lasted for hours. It always began simultaneously, although the women who were affected often lived in rooms far apart. This phenomenon appears significant, and discloses a central causative being, which influences a whole collective with similar intentions.

"Even a drink from a container made of the skull bone of St. Cornelius was ineffective. Finally, the nuns began to bite and beat themselves and each other, but didn't feel anything and felt it was right and fair — in fact, necessary. Satan sometimes lifted them up from the floor and then threw them down again, but without any harm or handicap to them,

---

[12] Joh. Bodini, *op. cit.,* part II, p. 232.

[13] Joh. Bodini, *op. cit.,* part II, p. 234.

during which they imagined they were as light as down; from which they clearly noticed that they were no longer their own but had received, superior to them, a stronger lord and master. . . . When they were finally exorcised, they lost an immense amount of blood from their throats, but suffered no injury." [Similar to the case of Gottliebin Dittus. (N.)]

The women felt as if their throats had been singed. Even the cook, who was accused by a fortune-teller of magic and having caused this, was affected by the event, but nevertheless was later burned to death. After her death, nothing improved, but the pestilential possession spread to two neighboring towns, where men were mainly affected. During an exorcism, one of them supposedly rolled into a ball and slammed against a tightly locked door, which then opened as if by the hand of a ghost. The possessed fell down the stairs but suffered no injury.

Again, the close relationship to haunting by poltergeists is apparent. As I experienced myself in one case, doors often open in spite of being tightly locked.

The Possessed Servant[14]

"The servant of a nobleman in Bontenbrouch castle near Jülich was, in spite of spiritual encouragement and preventive measures, more and more affected by inexplicable bodily symptoms. The possessed's neck first began to swell so much that his face turned as black as coal from it, and one worried that he might suffocate from this swelling."

Then an especially God-fearing lady began questioning him very closely.

"After this happened, there came from this man's mouth, aside from other junk: a shepherd's piece of sheepskin, whole and broken pebbles, women's hair, rolls of yarn, thread, needles, a piece of lining torn from a child's skirt, and also a peacock feather, which he himself had torn from the peacock when he was still well and healthy. . . . He thereby confessed that none of the strange objects reported earlier had been in his body, but were pushed into his mouth by an evil spirit. For a time he behaved rather happily, because he had been given a filled bag by Satan, which he had hidden under the straw of his bed. But when it was searched for, it was found empty. This is not dissimilar to what one reads about the life of St. Francis. When he and his companions found a big sack with money, St. Francis immediately noticed that it was only a temptation and delusion by the evil foe, and for that reason, did not want to take it. When one of his companions asserted that the money should be taken out of the sack and given to the poor, he opened the sack, but found a snake in his hand, which instantly disappeared. But to return to our servant, it was once observed that a little mouse jumped

---

[14] Joh. Bodini, *op. cit.*, part II, p. 238.

out of his mouth, whereupon he crept under the bed and lamented about having lost a little mouse. Soon he came out from under the bed and told them, he had caught it again. . . . Once he was found in the pig manure. His eyes were so tightly shut at times, that they could not be opened by force. . . . Once, when he rudely and roughly attacked the kitchen maid, for which he was severely punished, and addressed by name, he answered in a terribly hoarse voice that his name was not Wilhelm, but, on the contrary, Beelzebub."

Wilhelm's caretakers told Beelzebub that they were not afraid of him, since God was so much stronger. The nobleman read parts from the Bible in everybody's presence and told Satan to leave. The servant fell unconscious, was quiet for one whole night and felt well the next morning. He was sent home, but the wagon in which he was riding fell over on a smooth road. Nobody was hurt, however. That was the last prank of the devil. Later, the servant married and fathered a child.

This occurrence contains several notable details. First, it seems to demonstrate again that the demonic is constellated by the positive divine. The nobleman, as well as other participants, were judged as very positive. Let us remember that the essential phenomena of possession in the case of Gottliebin Dittus first began to appear when Pastor Blumhardt came on the scene.

The materialization of women's hair is seldom found in the literature on possession but it is not infrequent within the field of Philippine psychic surgery. A particularly impressive case, in which the healer and exorcist Alex Orbito in Manila, was photographed and filmed by two well-known researchers Oscar Marcel Hinze and Doctor of Medical Dentistry Walter Früh to document the phenomenon.

The details regarding the mouse which jumped out of the mouth, and was found again under the bed, must certainly appear to the psychiatrist as a delusion of a mentally ill person. In principle, this could be possible in someone who is possessed. However, the occurrence was observed by other persons present. Considering the numerous materializations, which were visible to bystanders, one could also consider it a genuine phenomenon. The person who is familiar with the literature on magic or possession also knows about the materialization of living animals, just as during serious spiritualist circles at the turn of the century, the spirit beings of deceased persons materialized for a short time. All other materialized objects were probably not, as the servant believed, pushed into his mouth but very likely were, as in many other cases (for example, the girl from Löwenberg) materialized inside it.

The case of Wilhelm illustrates the point that exorcistic efforts are not restricted to the church and the priesthood, but, on the contrary, strong people with an honest desire to heal are also capable of the task when called upon. A belief in God may help.

Agnes Katharina Schleicher[15]

In the hometown of the schoolmaster Schleicher, in Wetschgershausen in 1680, cows were bewitched, giving spoiled milk or no milk. Pigs also perished and poultry was found weak or strangled. Finally, the 8-year-old daughter Agnes was affected. She reported to her mother that to her immense shock she had heard something producing a rushing sound above her and got the feeling that it had slipped into her. She was then forced to swallow something (choke it down) and finally was forced to say "hack, hack, hack," which, in the following months, she felt compelled to say again and again.

The parents at first heard a "voice" from the area of Agnes's stomach, without movement of the tongue. But then an extraordinarily rude male voice could be heard from her larynx. In addition, something in her stomach began to sound like the "purring of a turtle-dove." In addition, the parents, and at another time the clergyman, heard the grunting of a herd of pigs when none were nearby. The girl was placed under the care of the church and three clergymen concerned themselves with Agnes Katharina. They disputed with the devil dwelling within her, and with intense praying and singing of religious hymns, attempted to drive him out. After about four months they succeeded, even though there was no visible sign of the devil leaving. The girl appeared unaffected from then on. This case — described in very abbreviated form — is remarkable because of the haunting in the barn which preceded it, and it shows again the close relationship between haunting and possession. Agnes had also had the sensation that something had slipped into her. To put this down as hysteria makes no sense, in light of the extraordinary appearances and the girl's freedom from symptoms before and afterwards.

A rude man's voice emanating from the larynx of an eight year old girl is physiologically impossible. Perhaps for a limited time a deformation (psycho-plastic) of the larynx of this immature child took place, or the demonic ethereal spirit was capable of temporarily materializing its own larynx and creating the corresponding sounds. The Protestant method of exorcising by singing religious hymns and having a large number of clergymen and parishioners pray intensely together, is also of particular interest in the exorcism of this child.

Germana Cele

The description of Germana Cele's possession, mentioned previously, can be read in its entirety in the book by the Jesuit, Father Adolf Rodewyk.[16] This author is probably the best known contemporary expert on problems of possession, although he was not consulted at the trial involving the death of the possessed girl, Anneliese Michel in 1978.[17] Germana Cele, in 1907/1908,

---

[15] Joh. Bodini, *op. cit.*, part II, p. 87.

[16] Adolf Rodewyk, S. J., *Die dämonische Besessenheit,* [Demonic Possession] (Aschaffenburg: Paul Pattloch Verlag, 1960), p. 139.

[17] see chapter 15.

presented well-verified phenomena of an extraordinary nature.[18]

> *"In the case of Germana, peculiar manifestations of fire took place: she came into the children's kitchen where some coals were still smoldering. Suddenly a huge burst of flames shot up. Everybody screamed and ran away. Germana laughed and moved away, and a few half-extinguished coals continued to smoulder underneath the ashes. At times the whole room was full of fire."*
>
> *"Once when Germana was resting on her bed, and left and right from her were over twenty grown girls, all in their beds, Germana suddenly screamed for help. All sat up, including Sister Juliana, who had been resting on a chair in the same room. Germana's bed cracked and shook, and a huge fire flared up from it. Sister Juliana sprinkled some holy water, and all activity stopped. When they checked, they found the boards and the bedposts were badly scorched, the covers and Germana's clothes were undamaged, while Germana complained of pain from burns."*

This event seems almost unbelievable. Two effects of fire took place, completely isolated from one another. The woodwork was scorched, but the bedclothes and Germana's nightdress remained unaffected, while on the other hand, Germana complained of pain from burns on her body. Such selective or atypical effects defy logic and coincidence and strengthen the case for possession.

A phenomenon which was filmed several times during psychic surgery in the Philippines may shed some light here. Mental imagery by the psychic surgeon, and his symbolic imitation of cutting in free air, result in a cut on the skin of the patient, while an interposed layer of plastic and the patient's shirt over it are not damaged. The mental image of the psychic surgeon, together with his guiding spirit, affect the skin only on the body surface of the patient and nowhere else. Similarly in Germana's case, the demonic spirit did not manifest itself on relatively unimportant matter around the patient, but on Germana and on the material of the bed (causing the housemates to be frightened). Transcendental intelligences, influencing matter, appeared to be involved in this case.

Manifestations of fire within phenomena of possession and haunting are seldom encountered. They are mentioned in the case of Magdalene Gronbach of Orlach[19], in which the phenomenon, researched by Justinus Kerner in 1842, should be categorized as something between haunting and possession. The materialized red-hot coals rested on a cloth which did not get singed where the coals touched it but only on the upper part. Fire also began to burn in inexplicable ways when the house was surrounded by guards. Several of these glowing coals were buried in the ground, but when an attempt was made to

---

[18] A. Rodewyk, *op. cit.* p. 100.

[19] Heino Gehrts, *Das Mädchen von Orlach* ["The Girl from Orlach"] (Ernst Klett Verlag, 1966), p. 16.

find them again, they had disappeared. This appears to be a clear case of de-materialization, since a complete combustion of the coals would have been prevented by the lack of air as a result of being buried.

In the case in Orlach, two spirits, one more positive and one more negative, manifested themselves through the mediumistic Magdalene and played an essential role. Whoever takes the existence of "poor souls" seriously, will acknowledge that their mental-spiritual potential has a much greater determining influence than the (hypothetical) unconscious conflict within the girl. I am inclined to disagree with Jung's opinion that haunting phenomena are the result of "exteriorization" of psychic conflicts. Within this context, for example the phenomenon of the branded hand, which was experienced by Magdalene of Orlach, should also be mentioned.

The Kaffir[20] girl Germana, of uncertain parentage, but herself beautiful, intelligent, and despite a violent temper, good hearted, was supposedly seduced by a sorceress at an early age. Most likely, this created an entry into Germana's psychological constitution for demonic spirits. At age 16, for unknown reasons, she sold her soul to the devil.

Germana exhibited practically the whole range of *Signa* (signs) of possession mentioned in the *Rituale Romanum,* but her snake-like nature was a special case.

> *"At times, she came slithering over her bed exactly like a snake, as though her whole body were made of rubber: sometimes on her back, sometimes on her belly, in all forms of snakelike twisting. . . . When she crept backwards, her head was presented like a foot, and the whole body followed slithering like a snake. . . . When she was held fast, while standing, during an exorcism, Germana's neck turned longer and more snakelike in front of everybody's eyes, and she struck like a snake and bit the nun — who knelt on the floor in front of her — on her arm, which was covered by a habit. The wound developed as many burn-like blisters as there were teeth, with a reddish puncture wound in the middle . . . a little red wound like the bite of a snake."*

It was also notable that she ran up a wall, 2.5 meters high, with great speed "as though she were on solid ground." She often exhibited a speed like lightning, especially when she was attacked by someone.

The following was also unusual:

> *"Sometimes something wound itself like a rope the width of a finger underneath her skin and around the whole body, across the arms, shoulder, neck and down one side to her feet. Holy water helped against it."*

One is reminded of Gottliebin, where Blumhardt and his wife pulled out an iron wire, which had been wound around her whole body *under* the skin.

---

[20] Kaffir: a member of a South African tribe.

From the description in the case of the Kaffir girl, it could not have been merely muscle spasms, but an unknown type of materialization, which dematerialized when sprinkled with holy water.

Materializations of animals, visible to all present, are reported as follows:

"A nun saw a pretty kitten sitting on a bench and wanted to pet it. Suddenly the kitten turned into a huge black dog the size of a calf, with glowing eyes. Then there was an explosion like thunder and everything was gone. By day and at night, the nuns and girls and others often saw outside the windows, shapes of frogs and toads, big and small (some the size of a hand) with bulging eyes, glowing like fire. After five to ten or fifteen minutes everything disappeared again. We went outside and looked around, and nothing could be seen. Only something like a sneering laughter could be heard all around."

"One morning she said laughingly: 'Look under the altar box!' I did not respond, but she looked with such fear that I thought of a snake, which so often come into the houses, but I was greatly astonished — there were about 50 frogs. She did not let anybody touch them, but she herself put them into a container and they were thrown into a hole far away. By noon, just as many had appeared again. I had them removed; and at a time when nobody was looking, I put a medal in the place — and it was quiet."

Often, it was not clear whether Germana herself or the demon spoke from her mouth. The report goes on:

"She was once given strong doses of opium, in order to break the crisis. She took the tablets laughingly and then screamed: 'Oh, the long-legged fool gave them to you for me so that I should sleep! Has anybody ever made a spirit sleep?' Then she raged hours on end. The pills had no effect. During her crises, she felt no physical pain."

Every orthodox physician would ascribe this to auto-suggestion. But to the person who knows about spirits, it is clear that they cannot be influenced by chemicals. They obey their own transcendental laws.

Germana was exorcised over a period of 7½ months. The Bishop of Natal finally succeeded in the definitive exorcism, which brought on a stench which "cannot be compared to anything else." Thereafter Germana was completely normal. Many who have been possessed die at an early age, and this girl died (of consumption) at age 23.

The Possessed Cat

Professor Dr. Vintila Horia, of Madrid, Spain, described the following to me in a personal conversation:

"Originally I came from Rumania, and in my home country I knew a very well-educated lady who told me about her cat to which she was

attached in an ambivalent relationship — that is, she loved as well as feared her cat. The cat was dark brown, not black, and at the time of the events was eight years old. At that time, the cat urinated on every religious book, even if they were lying underneath other non-religious books. Once, the lady wanted to hang up an icon but hammered the nail in crooked. She put the icon on the table and while looking for a new nail, left the room for a short moment. In her absence, the cat jumped on the table and pawed the icon until it fell and was badly damaged. This cat also behaved strangely in other ways. An automobile once rolled over her and she suffered no injuries."

It is difficult to comment concerning this case. Although cats tend to be solitary beings, they do have close relationships with significant contact persons. Thus, the demonic in the owner may have transferred into the cat, but this can only be a matter of speculation since no more precise information about that incident is available. Its significance lies in the fact that it suggests that even an animal can be infiltrated by the demonic in some way.

Although many of these extreme cases are drawn from earlier times, again and again we see similar patterns and forms of appearances, sufficient to strongly suggest that possession is a unique phenomenon, not to be confused with clinical schizophrenia, or other syndromes with some overlapping features of ego-splitting.

14. CULTS AND CHARISMATICS

Cultic Possession

Information about the character and form of possession can be found today in Voodoo cults in West Africa and Haiti, and especially in the Afro-Brazilian syncretism (the mixture of Christian and animistic religions) of the various places of worship, "Macumba," "Candomblé," "Umbanda" and "Quimbanda." From Quimbanda to Macumba we observe nuances from black magic to white magic. In the true sense of the word, these are worship services, during which the initiated make themselves available to their gods by rendering their own bodies to them for material manifestations. Even if one does not participate in these services as mediums, the whole being is affected. I visited a number of *terreiros* (worship houses) in Rio de Janeiro and also in San Salvador (Bahia), where I was introduced by disciples and physicians and was provided the opportunity to experience genuine events. But I gained meaningful insights only after reading Serge Bramly's book *Macumba*[1] and then Gert Chesi's work *Woodoo* (Voodoo).[2]

First, a brief description of cultic events:

The *terreiro* as a place of worship may have an old tradition or be established anew by members of a traditional one. The rites adhere to unwritten laws, and resemble one another, whether white or black magic. In the Macumba or Quimbanda cults, the same numinous entities (gods) are worshipped, but since they, like all gods of nature and man himself, have ethically antipodal character, they have to be categorized differently depending on the way magic in the cult is practiced.

The *terreiro* is sometimes headed by a male leader, "Pae de Santo," but more often by a female leader, "Mae de Santo." They are supported by male or female assistants. The spirit of the worship place obeys them. Persons gifted as mediums are recognized by the leader or by an initiate during a trance, and become first novices and then initiates, through months of training, while cut off from the social milieu.

Under strict control by the Pae or the Mae de Santo, through drumming and singing, the orgiastic event is played out during the actual worship as the intervention of a particular and often stern personal god, who rides his "horses" quite properly. Most varied paranormal events thus take place. The desire of individual "gods" for energy-laden liquids — highly concentrated alcohol — makes the person under their spell drink liters of it; but this amount, which would normally be fatal, dematerializes, i.e. is transferred by the god into the transcendental sphere. The phenomenon of Indian Yogis,

---

[1] Serge Bramly, *Macumba,* (Freiburg Breisgau: Bauer Verlag, 1978).

[2] Gert Chesi, *Woodoo* (Perlinger Verlag, 1979).

who remain uninjured despite the ingestion of hydrochloric or sulfuric acid, should be interpreted in the same way.

The Mae or Pae de Santo always prevents the most flagrant excesses by muffling the drums, by blowing smoke from herbs grown according to cultic guidelines, and sprinkling with cold water which was drawn from the well of the *terreiro*. Here, again, we find a parallel to incense and holy water during Christian exorcisms.

During later phases of the rites, the entranced mediums are available as psychological counsellors, most often prescribing magic to resolve problems. In the circle, which is not accessible to tourists, all the participants finally meld, as I myself experienced, into a brotherly and sisterly union. Due to a pronounced receding of the egos, this experience was extraordinarily freeing and joyful.

The above description shows clearly how academic and intellectual our contemporary scholastic psychiatric perception appears with regard to demonic possession. A lack of ethnological knowledge makes it impossible to compare these phenomena. Thus, there is a tendency to fall back on the characteristics of epilepsy, schizophrenia and hysteria — clinical appearances familiar to psychiatry. In addition, the lack of knowledge about the *corpus subtile* (ethereal body) inhibits the comprehension of the real connections. That is why every possible interpretation of the event is reduced to physicochemical activities in the brain, even though this can never lead to a complete view.

Except for epilepsy, which, compared to cases of possession, exhibits a completely different character, the picture of brain waves in schizophrenia and hysteria presents nothing pathological. Thus, no scientifically relevant proof of an organic involvement of the brain is evident. For a century, research on mental illness oriented in natural science has sought in vain for such evidence.

Cultic possession affects people who, outside of the cultic event are considered normal, but exhibit all the criteria of possession during such episodes. *Therefore, this cannot be explained as pathological organic occurrences in the brain.* The phenomenon of cultic possession renders invalid academic psychiatry's attempts to explain possession. We should look anew at cases of possession, such as the cases of Anneliese Michel and Gottliebin Dittus. They, like so many other possessed people, exhibit normal or adjusted personalities when not under the influence of external forces. Reference to extremely negative split personalities, appearing like seizures, cannot help us here. This is because, in the person possessed in the context of a cult, as well as the demonically possessed person, every assertion of the person's will is rendered impossible. The possessed person has lost so much of his/her individuality that after the event he/she has no recollection whatsoever of it. Harassed and infested persons, on the other hand, always are capable of recall.

Resistance to fire, often manifested during cultic possession, cannot be explained by natural science. We can observe such phenomena in many cultic events. Sigrid Lechner-Knecht[3], for example, reports on Indonesian horse

---

[3] Sigrid Lechner-Knecht, *Reise ins Zwischenreich.* (Herderbücherei), p. 182.

dancers, who, during the cultic trance, eat splinters of glass and prove to be fire resistant.

During events within the Brazilian *terreiro,* after having passed the novitiate, those who are newly initiated have become immune to the effects of fire. Fire resistance is tested with a burning candle held directly under the arm pit. The fire is not felt during the time an initiate is filled by some deity, and leaves no marks on the body.

The fire cult of the Indian avatar Sri Ganapathy Sachchidananda in Mysore is especially impressive. Ganapathy opens himself to the god of fire after previous ceremonies and prayers lasting many days and then is seized by this god on his anniversary, the 4th of March. In 1981, when I was present, he stood for 13-½ minutes in a fire pit and, his head directly above the layer of fire, materialized a cultic object for two minutes. He then climbed out of the ditch with his body and clothes unaffected. This phenomenon has been filmed on many occasions, and it is not the result of collective hypnosis.

In Ganapathy's case, I assumed that the avatar was capable of activating his ethereal body, extended about 20 to 30 cm, so that its energy surpassed the energy of the fire. The skin as well as the clothes were thereby protected. I asked Sri Ganapathy for his opinion; he did not confirm my hypothesis, but instead referred to the grace of God. Whereas my attempt to explain the phenomenon still hinges on physical factors in the ethereal range of the ethereal body, Sri Ganapathy emphasizes a purely spiritual (numinous) influence from the astral region. At some level both explanations are complementary to one another, and both are necessary to understand such phenomena.

In the light of cultic possession, it is especially apparent how much the human being is bound up in two worlds, the material and the spiritual. His *corpus subtile* (ethereal body) connects him to the non-material world, and through precisely this ethereal body, the transcendence also is enabled to enter into physical existence. Immaterial spirits, often connected with the archetypal, but also changeable — especially when influenced by the human from the physical sphere of existence — are able to approach and join him. Transcendent spirits possess the ability to guide the physical body of the influenced person according to their intentions, whether in ritual dances or in undisciplined behavior.

In Macumba, we become aware of spirits which are worshipped as gods there, but seem to be extraordinarily ambiguous entities. They understand how to dominate a person, but can also be dominated by a spiritually strong personality. Close association of man with the "divine," i.e. transcendental spirits, becomes especially palpable in that situation — an experience unknown to present-day Christianity, where God "reigns in lonely majesty."

Perhaps we are dealing with the concept of deities in the *terreiro,* who, like "elementals" — forms of thought awakened to corporeality and independence — evolve, but disintegrate as soon as the human energy impulse weakens. Biblical accounts of Jehovah (who most certainly should not be considered as belonging to the elementals), state that if His followers did not offer flesh sacrifice to Him, He would fly into a rage, because He was otherwise threatened with destruction. *Transcendence forms a unity with the material world and is dependent on it.* In the same vein, although on a more sublime level, the Christian mystic, Angelus Silesius, sings:

> I know that without me, God cannot be; And should I
> cease, Imperiled, so must he.

Pan, the Greek god of nature, the only mortal god beloved in the Greek Olympus, lost his influence, it appears to me, because mankind's spirituality changed from being rooted in nature to intellectual concepts. The cosmos, and our small world too, does not exist in linear developments, but in rhythms, and therefore everything at times strives toward a lowest point, only to rise again. Pan also returns. Today he does not conquer European Greece, but rather Africa, and Central and South America. He may win back more continents, perhaps even his Mediterranean homeland, but whether this requires decades or centuries is not important. It appears important to me that mental attitudes may dominate at times, but they always contain their polar opposite to which they strive to return. Thus, the fate of the sovereignty of the natural sciences today is sealed; not because their doctrines would lose their validity, but because their polar opposite is equally valid. The inquiring person will only come closer to the truth by considering both polarities. But first, as a condition for total knowledge, the world of magic, as well as the world of natural science, has to be *experienced.*

There is an essential difference in that the demonically- possessed person is seized by the negative numen *against* his will, whereas the person possessed in the context of cult worship, after months of preparation, *volunteers* his body to the transcendent beings. These beings — according to Maria José — crave to enter and experience the physical body. They are just as divided in their aspirations as humans themselves, and they need a person spiritually their equal, in fact, superior to them: the Mae de Santo or the Pae de Santo, who, depending on their ethical outlook, lead a Macumba *terreiro* in white magic or lead a Quimbanda cultic place of worship in black magic.

For an understanding of demonic possession, the procedures within the Macumba are of great importance. Some insights can be gained from the words of Maria José, the Mae de Santo mentioned in Bramly's book:

> *"It is my job to insure that the gods benefit from the trance as much as possible. I do my best to keep the trance under control. I make sure it is neither superfluous nor dangerous. Sometimes the gods are not aware of their power. They forget that their mediums are not invulnerable. Then I comfort them. If they react too strongly to the call of a song, I soothe them. Sometimes an uninitiated person goes into trance. However, she is not yet prepared to receive her god. Such a god (called Santo Bruto) holds no claim to the medium. I therefore demand of him to be patient and wait for the initiation of his child. I calm him with prayers, I change the rhythm of the drums and initiate different songs until he leaves again.*
>
> *"You see, the gods are not much different from us. They follow their nature. They obey their needs. Therefore, they can be influenced like*

humans by cunning, flattery, reason, prayer, or also with presents."

This last statement, understandably, will move the parapsychological animist to denote such events in the *terreiro* as a projection of the human imagination into an imaginary plane beyond. Only the person who has experienced the transcendent and is at home in both worlds, will be conceptually open to both possibilities.

The seizure by a *Santo Bruto* ("holy animal;" brutal, primitive being) corresponds most markedly to experiences with demonic possession. The cultic exorcism and treatment in the *terreiro* takes place primarily on a psychological and humane basis and then permits the possessing entity an honorable retreat.

In my opinion, the separation between Good and Evil, Christ and Devil, during Christian exorcism by a priest, is too drastic. It leads to a humorless power struggle, lacking any kind of love and any kind of understanding of the opposite side, which, in the last analysis, also owes its origin and existence to a divine decision. Such practice provokes the spirit — whatever kind it may be — to put up a desperate fight, and to seize another victim when it is driven out by psychically stronger forces. Even Jesus Christ himself made concessions in the case of the possessed man from Gadarene and permitted the escape of the devil through swine — a courageous behavior, since naturally it brought him little gratitude from the populace.

A parallel between cultic and demonic possession is found in the fact that, in both phenomena, not only numinous entities but also spirits of the deceased are involved. The difference lies in whether the "possession" is invited or imposed.

To quote Bramly:

"At a particular moment, a rather young woman suddenly collapsed. She began to limp and supported herself with a stick. Her voice sounded like that of an old man. The *Mae de Santo* explained: *'The spirit of a "Preto Velho" (old black) had descended into her. Pretos Velhos are spirits of old slaves or long-deceased blacks, who, during their lifetime, possessed great wisdom, the gift to heal, a great knowledge about the nature of things. They return to earth in order to help us, to guide us, and to counsel us. A spirit is capable of taking possession of any medium. He uses the body of the medium, to come to our help.'"*

Bramly: "But why the stick, the pipe, the hoarse voice?" *"Because in this case, it was an old man. The age of the medium no longer counts during the trance. A Preto Velho can take possession of a young man. He too will limp, and drag himself along with a stick, and smoke his pipe. When gods or spirits come down to earth, they always remain themselves. They do everything they enjoy. They drink, if they are addicted to alcohol. They smoke, if they wish; they speak like an old man, because they simply are old."*

Bramly: "Are you trying to say that the behavior of the mediums in trance last night represented that of the gods and spirits who possessed them?" *"Exactly so. Xangô for example speaks with pride, Oxalá is wise and majestic. Oxum is coquettish. The daughters of Oxum often put on makeup while in the trance, and they boast in front of the mirror. Sometimes, the gods again take up old quarrels here. Oxum and Iemanjâ, for example, fight out of jealousy. The gods, as usual, have their own personality, their own way of behavior. They have their qualities, but also their faults. The children of the gods, those who have fallen into trance, are not movie actors. They absolutely do not play a role. They themselves do not exist at all during a trance."*

Natural religions are maternalistic religions, monotheistic are paternalistic religions. Motherly understanding and fatherly strength of will are their characteristics. Monotheism is often represented as a progression of the spirit. I consider this to be incorrect. Both types of religion merely correspond to two partial polar aspects of the cosmos and thus also the divine. The *syncretism[4]* of Christian paternalistic religions and animistic natural religions of Africa appears to me to be an understandable development, and helps to explain its success in recent decades, marked by an increasing importance of women. The Christian paternalistic religion was not capable of preventing our Western psychic degeneration, addictions and ruthless materialism to the point of the destruction of man and nature, or the rise of pseudo-father figures like Hitler and other dictators. A mix of Christian and animistic exorcisms appears to me appropriate from a psychotherapeutic standpoint. The "mix" that would be most effective would presumably depend on the beliefs of the possessed.

From phenomena of cultic possession and the practices of syncretistic worship services, decisive impulses could affect our theological as well as natural scientific dogmas. The former, in my opinion, has lost its credibility and its ability to be widely understood. The latter are called into question with numerous problems which have recently been opened for discussion, such as the fortune telling arts of the I Ching and Tarot, astrology, the phenomena of precognition and materialization, acupuncture and psychic surgery, and especially the phenomenon of voices on tapes. Psychotherapy could benefit from considering such experiences and would thus not be limited to an atheistic and materialistic view of life.

Phenomenological Similarities Between Charismatics and the Possessed

As objective scientists, we must presume that the good as well as the evil in men express themselves in similar ways and according to basic spiritual and physical structures of life. There are certain parallels in the physical experiences of charismatics, i.e., persons imbued with positive ethical impulses as well as those who are demonically possessed.

Paranormal events — levitations, penetrations, materializations, apport phenomena, odor manifestations, etc. — can be found associated with saints

---

[4] Syncretism: the attempted reconciliation or union of different or opposing principles, practices or parties, such as in religion or philosophy.

as well as the possessed. Most modern psychiatrists and psychologists, unfortunately still caught in the prevailing diagnostic schemata and materialistic- rationalistic concepts, believe they recognize epilepsy and hysteria in the charismatic as well as in the demonically possessed person. The charismatic, too — if we think of Padre Pio[5] or Therese von Konnersreuth — is a seized person, although seized by positive powers. Particularly in the case of Therese Neumann, psychiatrists suspected mechanisms of hysteria. Witnesses who knew Therese since her youth unanimously report characteristics which contradict such an assumption.[6]

Therese von Konnersreuth's stigmata represent neither artificially inflicted wounds nor hysterical mechanisms of her body. They were expressions of spiritual imprints on the body in the sense of an identification with the martyrdom of Jesus Christ, whereby it does not matter whether this corresponds to the historical physical reality. The spiritual content is always the essential factor. Today we know that the nails with which Jesus Christ was fixed to the cross had to be pounded through his wrist bones; otherwise the muscles and tissue of the metacarpus, not hindered by the resistance of the bones, would have torn, and the body would have fallen. But in every ecclesiastical pictorial description, the nails are put between the bones of the metacarpus. Correspondingly, this is where we find, contrary to reality, the stigmata of the saints. This points out that the stigmata of a charismatic person did not develop as a consequence of retrospection into historical reality but are based on a collective concept within Christianity. Whatever is imprinted on the mind develops into psychoplastic reality within the physical events of the body, even if it is a collective misinterpretation.

Which poses the question: if the possessed (perhaps unconsciously) should imagine he is being whipped by the devil, are the welts on his skin the psychoplastic result of his imagination, or do demonic beings whip with *ethereal* torture? An objective scientific conclusion is impossible for the time being. We have neither reliable data on the unconscious powers of the soul at our disposal, nor are we able to objectively comprehend transcendental beings. The phenomena of paranormally-produced odors speak in favor of a *direct* influence of transcendental forces. In the presence of charismatic persons, the fragrance of flowers, and in the presence of the possessed, smoke and stench — especially the smell of sulfur — are perceived. Several reliable persons acknowledged to me that in a Swiss health resort during a class about magic, taught by a teacher of black magic, they noticed a penetrating stench of sulfur. It can hardly be assumed that this could merely have been the result of physical perspiration. According to my own experience and the references in literature, demonic forces can manifest themselves indigenously. The teacher

---

[5] *Padre Pio* was an Italian Capuchin monk (1887-1968) who, among other things, became well known for his healing abilities, piety, bi-location and ability to levitate. (For more details see *Tales of Padre Pio: The Friar of San Giovanni* by John McCaffery — originally published in Great Britain in 1978 by Darton, Longman and Todd Ltd. as "The Friar of Giovanni" and by Image Books (pb) Doubleday & Co., New York, in 1981).

[6] An excellent study of Therese Neumann was written by Dr. C. Sträter in *Grenzwissenschaften* ["Scientific Frontiers"] 1-1977.

referred to is well known to me. When he called up demonic spirits during a seance in my own rooms, all persons present could hear grinding and knocking sounds from the beams in the attic. Although I am often in this room, I never noticed this at any other time. Demonic spirits are capable of manifesting themselves materially. This and many other personal experiences lead me to the assumption that mental potentials can transfer into matter, both through the power of imagination of the possessed or the inspired (i.e. the bloody tears of Therese von Konnersreuth) as well as directly. In both the case of a mentally inspired person as well as a transcendent force, it is a matter of energetic phenomena. The penetration of blood through the scalp of Gottliebin Dittus, as well as Therese von Konnersreuth, is interesting. In Therese's case, however, it occurred under completely different psychological conditions. Levitation, too, occurs in saints (Therese von Avila, Padre Pio) as well as in those who are possessed (lads of Illfurt, Nicole Obri).

We find materializations in those who are demonically possessed and also in psychic surgeons (psychic healers), where the latter believe themselves to be — and possibly are — guided by angels; Indian avatars (incarnations of God) also materialize thoughts or archetypical structures.

These few and incomplete references may explain how the spiritual-mental and the physical are basically one and adhere to the same laws. According to old Christian tradition, God created a spiritual as well as a material world — worlds which not only correspond to one another, but also influence one another.

15. ANNELIESE MICHEL —
A CASE THAT WENT TO COURT.

Again and again we encounter exorcists — especially lay exorcists — who in no way exhibit the humanitarian prerequisites for a treatment which demands love and integrity. They often dominate sectarian churches and manifest a sadism of which they are not even aware. Should their actions lead to severe damage, or even to the death of the victim, judicial intervention is required. In such cases, their exorcistic activities reach public attention, which, according to my experience, always leads to a branding of exorcism and the problem of possession as a relic of the Dark Ages. Rationalism then celebrates a new triumph.

Such an event occurred in the case of Anneliese Michel, in 1978, at the county court of Aschaffenburg, Germany, on the occasion of the trial of the priests and the parents of the girl, whose death was charged against the defendants. Although neither their human integrity nor the ecclesiastical legality of their act was doubted, they were accused of stubbornness and being caught up in medieval ways of thinking. In the opinion of the court, they should have initiated clinical treatment. In my view this would have been equivalent to "psychic rape," since the patient, who was not a minor and was mentally lucid, firmly rejected such treatment. High regard of Germans for the infallibility of the dogmas of natural science and modern medical knowledge became apparent. Even if a university professor characterizes the events of a case quite inadequately, and from an unbiased physician's point of view, incorrectly, the court must adhere to the diagnosis. This is understandable, because the judges are not physicians. But in the case of Anneliese Michel, this led to a striking misjudgment. This case was not appealed because the defendants felt overwhelmed by an ideologically superior authority.

As a physician and psychiatrist who also received neurological training at the Salpétrière University Clinic in Paris, I will try to judge the reports available to me and compare these with my experiences and studies of possession and exorcism.

At my disposal are: 1. A detailed article by Gerhard Moss in the Züricher *Tages-Anzeiger* of 4-24-1978, with the title "Bewährung um jeden Preis" ["Trial at any Price"]; 2. A paper by Kaspar Bullinger, Bamberg, 1929: "Unschuldig verurteilt" ["Convicted Though Innocent"], 62 pages; and 3. The book by anthropologist Felicitas D. Goodman, PhD, *The Exorcism of Anneliese Michel* (New York: Doubleday).

The family history of Anneliese Michel is rather ordinary. Her ancestors were artisans; honest, industrious and resolute. A psychiatrist suspected that the girl suffered under the dominance of the father, but Anneliese never confirmed this and it appears to me to be one of those frequently offered explanations in psychiatry, in which psychic behavior is traced back to

Anneliese Michel

experiences in childhood. External reasons and research into causes are used to explain characteristics which do not correspond to the norm.

Shortly before she turned 17, Anneliese, (until then a normal teenager), suffered a seizure of a few minutes duration, leading to unconsciousness, followed the next night by a condition of extreme psychic and physical depression. Goodman (pp. 36-37) described it:

> *"Anneliese woke up and could not move. An overwhelming force held her arms pressed together. She spilled urine in her bed. Her tongue seemed to be paralyzed, and she thought, 'now I must die.' But when the tower clock struck, everything was over, the pressure was gone as if carried away by the wind. Only her tongue hurt somewhat."*[1]

Exactly the same thing happened a second time one year later, causing the mother to consult a neurologist, Dr. L. During the trial he mentioned (Bullinger, p. 11) "bitten tongue and foaming from the mouth," which would suggest the diagnosis of epilepsy, but the electroencephalogram did not confirm this diagnosis. Dr. L. never had occasion to observe an attack.

Subsequently, colds and an incipient tuberculosis became apparent, which suggested treatment in a sanatorium in the Allgäu mountains. The girl was not happy in the Allgäu mountains. In 1970, the third attack, which resembled the previous ones, occurred. Once her friends noticed a condition in which Anneliese stretched out her fingers spasmodically like the claws of a cat, which was undoubtedly a first manifestation of demonic influence. Then one day, soon after a short religious experience, she experienced the polar opposite: the vision of a devil's grimacing face. For some time thereafter, any prayer became impossible for her. One is reminded of the constellation and provocation of evil by the good. In a neuropsychiatric examination, which took place soon thereafter, the electroencephalographic tests showed no signs of epilepsy.

Barely recovered, Anneliese went back to high school and graduated. In 1972, an anti-epileptic drug (Zentropil) was prescribed for the first time, although no pathological neurological diagnosis had been established. The subjective and objective disturbances increased. Aside from transitory loss of consciousness and stiffening, Anneliese noticed more and more often an unpleasant stench, which her relatives at first could not identify. She often saw the grimacing face of a devil — often more then one — and then not only she, but also her siblings, noticed poltergeist phenomena such as knocking sounds and noise in the cabinet under the floor and on the ceiling of the room. An observation by the mother, who became seriously disturbed about this, appears characteristic to me. Anneliese stood as if in a trance in front of the statue of the Madonna in the house, stiff, her face distorted with hatred, with black instead of blue eyes (Goodman, pp. 52-53). (These black eyes probably were caused by extremely dilated pupils). The mother noticed

---

[1] This description vividly reminds me of my own experience in a castle plagued by a ghost, although it did not lead me to empty my bladder, nor did my tongue hurt.

how the hands looked like clawed paws. Who would not recognize here the aversion to the divine which only occurs during a demonic attack — described in all the literature on possession? The same thing occurred at San Damiano, a place of pilgrimage, in 1973. Before the fenced-in statue of the Madonna, Anneliese bared her teeth and could not step in, because the ground supposedly burned her like fire. On their way home she behaved indecently toward her travelling companion, tore a religious medal from her breast, spread an unbearable stench and spoke with an unnaturally deep voice.

Anneliese had always obediently taken the prescribed Zentropil. An EEG, taken in December of 1973, showed only a pattern "like epilepsy" with localized brain damage, which was diagnosed as being a result of the Zentropil medication. Therefore Tegretol (also a medication for epilepsy) was used, whereupon the EEG became normal.

The psychological condition of the girl nevertheless deteriorated further. More and more, depressive states became apparent and the patient always saw herself pursued by the devilishly grimacing faces. Contrary to her earlier inclination, the girl now developed a growing aversion to religious and consecrated objects. She began exhibiting manic rages and made physical attacks on members of the family. The stench was also noticed more often. Since the physicians could not do any more for her, the family concluded that Anneliese's case involved a religious or psychic component. Reverend Alt and Chaplain Roth were called, but even before Reverend Alt, who — as will be reported later — lived in the parsonage at Ettleben (which probably was haunted by the spirit of Valentin Fleischmann), came into contact with Anneliese, occurrences which are of immense scientific significance happened within and around him. He was a mature and irreproachable man. His talent or ability as a medium appears to be of crucial importance here. He is known to be an excellent dowser and his clairvoyant abilities can be noted from the following reports to the bishop:

> "Suddenly I was able to describe the whole family: father, mother, siblings, grandmother. But I could not "know" it, because I had not yet seen the family. I also could ascertain that Anneliese had an enormous radiation from her neck, or, as the case might be, her thyroid and her head. I did not notice anything compromising. Naturally, this did not allow one to draw any conclusion as to the possibility of possession.

> "Two days thereafter, another Brother (Reverend Herrmann, who was entrusted with the case) visited me. He put two letters in my hand, one from the mother and one from the daughter Michel. I had not read the letters, when suddenly I felt nauseated, as if I might lose consciousness at any moment. I felt a strange agitation never experienced before — all of this to the horror and astonishment of my fellow Brother who was present. But even this did not seem enough to prove possession.

> "In the evening during mass, as I prepared myself mentally for the holy transubstantiation and as I included this girl, not yet known to me, in the offertory, I suddenly received what seemed like a blow on the

back. A cold current of air blew over my head from behind. At the same time there was a strong smell of burning. I had to lean against the altar. With an enormous effort and concentration, I spoke the words for the transubstantiation and the rest of the canon. Somehow I was in distress — confused. I felt as if a negative power surrounded me, which could not harm me but could torment me.

"After the service, I immediately went to see a fellow Brother, to whom I described everything calmly and in detail. The following night was the most restless of my whole life. Although I had taken a strongly acting sleeping pill, which normally always helped, I could not find rest. A whole gamut of stenches filled my room: smells of burns, manure, sewer, and feces. As I reached for the rosary, when I recited another prayer — it stank horribly! In addition, several loud rumbling sounds occurred in my filing cabinet. I was lying in bed extremely oppressed and tried to pray; and then I was reminded of my priestly powers. In my own words, I said an exorcism. For a few moments, it became easier for me. I was icy cold, but wet from sweat. In my distress, I called on Padre Pio in my mind, who I knew had had similar experiences. Nothing happened. I repeated my invocation — and suddenly an intensive fragrance of violets filled my room. At first, I believed that perhaps it was shaving water on my pajamas, but everything reeked of sweat. Strangely, the sweating was over in an instant — my body became warm. I exhaled in astonishment, and only now noticed that my field of view had been narrowed and my perception of colors had been reduced. I was now able to perceive the colors in their normal intensity. The pressure on my head had suddenly disappeared. Until it was time to get up, I was able to sleep quietly and with relaxation for one hour.

"On the following evening, as I reported this to my fellow Brothers, they suddenly could also notice this strange stench. The whole parsonage of the neighboring congregation [The Parsonage of Unserer Lieben Frau, where he was visiting] smelled of burning, although all the windows were open.

"These 'seizures' repeated themselves a few more times. They usually diminished and stopped, for the most part abruptly, when I prayed the exorcism. Sometimes one could speak of a struggle.

"In conversations about Anneliese Michel . . . I smelled — it was during an evening walk with my friend Chaplain Roth — the gamut of stenches already experienced and learned more details. . . . A few weeks later I met Anneliese Michel personally."

Father Alt was convinced that this was a case of demonic possession. The patient growled like an animal in his and Chaplain Roth's presence. She bared her teeth and when she left the room a horrible stench, mixed with a burned smell, was often left behind.

Both priests recited the *Exorcismus probativus* (a trial exorcism to determine demonic influence) over the girl. The behavior of the victim convinced the priests, but at the beginning they believed they had been successful after this first try, because Anneliese felt strangely free. However, the condition soon worsened. She ran naked through the house, put flies and spiders into her mouth, chewed coal, urinated on the kitchen floor and licked the urine. Often, she hit her relatives and bit her friend in the arm. Swarms of flies appeared and disappeared again and shadowy little creatures flitted around in a dark and threatening manner, frightening the tenants. [Goethe calls the devil the "Master of Flies and Mice" (Faust), so this detail, so to speak, exhibits archetypal character].

On the other hand, small oval-shaped wounds opened up on Anneliese's feet, which the family, in awe, interpreted as stigmata (wounds of the crucifixion). This detail clearly shows the tough struggle between the good and the evil in polar confrontation in the body and being of the girl.

As a Catholic, she was convinced that she was being representationally subjected to an atonement experience for the benefit of alienated German youth and many renegade priests, which shows, especially in these significant details, how wide- ranging and bitter was the struggle between good and evil. Father Rodewyk, too, became a witness to the possession. He succeeded in inducing the "devil" Judas to name himself.[2]

The three clerics petitioned the Bishop of Würzburg for permission for an exorcism which the Salvatorian priest, Father Superior Arnold Renz, was prepared to perform.

For the parapsychologist, the following fundamental questions are raised:

1. Did Father Alt, as a clairvoyant [better: as a "clairflairant" — "clear smelling"] perceive the odors which were produced by Anneliese's demons — especially, it is presumed, by the late Father Valentin Fleishmann who had officiated earlier in the parsonage? Or did they come into the picture by themselves? The latter appears more probable, since Father Alt's fellow-priests were also confronted by the stench. A mental induction (mental transmission by telepathy) on the priests by Father Alt appears improbable because the stench occurring around Anneliese and other possessed people was also always noticeable by all persons present.

2. Were the poltergeist activities which Father Alt heard in the filing cabinet triggered by the psychic tension within him? Or were the demonic spirits who threatened the possessed capable of having the same effect in Ettleben?

I do not believe that this question of alternative explanations can yet be resolved. The first version may be exemplified by C. G. Jung's experience, when during an agitated conversation with Sigmund Freud, a loud detonation was heard in the cabinet in the room. Jung believed he — perhaps together

---

[2] Here, I would like to suggest that the name announced by the demon could not have been that of the apostle, who appears to me not at all as detestable as the church would have us believe — but rather was adopted by a strong demonic spirit. I believe this to be rather generally the case for most names given by demonic forces during exorcistic rituals.

with Freud — exteriorized the tension, i.e. had transferred it into the environment.

On the other hand, we know that in cases of possession, poltergeist and barn spooks occur frequently. In the case of the possessed lads of Illfurt, haunting also occurred in the far-away parsonage and four other houses which were scarcely, if at all, related to the events. It has to be added to this that during later exorcisms, performed by Father Renz, the spirit of the criminal Father Fleischmann,[3] who formerly officiated at Ettleben, announced himself. It is plausible, therefore, that this spirit may be seen as causing the paranormal occurrences which took place within and around Father Alt.

The actual exorcisms were conducted by Father A. Renz, from September 1975 until Anneliese's death on July 1, 1976. The exorcistic struggle with the demons was preserved on more than forty cassettes which clearly recorded the diagnostic *signa* (signs) of possession, as noted in the *Rituale Romanum*. These recordings are of eminent scientific importance for research into possession and also leave room for critical reflection. Previously I have called into question that the spirit "Judas" was identical with the Apostle of that name, and I assume this to be the case for most of the demons who were asked for their names. The supposed occupants of Anneliese's psychical structure are not convincing that they are who they claimed to be, for it is unlikely that the (perhaps only mythological) spirits of Cain or Judas or Nero were still lurking around and got caught up in the psyche of Anneliese. I also assume that Lucifer, highest in the hierarchy of negative deities,[4] is involved in more important events — especially with regard to world affairs — than with this inauspicious high school girl. (Hitler also has been laid claim to in too many tape-recorded voices for his omnipresence to be credible). However, I accept that Fleischmann, a local spook, could possibly still be bound to a sphere close to earth, since the inhabitants of the Ettleben parsonage have reported that a ghost clad in black haunts the house.

Once when a rather casual reference was made to the spiritually-reprehensible Fleischmann (active in Ettleben 1572-1575) Anneliese screamed horribly and something similar occurred on a later occasion when she heard his name. This came as an unexpected reaction for the exorcists. Here, too, her clairvoyant ability, characteristic of most possessed persons, could have caused a connection between Father Alt's knowledge and Anneliese's unconscious.

I do not doubt, because of personal experiences, that demonic spirits acted within Anneliese, but as lying spirits, what they said should not be taken at face value. The same applies to the alleged positive spirits, whom even the possessed did not fully trust. The "Mother of God" stated as early as 1975 that the "Judgment" is near, and that the "Savior" suggests: "Hoard groceries in your house. Tell it to all you know." (Goodman, pp. 154-55). In addition, the "Savior" said to Anneliese, who also mistrusted the message: "You will become a great saint." So far, this has not happened, and it seems

---

[3] Murderer of a girl with whom he had sexual relations.

[4] This obviously is also speculative.

to me improbable it will happen in the future. Nor did the prophecy of the "Mother of God," that Anneliese would be completely released on October 1975, come true. Furthermore, Joseph, Padre Pio, Therese von Konnersreuth and other ecclesiastic celebrities appear, but only in the reports of the demons.

The following observation in F. Goodman's book (p. 142) is interesting: "The most effective weapon of the priests is the cross-examination by the interrogators." While the priests were versed in this, the demons did not possess this ability. The ability to ask questions supposedly is a human trait, and demons are not humans. As a matter of fact, I have never been asked a question by the voice of a demon through the mouth of a possessed person. The above observation is certainly remarkable.

I do not doubt at all the possession of Anneliese by transcendental demonic spirits. They probably were constellated by the almost saint-like character of the girl who imagined she was undergoing atonement. At first, they only manifested themselves in animal sounds, demonic grimaces and terrible contortions of the body. Then, through the priest, and especially through Father Renz, a new psychic force field was brought in, within which the demons — just as in the cases of other possessed people — were capable of expressing themselves through Anneliese's vocal organs. Names, as personal denotations of specific demons, and also the positive numina (Mary, Joseph, Padre Pio etc.), appear to me to be constellated (together with their expressions) through the combined energies of all participating psyches; that is, the priests, other participants, and Anneliese. The latter, as a possessed person, could have, in clairvoyant fashion, received and processed ideas of the exorcists.

I am of the opinion that there are angelic as well as demonic entities but that names frequently occurring in the literature on possession: Cain, Judas, Nero, etc., do not contain their immortal, spiritual individuality, but at most a mental identity.

Expiatory Suffering

The imitation of Christ by sacrificing one's own life, is, as far as death is concerned, a typically Christian phenomenon. Christ, who sacrificed his life to spread his message of salvation, was imitated by numerous martyrs as a witness for their Christian beliefs. As early as Job, we find the motif of a spiritual renewal and deepening of the knowledge of God through suffering leading to the boundaries of psychic and physical exhaustion. This motivation is spread worldwide, and is as much a determinant of suffering for the sake of atonement as it is of sacrifices for the salvation of one's fellow men.

In Mahaiana Buddhism, we find parallel concepts. Spiritual teachers who themselves are at a state of development where they need no rebirth as *Bodhisattvas* (enlightened individual, usually a Buddha), can continue to take on the suffering of a reincarnation to help others on their developmental paths.

Anneliese herself, in my opinion, was not always fully aware of her approaching destiny as an expiatory sacrifice. This perhaps explains why she strove for and accomplished her graduation from high school in spite of vicious demonic attacks. According to resources accessible to me, she possessed an unusually positive character structure, which made her martyrdom possible. As mentioned before, from a religious or positive orientation it is perceived that — especially in an unusually positive character — a provocation of the polar opposite principle can occur.

So here we encounter a religious drama, the conclusion of which — a sacrificial martyrdom — was already programmed in the unconscious. In my opinion, the anti-epileptic medication did not result in the physical death; Goodman appears too extreme with this opinion. But anti-convulsant, as well as anti-depressive and anti-psychotic medications, administered to attempt to control causes of physical agitation, impair, as we know, acuity and consistency of thinking and, in fact, all mental functioning. Academic pharmacology operates rationalistically and within the realm of philosophical materialism which presumes to control physicochemical causes. Spiritual healing, which is the goal of exorcism as well as of homeopathy, operates within the realm of imagination and attempts to re-establish lost harmony.

It would be conceivable, of course, that the strong anti-epileptic medication weakened the psychic structure of the girl and made it possible for possessing spirits, no matter what kind they may have been, to remain and may even have provided renewed entry. Presumably the exorcisms always failed when Anneliese was given a new medication, but since a positive correlation cannot be established, it should not be assumed.

The neuropsychiatrist with more than an academic knowledge of science who analyzes the tape recordings of Father Renz, will recognize that the symptoms of the patient were not in the least similar to an epileptic seizure. For example, an epileptic in a crisis cannot engage in a conversation or formulate sentences. Whether Anneliese in her first three episodes had a foamy mouth and suffered bites on her tongue, remains unclear, but this phenomenon is not only pathognomonic (typical for one illness alone) of epilepsy, but is also symptomatic of other spastic types of attacks. Demonic possession as such must also be considered.

The court's opinion that Anneliese's parents and priest had starved her to death does not appear valid on close examination. The girl had always begun to eat again, often after a prolonged food prohibition demanded by the demons. The caretakers took that into account and did not believe her to be at the end of her strength, since even shortly before her death she was capable of doing 600 knee bends, under the compulsion of demonic command. Death came apparently as a result of pneumonia which could not be combatted by the weakened organism (Goodman).

The attending physicians and medical advisors *had* to reach the above faulty diagnosis, because "demonic possession" is not considered a valid diagnosis in rationalistic professional circles. But life obeys other rules. One feels urged to remember Goethe's verse in the Walpurgis Night (Faust I):

> But you're still here! Oh! This is insolent! Begone! Why, we
> brought in Enlightenment! This Devil's pack, with them
> all rules are flouted. We are so clever, yet there is no

doubt about it: There's still a ghost at Tegel.[5]

Goethe expressed these words of biting sarcasm because even at the turn of the previous century in the wave of enlightenment, influence of non-corporeal beings on humans and houses was recognized as the darkest superstition. However in Tegel, near Berlin, such a massive and rationally inexplicable haunting occurred, that the case received great attention.

Let us briefly examine the question of the guilt or innocence of the defendants as well as of the physicians and judges involved. Although basically, psychology today is closer to the truth than it was 80 years ago, academic medicine is still of the opinion that matter dominates the mind, and thus the chemical strait jacket (chemotherapy) and electroshock are considered capable of restraining all mental activities. Both methods, with prolonged and intensive use, cause damage to brain and mind even though this effect is down-played by those who use these techniques. Clearly they impair the immediate language and motor responses. In individual cases during extreme agitation, it is often necessary to use these methods, but basic problems are not dealt with. I am convinced that no clinic could have prevented Anneliese's desired death as a sacrifice, either by anesthetizing her or by artificial nourishment. Elemental mental-spiritual intentions are, in the long run, always stronger then any external intervention. Therefore, although the judges decided most conscientiously, their guilty verdict affected *innocent people.*

The trial, which took place in Aschaffenburg, is significant because of its cultural-historical and mental-scientific perspective. In Great Britain, presumably the court might have arrived at a different conclusion. That country — perhaps because it did not have to undergo the inquisition and persecution of witches, with resultant destruction of many mediumistic gifts — is today more open-minded toward spiritual events. For example, at the turn of the century, Sir William Crookes, the famous naturalist and psychic researcher, had become president of the Royal Academy of Science.

The examination of Anneliese Michel's case of possession was especially important to me. In this trial, a mental attitude was expressed which lacked any flexibility and corresponded to thoughts of "forever yesterday." Spiritual and religious content is disregarded because it cannot be proven by natural scientific methods. How refreshing, in comparison, the statement by Claude Macy Hathaway (born 1902), the American physicist and inventor of the electronic brain, appears: "Modern physics teaches me that nature is not capable of bringing order to itself. But the universe constitutes a great mass of order. Therefore a great primary cause is necessary, which does not submit to the second law of thermodynamics, and which thus is supernatural [not material but spiritual (N.)]."[6]

---

[5] von Goethe, (trans. by Passage), *op. cit.,* pp. 145- 146. Used by permission.

[6] In: *Allg. Zeitschrift für Parapsychologie,* Vol. 7, No. 3, p.117.

16. Harassment and Multiple Personality Disorders

Multiple Personality Disorders (MPD)

Drastic, abrupt changes in personality are frequently encountered among patients receiving psychotherapy or psychiatric care. The behavior patterns of these patients change so abruptly that many mental health professionals now use the term Multiple Personality Disorder (MPD) to describe this phenomenon. Clinical case records often reveal histories of suppressed anxieties, fears and hostilities which can be traced to traumatic experiences, such as physical and sexual abuse and molestation, buried in the subconscious. From this it is hypothesized that one or more distinct, alternate personalities have been created by the patients to cope with their traumatic experiences.

In his book, *MULTIPLE MAN: Possession and Multiple Personality,* Adam Crabtree, a psychotherapist, wisely points out that this phenomenon should not be viewed exclusively as possession *or* multiple personality, but that some cases may be a result of dissociated personalities, while others are more likely to be cases of harassment by the spirit of a deceased person.

Crabtree's clinical experiences have led him to conclude that both multiple personality and harassment should be considered when viewing the entire range of such disorders. My own clinical experience has also caused me to conclude that the role of external entities should be considered. I know that the trauma of abuse and other shocking experiences results in scars on the psyche which are generally suppressed and emerge later in unusual disturbed behavior. In cases of weakened ego and/or extreme stress, external entities may invade or harass the person to the point where counselling or treatment is indicated to enable the patient to return to a normal state. Unfortunately, in my judgment, those clinicians who cannot conceive of a post-mortem existence, limit their diagnosis of such abnormal behavior.

Harassment Differs From Possession

Harassment differs fundamentally from possession. Spirits of all kinds, but most probably "poor souls," and less frequently, also angel demons of cosmic-archetypal origin appear to be involved. "Elementals," i.e. spirits developed from ethereally condensed images and emotional content, may also occasionally play a part. None of these beings is capable of conquering the body of the victim, but they harass it at a "distance," although nothing is measurable within the dimensions of transcendence. The ego of the harassed person seems to be strong enough to prevent complete surrender of itself; therefore, during exorcism no names or any other data can be obtained. The exorcised person remains mute, but nevertheless, the psychotherapist must try

Self-portrait, drawn during a trance, by a harassed patient.

to strengthen the ego of the harassed person, since, often for personal reasons, it has become susceptible to the whispering spirits of harassment. These internal reasons may be that the harassed person desires social contact, but his physical and psychological conditions make it difficult for him to make such connections.

The harassed person does not inflict injuries on himself. He believes that he hears voices in his environment, perceives odors and suffers irritating and sometimes painful touches on the surface of his body. Inexplicable changes in his environment, spatial displacements of household objects (telekinesis) cause him to firmly believe in spirits which are external to his psychosomatic reality. The situation here resembles what shall later be described as infestation.

In cases of harassment, mediumistic sensitivity seems to be an essential ingredient.[1] Many authors on the paranormal and especially Wickland, point out that the aura of a medium glows particularly strongly and attracts "unreleased" spirits, still bound to earth. They get caught in it or, if the medium's ego is still strong enough to resist complete possession, remain bound to the vicinity.

I have concluded from my own experiences with exorcism that the number of harassed persons appears to be much greater than the number of those who are possessed. During the last 150 years, the percentage of harassed and especially possessed appears to have decreased when considered as a percentage of the growing population, presumably because egos have gained strength with the increased intellectualization of Western nations. The psychiatrist who is open-minded about the problem, however, does not fail to recognize the phenomenon because of its less frequent occurrence. Only the academically-oriented scientist categorizes all these cases as schizophrenia, without noticing that the inflicted persons do not, in the least, exhibit the components of schizophrenia in their character structure. The person whose perceptions are not externally verifiable is considered schizophrenic, especially by the medical profession.

Jean Baptiste Delacour, the author of the book *Apage Satana,* points out that originally, the Catholic church did not distinguish between harassment and possession. The *Rituale Romanum* discusses only *obsessio.* Only in the 18th century was a more accurate distinction made between different categories of possession. Thus the differentiation into *possessio* (the actual possession), *circumcessio* (harassment), and *infestatio* was made.

Delacour's observation that harassed persons, in contrast to possessed persons, do not react to religious objects, corresponds with my own experience. In borderline cases, the only symptom experienced during contact with holy water is a sensation of heat, rather than complete inability to tolerate it.

Delacour reports further[2] on the opinion of the Catholic church that harassment, especially, constitutes a test by God. The person is tested by

---

[1] This suggests that mediumistic sensitivity is "neutral" and can serve in a positive sense for well-integrated personalities, but can cause problems for those who are under stress or emotionally unstable.

[2] *Apage Satana,* p. 18.

temptation, as was demonstrated in the stories of the lives of the saints. As a result, the state of harassment itself disappears after the test has been successfully passed, while possession requires exorcism. Since true saints are few, we usually encounter the average person afflicted by *circumcessio,* whose mediumistic sensitivity attracts spirits. In their cases, a special divine test is not required, but without counselling or treatment, as well as exorcistic rituals, these cases are not healed.

In the harassed person, we do not observe a "crisis," during which — as may be remembered — the dominance over psyche and body is temporarily lost. On the other hand, the patients report occasional emotional explosions, whereby, usually without witnesses, they rant and rage against the molesting spirits. The latter do not expressly announce their re-appearance, as is often the case in possession, but re-appear unexpectedly after occasional periods of calm. The strongly harassed person feels continually beleaguered and often experiences whispering and molestations by the spirits day and night.

The degree of harassment may range from massive oppression to occasional establishment of contact. In the case of isolated sensations, or special messages — often from divine sources — a pathological condition cannot be assumed, since we are all open to transcendental events in differing degrees. As in all physical illnesses, the change from health to illness is fluid. Nor should we speak of harassment when a person at chosen, regular intervals — usually while in a trance or semi-trance — intentionally seeks to open themselves to spirits.

One could ask the question whether Eugenie, Princess of Leyen, was harassed. In principal, certainly, but in her case the essential difference was that the "poor souls" did not torment her or use her for ignoble, ego-centric purposes. They came for help which the princess provided in a sovereign manner.

Hardly any report better establishes how the transcendental and material worlds are interwoven, than does the one of Eugenie. Possession and harassment are expressions of just this fact. The many facets of the psyche are expressed in qualitative and quantitative differences which the orthodox psychiatrist categorizes normally as schizophrenia (split personality), or in other cases as schizoid. Wickland, Bull and Van Dusen demonstrated how many schizophrenics confined to hospitals are actually possessed or harassed persons, whom they were able to treat successfully with their own methods, where clinical psychiatry had failed.

Formerly, during the time I was an assistant surgeon in the psychiatric hospital, only the most severe paroxysmal attacks in patients were treated with morphine. In all the other cases, a mildly sedating medication was considered sufficient. Today the psychically ill person is overwhelmed by constant and massive chemotherapy. What kind of damages the nervous system and psyche will suffer as a result of this has not yet been determined. The confirmation of such damage often requires decades of research. (The issue in question finds its parallel in chemical agriculture. Every year the ground is treated several times with poisonous chemicals, which not only destroy the pests, but also their natural "enemies." The result is the "Silent Spring." Nature and life, with their blessed polarities and rhythms, are gravely disturbed. With each species that becomes extinct, the spirituality of this world is that much more impoverished.) The spiritual foundation of the patient is weakened to such an extent that personal impulses for recovery and positive development are literally prevented. The healthy conflicts between the positive and the negative, strengthening spirit and soul, are forcibly interrupted. Although relative calm reigns, it is the peace of mental inactivity. A patient, declared to be schizophrenic (whom I had previously known as a gregarious person even when in a mental crisis, and not at all schizoid), after 1½ years of medical treatment — justified because she was suicidal — became a very dull person, although still able to work. Only 2 years later were the damages somewhat mitigated. All this applies only to patients who undergo massive chemical treatment; the usual drugs for relaxation and sleep in normal dosages do not cross over a certain threshold of tolerance.

Nevertheless, the question remains, whether the massive use of psycho-pharmaceuticals could perhaps be a blessing for the possessed or the harassed person, but strong pharmaceuticals, which anesthetize the mind of the afflicted person to a considerable degree, have no effect on non-corporeal spirits, and only impede their effect on the organs of human communication. This affects mind and body. Since these "therapeutic agents" always weaken the spirit, the soul and the ego of a person, the situation after treatment is worse. In fact, it is statistically established that although the time a hospitalized person spends in the institution has decreased, relapses occur much more frequently. It is not accurate to call this healing if the healthy defenses of the psyche have been weakened, for this makes possible the mental takeover by transcendent negative spirits.

The Treatment of a Non-Schizophrenic Delusional Patient, Who Phenomenologically Exhibited the Symptoms of Harassment.[3]

F. K. was born in 1900 as the youngest of 9 siblings. At the time of treatment she was 68 years old, and claimed to have had a happy childhood. Although almost dwarfish and slightly chondrodystrophic, she reportedly had always had a cheerful nature and had loved to sing. Mental illness and depression had, according to her knowledge, not occurred in her family. She was never held back in school and after graduation from the primary school, she successfully attended a vocational school. Sexually, she developed late and had never had intimate friendships with men. Although two men had sought to marry her, she never agreed. Being introduced to the practice of masturbation by a childhood friend, she had always satisfied herself after feeling strongly aroused from external sources, but never felt guilty about it. Between the years of 50 and 60 this habit definitely disappeared. She had never visited a psychiatrist.

Until she had reached menopause, reportedly nothing abnormal had happened in her life. She enjoyed life, but then something strange happened

---

[3] See also "Die Circumsession," in *Paraps* (1/76).

to her. While at work, she suddenly felt compelled to take a pencil and make drawings. It was as though an invisible arm had been guiding her. Suddenly now, in a much more gifted way than before, she predominantly began to draw people, whereby the question arises whether, at that time, the spirits of deceased persons were involved. In any case, this event indicates the woman's strong mediumistic ability. She regretted it when this gift slowly began to vanish.

Not much later, the current episodes began. She had lived with a family where she had unpleasant experiences. Three of the children were deaf and non-verbal. A boy, Heinz, about 12 years of age, always had a sullen personality; in the many years of her stay she had exchanged less than a hundred words with him. Gradually, when she no longer was living in the same house, she got the feeling as if he lived around her (somehow like a ghost), observed her sexually and committed mischievous acts. He tortured her with stabs to her breast, used sexually filthy language, produced odors and visibly rattled a cabinet. Her older sister had neither heard nor smelled anything and had instead concluded that these were paranoid delusions of the patient, but for F.K. everything was very real. She was convinced the events were caused by "Heinz." She had talked to him and he had answered. He was always better informed about her situation at a particular moment than she was herself. For example, he was able to name the exact amount of money in her purse or the right number of pieces of linen in the drawer. She herself could not have done that. He was supposedly able to see her body through the ceiling. Often he jumped at her as though coming out of the wall, and when she lashed out at him with her handkerchief, he felt it and scolded her for it. The voice never spoke from out of herself, but always from her surroundings. In time, other male and female spirits also appeared; often, deceased relatives too were fetched by "Heinz."

To the spirits who were neither deceased relatives nor recognized by her, she gave proper names since each of them behaved differently toward her and exhibited very personal characteristics. Although her range of experiences had broadened in an interesting way, she felt troubled and tormented by the spirits, especially at night. Noise, whistling, smoking, banging and hissing continually prevailed.

As the appearances continued day and night, this patient, in April 1968, was advised by an esoteric society to seek help and counsel from me. I fully empathized with the patient's descriptions of the appearances. Any other procedure, considering the subjective reality of the experiences, would have led to an immediate breaking off of contact. I did ask her to consider that the real Heinz, as a living person, could never — not even as a ghost — be around her all of the time. Thus there must be spirits which we call mocking and deceiving ghosts involved, pretending to be Heinz and his companions. Intellectually, this explanation appeared acceptable to her; emotionally, it seemed to me, not quite so. The patient was instructed to pray for the obviously unreleased souls. In addition, I treated the woman bio-electrically with magnetic "passes" from head to toe, while the patient was dressed and comfortably seated in the therapeutic chair. A partial success was achieved immediately. The nights were more quiet; medication became superfluous;

and often (even during the day) she had hours when everything was calm. The "ghost" gradually retreated, saying it no longer liked the situation. After 6 months, in December, 1968, the patient discontinued therapy, thinking it was finished. In June, 1969, she reported a very tolerable situation with the appearances occurring to a much lesser degree. At the end of April, 1970, when asked to give another report, the patient complained about a relapse into earlier circumstances. New ghosts, different from one another with regard to intelligence, temperament and viciousness, had supposedly joined "Heinz."

I had already realized for a long time that the patient felt ambivalent toward her "ghosts." On the one hand, while she was tormented by the noise, the smell and the filthy language, in her discussions she dealt with them with a sisterly undertone, especially with "Heinz." Often while describing his expressions she had to laugh heartily. Since she retired she was able to live a relatively normal life — under her own control — but not without the tension presented. The now reinstated psychotherapy had to take this fact into account. In addition, the *hypnotic* component had to be strengthened. This presented no difficulties, since the patient was always in the condition of *"abaissement du niveau mental"* during treatment, and thus open to verbal suggestions. The procedures resulted in a quick and obvious improvement.

The picture had also changed in 1971, inasmuch as the patient (according to her) was not so much the center of the infestations because the ghosts fought among one another. While Heinz had become less active and his sexual interest in her had also receded, the other ghosts often attacked one another, making intolerable noise and often causing a bad smell. One ghost in particular, "Charlotte," tormented male members of the group of ghosts by stabbing and thoroughly persecuting them. "Heinz" was the only one she had spared. She herself only occasionally received a stab.

In 1972, Heinz, and sometimes his companions, claimed they were tired of it. Whole days and nights allegedly remained quiet. The patient also had moved into a home for retired people in which, although she did not find much contact, she felt comfortable. Under these conditions, she gave up treatment a few months later.

The *differential diagnosis* must first exclude paranoid schizophrenia. Olfactory, auditory, and tactile hallucinations are part of the picture of schizophrenia, but are also found under other psychopathological conditions. However, the patient lacked any obstinacy, any true despair, any misanthropy. Her language is markedly syntonic (in accord with its meaning) her mimicry lively, her mood open. Although the beginnings of delusions were present (she thinks the minister alludes to her in his sermon!), they were lacking any kind of systematization which is characteristic in paranoia.

The question of certain kinds of "shared delusional systems" (Kretschmer) must be considered seriously, but this is also characteristic of an internal psychic alienation, a partial loss of personality. The egos of these persons belong, so to speak, to the alleged opponents, with which no truly emotional relationship exists. Not so in this patient. Her ego is clearly delineated, remarks and responses are provided, she makes suggestions, and has almost too much of an affective rapport with the subjectively experienced spirits, which animistically could be explained as parts of her own personality.

A striking resemblance to our case is found in the experiences of the German chemistry professor, Ludwig Staudenmaier, who extensively and critically described his observations in the book which became well-known: *Die Magie als experimentelle Naturwissenschaft* ("Magic as Experimental Natural Science") (Leipzig 1922). In his case, too, automatic writing occurred first, then pre-hearing the written material and lastly, hallucinatory occurrences involving all functions of the senses. He, too, was capable of clearly separating his ego from the appearances. He maintained a critical position ("lucid possession"). In his case, too, we find the separation of the hallucinative partner into personalities with different characteristics. He himself believed in "mocking spirits" and asked himself whether he was possessed. The difference between possession *(possessio)* and harassment *(circumsessio)*, it seems, was not known to him. Although the parts of the personality (personifications) — in a spiritualistic sense, the spirits of possession — had extensively taken control of his organs, his ego remained free. I would characterize Staudenmaier as harassed.

Even among parapsychologists, the differences between animistic and spiritualistic orientations are obvious. The latter is certain of the existence of extra-personal "ethereal" spirits, who, in their ways, can influence our material world. According to my own experiences, knowledge of the literature and experience with patients, the spiritual interpretation appears more likely. But, to the non-material forces of the human soul, I also attribute phenomena which cannot yet be comprehended from the perspective of natural science.

Whatever genesis the phenomena of the patient had, my own inner attitude facilitated the interpersonal contact. Since I, like Staudenmaier, attribute the appearances which were described to the magical potential of the psyche (and possibly to transcendental beings or entities), the treatment could only be effective on the level of magic. Any dialectical psychoanalysis, or even any purely verbal suggestive treatment, would have been ineffective.

At that time, I was unacquainted with exorcism. I was able to do without it, inasmuch as the life of the patient (F.K.), in the end, had become clearly tolerable. Complete recovery was not gained, but exorcism, too, as a direct verbal and liturgical threat toward the demonic spirits, often brings release only after many years, if at all. Exorcism is certainly more spectacular — particularly for the psyche of the possessed person — but all external phenomena are less important than the mental and spiritual efforts of the care-giver. This was demonstrated by Blumhardt.

17. THE ELECTRONIC VOICE PHENOMENON

The Potential Risk of Intense Preoccupation With Paranormal Taped Voices

Thousands of persons, in recent decades, have experimented with "capturing" paranormal voices on magnetic tape. Many have achieved success, some almost immediately and others only after weeks or months of experimenting. Some have become so preoccupied with making contact with a deceased relative or friend that they have become deeply involved emotionally and have become vulnerable candidates for harassment or even temporary take-over by invisible entities.

Friedrich Jürgenson, a Swedish artist and film producer, who died in 1987, is generally credited as being the first to record such voices on tape. Dr. Konstantin Raudive (who died in 1974), Bad Krozingen, Germany, however, became even more widely known for his prodigious experiments with tape recorders which he reported in several books which have been translated into English and Italian. As far as has been recorded in the literature to date, Atilla von Szalay was actually the first to succeed in recording paranormal voices with mechanical and later electronic equipment. The fidelity of voices on phonograph records in the late 1930's was too poor to be persuasive; the wire recorder (which preceded magnetic tape recorders) also proved ineffective. In 1956, three years before Jürgenson got voices on tape which were of extraneous origin, a long letter by co-experimenter Raymond Bayless was published in the *Journal of the American Society for Psychical Research* in January 1959 which brought no responses, apparently because most parapsychologists at that time were not able to imagine that invisible entities could somehow imprint their voices on magnetic tape.

In 1959, Jürgenson had gone into the woods to record bird songs; when he played back the tape he heard a male Norwegian voice say something about "bird voices of the night." The more he concentrated on listening to the tape, the more voices he heard and the less likely it appeared that radio signals could explain what he heard. He heard his name called, then "Friedrich, you are being watched!" His dog Carino responded to the calling of his name on one of the tapes, and other voices, in Swedish, German or Latvian appeared. Jürgenson has admitted that the discovery was not "pure chance" — he had experienced an overwhelming desire to establish contact "with somebody or something unknown."

After four years of careful and systematic experimentation, he decided that the implications were too important not to be shared with others. He consulted with technicians and parapsychologists and in 1963 called an

143

international press conference at which he played his tapes and discussed the implications of his findings. He published a book reporting his experiments, *Sprechfunk mit Verstorbenen* in 1967. Dr. Konstantin Raudive, a psychologist and author of a number of philosophical books, visited Jürgenson in 1965 and together with him made a number of successful recordings. Raudive returned to Germany and began the arduous task of recording, analyzing and cataloging what amounted to well over 80,000 paranormal voices.

Raudive obtained technical assistance from Prof. Alex Schneider, a Swiss physicist; Theodor Rudolph, a high-frequency engineer with Telefunken; Dr. Franz Seidl, an electronics engineer in Vienna, and others in the construction of diodes, goniometer, etc. which used as alternate devices for microphones or interfrequency settings on radio to capture the paranormal voices. The results of his years of work were published in his book *Unhörbares wird Hörbar* ("The Inaudible Becomes Audible") which appeared in English translation published by Colin Smythe, Ltd., under the title *Breakthrough: An Amazing Experiment in Electronic Communication with the Dead* and later was published in New York by Tapplinger Publications and Lancer Books. Not everyone achieved success, but many did, with time, and became convinced that the "voices" did, in fact, represent efforts to communicate on the part of some deceased persons. Many of the serious investigators I had come to know: Friedrich Jürgenson; Dr. Raudive; Fr. Leo Schmid, Oeschgen, Switzerland; Hildegard Schäfer, Goldbach, West Germany; Franz Seidl, Vienna; Fidelio Köberle, Düsseldorf; Gunter Henn, Brucksal, West Germany; Wolfgang Dreiss, Ludwigshafen; and Viktor Bättig, Aesch/Basel; were all convinced the spirits of transcendent realms could imprint voices.

At first, during the early experiments (tune-ins) with Dr. Raudive, I was, like Dr. Hans Bender,[1] of the opinion that the voices must somehow represent impressions of unconscious energies of one or more participants. Of course, even this "animistic" interpretation of this phenomenon was remarkable and inexplicable. As a result of continued involvement with these experiments, which include "tune-in" sessions with Pastor Leo Schmid and listening to tapes sent to me by W. Dreiss and V. Bättig, I felt compelled to change my view and concluded that the voices did, in fact, come from discarnate entities. Examining and evaluating the work of Dreiss and Bättig, before I wrote a preface for their books, convinced me that they were dealing with a valid phenomenon.

Today an "Organization for Research on Tape-Recorded Voices" *(Verein für Tonbandstimmenforschung)* (VTF), with headquarters in Düsseldorf, Germany (organized in 1975) has over 1,500 members in a number of countries, and a newer European organization, Research Association for Paranormal Taped Voices *(Forschungsgemeinschaft für Tonbandstimmen)* Mönchengladbach, Germany, (organized in 1983), already has hundreds of members, many of them trained in physics, electronics, etc. In the United States, the America Association: Electronic Voice Phenomenon (AA:EVP) of

---

[1] Dr. Hans Bender: Director of the Institut für Grenzgebiete der Psychologie und Psychohygiene (Parapsychology Institute), Freiburg, Germany.

which Sarah Estep, 726 Dill Road, Severna Park, Maryland 21146, is president, has over 200 members from a number of countries. Some of the early experimenters in the U.S. have included Mary Sharpe, Michigan; Joe and Michael Lamoreaux, Washington; William Welch, California; Daniel McKee, Illinois, and Richard Veilleux, Maine. In Great Britain, Richard Sheargold, Raymond Cass, Gilbert Bonner, Alex MacRae, and David Ellis conducted private research in the field for years with little attention or encouragement from organized research societies. Individuals in Italy and Spain have also carried on with experiments in the taped voice research.

The thousands of voices which have been recorded on magnetic tape by Raudive and Jürgenson and many others, though usually faint and brief, contain information which is very personal and relevant for the experimenter, and according to Bättig, have a quality which closely resembles human intonation. One significant difference exists between the voice recorded on tape and those emanating from possessed persons. The former appear to be discarnate, while those in the cases of possession could be characterized as from another dimension or as "angel demons." W. Dreiss, who was *not* schizophrenic, experienced hearing voices in his "inner ear" which he identified as transcendent spirits.

Prof. Alex Schneider, a physicist from St. Gallen, Switzerland, for years president of one of the Swiss parapsychology associations (SPG), gave a paper at the first conference on taped voices, arranged by Hanna Buschbeck in 1975. He postulated that the taped voices were most likely not a new development at all by merely an extension of "direct voice mediumship" to persons with some mediumistic sensitivity, generally not strong enough to produce voices audible to the human but with enough energy to influence magnetic tape.

Here is a brief excerpt from Prof. Schneider's paper:

> *"Let me refer to the case of G.S. who reported getting voices from beyond. This was a severe case in which experimentation with a tape recorder led to 'getting voices' directly (even though subjective) and eventually led to a suicide attempt. But we don't want to dwell on the pathological cases here, even though we should remind ourselves that problems can also occur with automatic writing, use of the pendulum, or engaging in table-tipping experiments, or if one goes into a trance without the necessary background and training. I would only say that I would advise against the use of any of these approaches if there is a strong personal or deep emotional involvement."*

The significance of the electronic voice phenomenon lies not in the fact that clear and detailed information is generally obtained, but that it shows that invisible entities can somehow influence materials such as magnetic tape to demonstrate their continued existence — a phenomenon that presented a challenge to skeptical materialists.

Researchers of the tape-recorded voices know that many of the voices are soft and often difficult or impossible to understand, but they have a quality which usually rules out stray radio signals. If emotionally distraught or bereaved persons turn to experimenting with tape recorders, they risk the possibility of being besieged or harassed by transcendent spirits and may become so involved that they lose contact with objective reality and may enter a state which psychiatrists, unfamiliar with the taped voice phenomenon, would immediately categorize as psychotic.

In late 1979, a Mr. N. came to me for professional help. He had been fascinated by the pioneer work of Dr. Raudive and Fr. Leo Schmid, and had acquired an abundance of tape-recording equipment. He spent countless hours, day and night, recording and listening, and got numerous male and female voices on tape. After four years, he began to hear voices without using the recorder and became distraught. The voices spoke directly and often in a contemptuous manner. At home he believed he was being teased by tenants on the first floor and actually called the police, even though his mother and daughter assured him that they heard no voices. Then he heard voices while he was on his job, which he believed to be the voices of co-workers whom he assumed were jealous because of the position he had attained. He felt so tortured that he took early retirement, but the voices continued to bother him. These voices not only irritated him, but he also experienced an inexplicable tugging on his earlobe, so real at times that he would look around for the person doing it. These acoustic and physical annoyances led to a condition resembling paranoia. Such a condition, as in the case of the "infested" person, and in contrast to the true paranoid, is at least to a degree, psychologically, empathetically understandable.

In addition to hearing voices with primarily negative content, Mr. N. was disturbed by painfully harassing noise. This manifested itself in hissing sounds of varying volume, often accompanied by a pure tone of between 100 and 800 Hz as well as trills and twitters, with or without accompanying pure tone. The differing volume of the voices was also remarkable. Individual voices seemed to come from far away and at times hardly to be perceived. Once, N. reported a long but unintelligible monologue by a male voice. Dialogues between male and female voices also occurred.

In the case of Mr. N., the voices do not resemble the voices of a schizophrenic. In the case of the latter, the content of the voices corresponds to unconscious concepts from the inner realm of the psyche, as compared with the EVP[2] voices which reflect events from the world external to the psyche, and subject to energies still not understood.

Single persons and groups of people whom the schizophrenic believes he knows are accused of being the originators. But the harassed person recognizes, in addition to unjustly accused contact persons, alien tormentors not known to him, who are often subordinated to an equally unknown "boss." In addition, the true paranoid constantly expands the circle of his adversaries, while the besieged person is always pitted against the same spirits.

In both cases of possession and in cases of harassment resulting from too intensive experimentation with taping voices, the third person is used in the languages. N., for example, heard: "He noticed it," "Now he is awake."

---

[2] EVP: Electronic Voice Phenomenon.

During an attack, different spirits possessing M.M. expressed themselves from her mouth: "The wretch belongs to us." These remarks obviously do not represent products of some internal subconscious but of an external intelligence. So-called "angel demons" expressing themselves in phenomena typically use profane and hateful language about everything divine.

While most experimenters recording paranormal voices have experienced no problems, the following is an example of harassment of one person (Mr. N.) during experiments with his recorder. His report was prepared January 7, 1980:

> *"1:20: A man's and a woman's voice (clearly without emotional content). 3:15: as at 1:20. 5:05: as at 3:15. 7:40: woke up. Very strong interfering hissing signal but no voices. 8:35: strong signal of interference, pressure in the top of my head. 12:30: strong hissing signal. Pressure in both ears, mild feeling of nausea. Voices of two men and one woman, loud, apparently quite close. 3:20: constant strong hissing signal of interference with a weak pure tone in the back of my head. Strong pressure on the· forehead and less so on the neck. Voice of woman in the distance: 'Scheme is not bad.' A man's voice, unintelligible. Two times in a row the 'Berner' circuit worked (an experimental circuit constructed as a defense). Result: voices stopped coming. Level of interference signal goes down within the next 5 minutes till it reaches a value of 'medium to strong.' Constant strong hissing interfering signal. Light high accompanying pure tone can be heard. At the moment no voices can be noticed. 11:45 P.M.: Constant, strong hissing interference sound. Two voices can be heard sporadically. 'Berner' circuit switched on. The voices can only be heard very far away after this attempt. Understand the exclamation: 'Madness!' Went to bed."*

I have heard many say that trying to record paranormal voices is a waste of time because many of the voices are weak, difficult to understand, and the content seldom tells much about "the other side." This is only partially correct, for there are many instances when specific, relevant names and messages are received. The phenomenal fact is that entities are able to influence magnetic tape so that voices can be heard.

The "SPIRICOM" Experiments
(*Spirit Communication*)

Established views of reality, as is usually the case, change slowly. Interest in the electronic voice phenomenon continues to grow slowly and has not yet become a household word. George W. Meek, a successful businessman, engineer and inventor, at one time an aide to U.S. Ambassador Averill Harriman in London, now living in Franklin, North Carolina, has had a continuing interest in research related to the meaning and continuity of life, and thus took an early interest in the work of Dr. Konstantine Raudive. Meek took early retirement so he could devote all his energies to this elusive question and during the past seventeen years has spent more than half a million dollars supporting the research of others, and on his own research and experiments.

He was convinced that the paranormal voices recorded by Raudive and others were genuine, but believed that equipment should be developed, if possible, which would make the voices stronger and clearer and result in better communication between the visible and the invisible worlds. Thus he coined the word, Spiricom (*spiri-t com*-munication) to describe his efforts. He has travelled frequently to Europe to keep in touch with researchers there and is also acquainted with experiments carried on in the United States.

A detailed, fascinating account of his years of investigation and his findings is contained in a book, *The Ghost of 29 Megacycles,* by John G. Fuller, first published in London (Souvenir Press) in 1985 and by New American Library (Signet Books) in 1986. It records the events which even many parapsychologists find difficult to accept, apparently because they too often try to measure phenomena by materialistic views of what is possible. Yet this is a story with far-reaching implications.

On July 23, 1977, George Meek wrote Prof. (Emeritus) Walter H. Uphoff at the New Frontiers Center, Oregon, Wisconsin, stating:

> *"A close friend and associate who is a very good electronics technician and a superb healer, has had recently an experience which shook him up both mentally and physically. A materialized figure about six feet tall and the equivalent of 190-200 pounds took him by the shoulder and in no uncertain terms and at length talked regarding possible collaboration on certain research."*

The entity gave his full name, George J. Mueller, his social security number, when, where and what he had studied at universities, etc. Meek asked Prof. Uphoff if he could check at the University of Wisconsin archives, since he lived near Madison, and he found that university records matched "Mueller's" claims. He had graduated in electrical engineering in 1928, had been a member of the Triangle fraternity (a fraternity for engineering students), and a member of a mens' choral group called "Haresfoot."

The "ghost" had also stated that he took graduate work in physics at Cornell University at Ithaca, New York, where Uphoff's son, Norman, on the faculty at Cornell, verified that "Mueller" had received a Ph.D. in physics at that institution in 1934. The social security number helped Meek track down the fact that a George J. Mueller had died at age 60 in 1967 while he was on the faculty of a California college. His widow verified the information gathered from a variety of disparate sources.

There followed a long period during which William O'Neill, Meek's friend, recorded numerous paranormal conversations with "Mueller" giving him technical information on the construction of more sensitive voice recording equipment which O'Neill constructed. O'Neill was challenged and at times frightened by these contacts with the surviving spirit of George J. Mueller. This was not a case of harassment, even though, at times, Mueller addressed O'Neill in a strong, imperious manner. The physics professor Dr. Ernst Senkowski, Mainz, Germany, has worked closely with Meek's research project which he has called the *Spiricom* and is fully convinced that the electronic voice phenomenon is an important breakthrough, as it was characterized in the title of Dr. Raudive's first book. Senkowski has also worked with Hans Otto Koenig, Mönchengladbach, Germany, who has developed equipment for more effective two-way communication with the invisible world. Koenig has been successful in demonstrating his equipment on live television on RTL-PLUS, Luxembourg, as early as 1983.

Although the Spiricom phenomenon is challenged by some parapsychologists, who always look for the "repeatable" experiment, there is every indication that Meek's efforts have made an important contribution to a better understanding of the nature of life and the survival of physical death — a fact which will be helpful to all mental health professionals who are, from time to time, confronted with cases which do not fit conventional concepts of emotional illnesses. It should help to give them more courage to at least consider the survival hypothesis and not be restricted to diagnoses which result in treatment by incarceration and/or chemotherapy.

In 1986, Senkowski investigated the case in Aachen, Germany, where Herr Klaus Schreiber succeeded in getting images of his deceased relatives on a TV screen, following instructions via taped paranormal voice messages from his deceased daughter Karin.

Since the German edition of this book appeared, new developments associated with the paranormal taped voices (EVP) and the Spiricom experiments have come to public attention. Rainer Holbe who moderated a weekly program, "Unglaubliche Geschichten" (Unbelievable Stories) on RTL-PLUS television, Luxembourg, for the past five years, presented a program on the electronic voice phenomenon in 1985. Among his viewing audience was Klaus Schreiber, Aachen, West Germany who had lost a number of family members through death. Skeptical as he was, he decided to experiment with a tape recorder and was astonished to get a voice he recognized as his deceased 18-year-old daughter Karin. She told him "we will try to get our images on TV" so he tuned his TV set to an open channel and saw nothing. Karin then instructed him to get a video camera, which he bought, pointed it at an empty chair and again got nothing. A further message told him to point the camera at the television. (When the same power source is used, the camera will photograph the television screen which will be picked up by the video-recorder and played back over and over. Eventually, recognizable images of Herr Schreiber's relatives appeared, as well as those of some well-known personalities.

Holbe's book, *Bilder aus dem Reich der Toten* ["Images from the Domain of the Dead"], a detailed account of the experiments of Schreiber and an electronics technician, Martin Wenzel, was published by Knauer Verlag, Munich, in July 1987. The book, illustrated with about a hundred photos, is the story of a new breakthrough in psychic research.

If Schreiber were the only person who obtained paranormal images, skeptics could easily dismiss it as deception, but three experimenters in Luxembourg (Jules and Maggy Harsch-Fischbach and a Mr. Seyler), and Luise Fuchs, Billigheim/Alfeld, Germany, have also succeeded in getting images on television. Similar successes have also been reported from Italy.

18. INFESTATION: THE THIRD AND MILDEST FORM OF POSSESSION

Infestatio (Latin: molestation, disturbance, persecution) represents a third form of demonic infiltration into the human sphere of life.

Delacour observed that the differentiation of *obsessio* into *possessio* (true possession), *circumcessio* (harassment) and *infestatio* first took place in the 18th Century. In *Apage Satana,* p. 19, he also equates the concept of *infestatio* with poltergeist phenomena and then adds: "Infestations always occur in combination with *possessio* or *obsessio.*"

This remark appears contradictory to me. *Infestatio* would then only belong to the symptomatology of *possessio* or *circumsessio.* Presumably the boundaries between *circumsessio* and *infestatio* cannot be clearly defined. The infested person often suffers physical torture — a fact which clearly contradicts Delacour's definition of *infestatio.* As a rule, objects and appliances in the environment of the infested person are particularly the target of the demonic agents. This is also emphasized by Delacour. Unlike haunting by a poltergeist, which is primarily a short-lived event, infested persons are plagued for years. The barn ghost, related to the poltergeist phenomenon, is often, especially when treated with a blessing, also of short duration, and mostly affects animals and barn equipment. Here too, the view of most parapsychologists that the inexplicable events can be explained as being caused by tension in the unconscious of the barn personnel — by which active energies are mobilized — appears to be grossly inadequate. Aside from certain exceptions in haunting by barn ghosts and elsewhere, the content and type of psychic tensions of persons who supposedly cause the haunting are almost imperceptible. The supposed tension is used to support the animistic thesis. The hypothetical carrier of the tension, however, serves as a mediumistic source of power. Haunting in a barn often appears to involve witchcraft, whereby through appropriate rites, perhaps only in thought, demonic spirits are mobilized to cause patterns of haunting which are almost identical in all countries and cultures. Nevertheless, I believe barn ghosts are a form of haunting which is close to actual infestation.

I have observed quite a number of cases of haunting by poltergeists. I noticed that the persons who presumably were causing the disturbances, although they often felt uneasy, did not otherwise actually suffer. There were also some, namely children, who did not even feel uneasy, but continued their life as carefree as before. In haunting by poltergeists as well as infestations — in my view — the demonic comes into play, especially when destructive behavior occurs. The person with a mediumistic sensitivity who makes the haunting possible, appears to be, as said before, the transmitter of power. It is conceivable that such demonic spirits, probably mostly "poor souls," are merely interested in gaining recognition and causing trouble, which they may already have done during their lifetime on earth, and may possibly also have used magic to do so during a previous life.

I agree with Delacour in the following: haunting by poltergeists often occurs in connection with later possession (Gottliebin Dittus) and sometimes also as a concomitant phenomenon of possession (the girl of Orlach). However, in poltergeist phenomena, the involved persons, who presumably cause the haunting, generally do not appear possessed and behave in relatively normal ways. The haunting occurs for the most part around these persons, who are, however, not completely spared from it.

Regarding *Infestation,* a third and minor form of possession, *I will limit my remarks to cases where one individual, most often a woman, is being molested in her solitary home environment.* Bonin's[1] *Lexicon of Parapsychology* defines *infestatio* as a light form of possession; no reference is made to a poltergeist.

The appearances are relatively minor in scale, and are not spectacular, as was, for example, the famous haunting of the house of the politician and lawyer Joller in Stans.[2] Small, often physical, effects, such as nearly inexplicable damages or changes to furniture and household items can be noticed. Papers, keys, or fabric may disappear, only to suddenly reappear again, often under most unusual circumstances.

I venture to pass a definitive judgment only when I have had the opportunity to observe the involved person during months or even years, so that I can draw conclusions about his personality. Only then can the possibility of deception be excluded, even though such cases which come to the attention of a psychiatrist are relatively few. I am confronted with infestations in increasing number; consequently my colleagues are apt to shake their heads, but as president of the Parapsychological Society in Switzerland, I have had occasion to learn about many such paranormal events.

With respect to infestations, the inexplicable changes in the furniture of the house are mostly noticed when the owners return, and probably thus occur during their absence, but it often suffices for the person concerned to be in another room of the dwelling. Occasionally, all that is needed is a short time of inattention or incidental preoccupation in order to elicit paranormal phenomena in the same room. The changes not only affect all sorts of objects within the dwelling, but frequently also washing machines and other electrical installations in adjoining rooms of the house. Frequently, the infested person, who may be somewhat conspicuous or asocial, is accused by housemates of mistreating appliances used by all, since the disturbance appears in connection with her. Part of the total picture is that professional repair persons who are called in often find no cause for the disturbance, and the machine starts working again by itself. This then often leads to a further deterioration of the relationship with the housemates and not infrequently causes them to believe the affected person was using witchcraft. The affected person believes the

---

[1] Bonin, *Lexikon der Parapsychologie* ["Lexicon of Parapsychology"] (Scherz-Verlag, 1976).

[2] Fanny Moser, *Spuk* ["Haunting"] (Baden-Zürich, 1950).

same of her housemates, and she herself in turn accuses them of being witches.

Although this view is not present in all cases, I have had the impression at times that, in fact, demonically-inspired housemates also came into play, especially when they were also viewed in that way by their fellow lodgers. Such an hypothesis always remains doubtful, but I can imagine how two persons, gifted as mediums and demonically imprinted in some way, could build a stronger field of influence than only one person. Thus the notion that directly affected persons were targeted by a neighborhood witch could be quite true, but without the negative form of a magic potential on the part of the directly affected resident of the dwelling, I cannot imagine that such occurrences would be taken seriously in our world dominated by rationalism. Within a population still oriented toward sorcery, a completely one-sided action by a magician is quite imaginable. Today, for example, we do not find a "folie à deux," in which a positive relationship is always at play, but rather an "action à deux," of persons who actually oppose one another in hostile interaction.

In any case, in the homes of such people, and often, too, in the common rooms of the house, most unusual occurrences may take place, which cannot simply be put down as a lively imagination or a pathological misinterpretation by the affected person. This last conclusion could certainly be drawn by a psychiatrist who heard of only one such situation. In fact, in the beginning, this is what also happened to me, but when such evidence is repeated, as in my case, it provokes the recognition of certain "rules of the game," which seem to be rooted in the psyche.

Cases of infestation affecting completely lucid people are illustrated in the following:

Mrs. L. in B.

This nearly 80-year-old lady, with education and intelligence far above average, looks younger than 70 years and enjoys continued liveliness and presence of mind. No signs of mental aging can be found; on the contrary, she has a flawless memory inclusive of recent events (short-term memory). She cultivates little contact with other people, but does not feel any lack of contact. The lady worked until she was 70 years of age and has lived financially secure, but modestly, for the last 2½ decades in her elegant apartment.

For a long time, her conflict with "the witch" remained latent, but previously, different tenants who had lived there earlier — according to her report — had felt ill at ease and also had complained about compulsive coughing, shortness of breath and migraine whenever the suspected "witch" was present. The accused witch had already lived in this apartment community for 25 years, and although they lacked personal contact, both women felt dislike for one another. Only in 1973, handwritten essays disappeared in an inexplicable way.

The infestations, described by Mrs. L., are typical and generally correspond to a pattern which in such circumstances always recurs, although in every case, some singularly striking phenomena seem to crop up.

At the beginning of the actual events, in 1977, the homeowner was disconcerted by a strange rearrangement of objects. A bronze statue on the dresser suddenly was facing the wall, although she could not remember having touched this sculpture in recent times. Water spots, that appeared under the always-dry carpet, although she had wiped the floors a few days before, seemed more unusual. Then objects which were not even valuable disappeared, such as a notebook for the entry of interest on the rent, so the lady bought a new book. A short time later, she found the old as well as the new note book in the usual place in her desk drawer, carefully placed on top of one another. A string hanging from the light fixture in the living room was suddenly knotted into a loop. The same thing happened a year later to an unattached string. This can all be viewed as parallels to the braided tails of the cows in the occurrences of barn ghosts. The television set tipped over when barely touched and fell to the floor, in contrast to its previous stability. Later, the T.V. went completely haywire and a repair man who was consulted could not explain it. Almost all technical appliances, such as the hair dryer, the ironing machine, the washing machine used in common, etc., refused to function at times. Keys which had previously been held together by a key ring, were suddenly found separated.

Mrs. L. became seriously troubled by many different kinds of damage to the carpet. Most obvious was the severing of the carpet fringes as if they were cut by scissors held at a slant. Single strands of the fringe were found, but not all of them. After quite some time, without any obvious sign of repair, the fringes were suddenly intact again.

Even less explicable was the following occurrence: the enamel on the bottom of the bathtub suddenly was massively damaged. The craftsman called in to evaluate the damage was unable to explain what could have caused it. Months later, the damage disappeared all by itself.

Practically all antique tinware, including rare and valuable pieces, were inexplicably dented on the body, the lid and the bottom. Since the edge of the lid as well as the top edge of the container had lost their original circularity, lids no longer fit exactly onto the pitchers. After more than two years, one of the pitchers was again completely free of defects. The lid was again circular, as was the edge of the pitcher, on which it fit correctly.

In a previously perfect glass art work from Bohemia, an air bubble suddenly appeared. Silverware was dented. Furniture showed discolorations in the wood, holes, sticky smudges and minor damages. Scales suddenly stuck, thermometers showed incredible readings. A hot-plate, although not turned on, suddenly began to glow. The floor of the refrigerator unexpectedly radiated extremely cold temperatures, while at other times it felt warm in a strange way. Even a teapot abruptly began to radiate cold. The number of paranormal changes recorded amounted to over 100 individual events.

The lady herself was physically affected. For example, she suddenly lost large bunches of hair. Other annoyances — according to the infested woman — included a dry mouth, the mucous membranes of her cheeks sticking to her teeth, cuts in the corners of her eyes, weakness, pain in her legs, and welts on her thighs. She frequently had a feeling of extreme cold on her knees, and she had the sensation that a hand was pressing on her shoulder at which moment, she felt a puzzling threat.

In several control visits to the lady's home, I saw some of the evidence described. The lady, who had already visited me more than a hundred times in my office, showed no symptoms of hysteria. She always appeared composed and mentally interested. Paranoid thoughts were exhibited only in relation to the accused witch.

When I think about the cases known to me, the following theses of causal connections become apparent.

1. The contemporary view within academically oriented parapsychology, according to which paranormal events are caused by a bioenergetic field of energy of a consciously or unconsciously restless, and perhaps insecure person.

In over 40 years of practice as a psychiatrist, I have met numerous patients who, in comparison with the persons molested by ghosts, showed much more extreme tensions, but nevertheless caused no haunting, or the least sign of transformations into matter. In the case of the ghost in Rosenheim — investigated by Resch and Bender — the psychic tensions of Annemarie S., said to be the focus, appear insignificant compared to the ones many of my patients exhibit. Although her strong powers as a medium are noted as an additional cause, this does not suffice to explain the extensive phenomena at and away from the law office.

> *[In the fall of 1967, German newspapers carried stories about mysterious happenings in the office of Attorney Adam, Rosenheim, West Germany. Fluorescent lights turned in fixtures and exploded; fluid gushed out of the photocopy machine when no one was near; phone connections were broken and phones rang when no one was near; over 500 calls to 0119 (time-of-day) were registered at the telephone company during late afternoons.*
>
> *Completely baffled investigators called in Dr. Hans Bender, director of the Institute for Parapsychology, at the University of Freiburg. He concluded that an employee, Annemarie S., showed characteristics of the adolescent poltergeist personality around whom such disturbances usually center: an intensely unhappy emotional life without satisfactory outlets, high irritability and frustration. Dr. Friedbert Karger of the Max Planck Institute videotaped a phantom hand which came through a wall, striking the corner of a large picture and turning it 320 degrees on its hanger.]*

2. The person afflicted is always gifted as a medium. This, I believe, is pertinent, but the ability as a medium cannot be a cause by itself.

3. A magic spell (witchcraft) is involved. For barn ghosts and related types of haunting, such as in infestation, this appears probable and constitutes at least one source of phenomena.

4. Demonic spirits of transcendence (angel demons, "poor souls") wish to and must make themselves known. With regard to the phenomenology of

cases of haunting, including the ghost bound to one locality, this appears to be the main source.

5. Whereas these elements seem to be required for any kind of possession, certain qualities seem to emerge which distinguish primary possession from the lesser forms of harassment and infestation. Witchcraft could activate the energies involved in haunting by demonic entities.

Let us consider the case of L.: the house-mate, perceived as being a witch, is perhaps the primary cause. It is not likely that she knows exactly the many objects in the apartment of L. and thus would be unable to change them psychoplastically by imagination alone, as, for example, happens in cases of psychic surgeons in the Philippines. Learning about the objects through the power of clairvoyance (almost always as an astral journey) on the part of the "witch" appears to be too complicated an explanation.[3] However, it is imaginable that the hostile house-mate, by the power of her thoughts, creates a negative potential in which demonic spirits can function in a way possible for them — at least the pattern of actions is always similar.

The patient, who according to many of my observations has to be described as an able medium in spite of her advanced age, represents a source of energy. In addition, I suspect in her a certain ambivalence toward the events. Owing to her age, her range of activity is greatly reduced despite her retained mental flexibility, which creates a need to experience the occurrence of events. From long observation, it is my impression that animals, too, and especially dogs, prefer to be abused rather than remain unnoticed. This ambivalence greatly impedes the liberation from demonic events.

Treatment, in this case, too, took the form of a personally tailored exorcism. The wording, *"I give you the coat of protection against all bad forces from without and from within"* attempts to take all causes into account. The request that she pray for the adversary is theoretical, since the intensity of the praying is questionable. Partial success is little proof, but provides both parties, i.e., the patient and the exorcist, encouragement. In L.'s case, a pronounced atheism had to be overcome. Partial success was registered only through a lengthy exchange of views lasting over two years. An honorarium had to be rejected, because it denigrated the unconditional personal commitment.

This case is not yet closed. But much has been accomplished when those who are suffering — including Mrs. L. — report that they have regained a certain enjoyment of life, since the darkening of life is the main purpose of demonic powers.

The Events Surrounding Mrs. F.

Mrs. F. comes from a lower middle-class milieu. Her mother, depressed from time to time, wanted to drown herself shortly after the birth of her only child.

---

[3] [*Publisher's Footnote:* Some persons apparently can astral project at will and affect others, even without evil intent. Robert Monroe in his book, *Journeys Out of the Body,* (Doubleday, 1971), p. 56, describes how he projected to the location of a friend and pinched her to confirm his presence. She later confirmed the pinching, verified by the black-and-blue mark. The limits of this phenomenon are not known or understood.]

Under this caretaker, who was tyrannical and choleric but at the same time gifted as a medium, Mrs. F.'s childhood did not stand under a lucky star. Her school grades were average-to-good; grades in vocational school were good to very good. Because of her mother's resistance she married late to her husband who was twice her age, tyrannical, sex- and loveless, whom she continued to semi-worship even after his death. This reveals, in connection with other signs, her pronounced masochism. In addition, however, Mrs. F. possessed an inherited ability as a medium. While her husband was still alive, she had attempted to participate in a demonstration by the most famous Swiss hypnotist of that time. He chose her while selecting mediumistic persons and asked her to come to the stage, since she seemed to represent the best medium among the participants. But her partner, due to jealousy, had dragged her out of the lecture hall.

Mrs. F. was frugal and wherever she was employed, competent, so that she was able to save up a modest amount of wealth. In 1968, allegedly due to an intrigue, she lost a highly valued job. Since then she found, for the most part, only short term employment and felt uprooted. Personal relationships in her environment were lacking, although she could still be described as attractive. Of stocky build, which is rare for a schizophrenic, she appears to enjoy contact, once her trust has been won. Her masochism, however, seems to have caused difficulties everywhere. Since 1969, paranormal occurrences are supposed to have taken place in her apartment, including physical tortures. Out of this developed a number of delusions and ideas of reference for which she was hospitalized in 1972 in a clinic for nervous diseases. Her problems were interpreted as a schizophrenic disorder. Since the term "infestation" does not appear in the psychiatric terminology, the diagnostic expression "shared delusional system" (Kretschmer) would appear to be most appropriate.

Today, she still exhibits flourishing delusions and misinterpretations of earlier events, especially in hospitals. The misinterpretations of events of a ghostly nature in her apartment, and the torture which she often experiences intensively on her body, permit one to understand her paranoid ideas. Since most people today do not believe in influences by transcendental spirits, they assume that the effects were produced by living humans, who are suspected of invading the home. From time to time, the patient expresses the suspicion of a magic influence in the form of sorcery by certain persons. From my own experience, I know that it hardly ever helps to make clear to the afflicted person that sorcery requires energies from the practitioner, which seems not to be worth the effort in the case of a victim with no particular importance to the public and the neighbors. These isolated people usually play insignificant roles in their social environment, and thus try to compensate — totally unconsciously — by suffering from partial ego-inflation. Whether through them, such a great energy potential develops that, independent of transcendental forces, they influence matter in a psychoplastic way, can not be proved or disproved in this case. In any case, I believe this possibility is quite unlikely to be contradicted. Indications that it is possible for people to cause a psychoplastic effect are supported by the successful experiments made by engineer Franz Seidl[4], in which thoughts alone affected tape recordings in an adequate fashion.

The infestations which occurred in connection with this patient also demonstrate a wide range of phenomena which we often encounter in haunting by poltergeists. On the 9th anniversary of her mother's death, there was a very unusual loud knocking on her bedroom doors, although Mrs. F. was alone in her apartment. The mother was said to have been an evil woman, who as long as she lived, had dominated and tormented her daughter. The infested daughter's opinion that her mother had not yet been able to separate from her cannot be rejected out of hand.

Mrs. F.'s character must be described as emotional and hot-tempered, to which she freely agrees. She suspects sorcery when the paranormal phenomena happen in close vicinity to her and she is alone in her apartment. After she sets the table in her kitchen, she may find, after being busy at the stove for a short time, that the knife and fork are arranged crosswise, or the silverware pushed so far out over the edge that they barely remain on the table. This occurs quite frequently. She often finds her silverware to be damaged or bent, as occurs in the case of people who intentionally bend spoons by the power of their minds. Once, after a short absence from her kitchen, she found some sauerkraut, which had been in an unopened package, sticking above the kitchen door. With her pencil, she had drawn on the wallpaper the place and shape of the sauerkraut stuck above the door.

After a short stay in the hospital, she had found a cross added under her drawing. During food preparation, tomatoes, leek stems, and other parts of vegetables disappear again and again, only to return in the same place a short time later. Over and over, she found her clothes or mattress cut. Her right shoe was pierced in several places and entire parts of the sole were torn off. Angry, she put the left, slightly damaged shoe, into a plastic bag and placed that in the cabinet, but 10 minutes later, she could no longer find this shoe. Other objects would also disappear for some time or altogether. Furniture was damaged; chairs fell apart when touched — the seat, back, and legs falling off separately. Edges of fabrics were often unraveled, fringes of the carpet were cut off and — though less often — returned to the former condition at a later time, just as was described to me by two other infested persons. Pans and their lids were damaged. The wooden floor showed spots and the wood grain changed all the time. A colleague tried to take photographs of the changes, but for the second picture, needed for proof, the camera failed to function. Similar problems were encountered by some investigators.[5]

Three thick wax candles which Mrs. F. had placed on her table at a considerable distance from one another and lighted, had burned down completely while she had taken a 15-minute nap which had unexpectedly

---

[4] Franz Seidl, Vienna, Austria: electronics engineer, developer of the "psychophone" for reception of the paranormal taped voice phenomenon.

[5] Dr. Alfred Stelter and Lyall Watson, among others, who have observed the psychic surgeons in the Philippines. Lyall Watson mentions the "barriers" which are raised by unknown entities.

overcome her. The wax had run off the table and onto the wooden floor, but when she removed it no spots were left, as would have normally been the case. The list of paranormal phenomena is long indeed. As already mentioned, many infestations resemble a prolonged form of haunting by poltergeists, and certainly must be interpreted similarly with regard to their causes.

Mrs. M.G.

Mrs. G.'s life did not begin well. Reportedly conceived by an alcoholic father while he was drunk, the baby was rejected by her dominating mother. When the mother had seen her child immediately after birth, she was horrified, and had screamed: "Just like the old man" (father), and she cursed her daughter then and there. The parents hated each other. In her early childhood years, M.G. heard again and again: "You are cursed, you are a cursed creature!" The only positive characteristic of the father, who was a gardener, was his love for his plants, which flourished under his hands, but the tavern was his home. He either beat his daughter or neglected her, so she kept out of his way. To the mother's and child's relief, he died when the child was 9 years old.

As an infant and small child, she cried uninterruptedly during the night, so that her father in desperation once grabbed her by her hair and threw her into a basket. The patient believes it is possible she was "plagued" by magic or a demonic spirit, or perhaps simply had a reaction to the desperate conditions at home. Beginning as early as age 5, she maintained a good friendship with another girl until dating men became more important to them both.

After three years of secondary education (no high school), she went for one year to a school for women and another year to a vocational school. Due to her unusual abilities with piano, violin and flute, she did not have to pay tuition, but without financial means, she could not continue her education in the conservatory of music. She failed to graduate from a school of theatre because her voice was not adequate for singing and she also had financial difficulties. When she told her mother about this, her mother laughed loud and maliciously. M.G. responded with a violent tantrum during which she ripped up her coat. As a result, the mother had her committed to a mental hospital, where she stayed for three weeks, and from there she was sent away, again by the mother, to a convent in their home town. Being a Protestant herself, she was mentally tormented and threatened with the devil there for over a year until she finally converted. When afterwards, she also consented to sleep with the priest, her life became pleasant. But after her release from the convent, she could not find her way back into regular life, which led to a renewed but shorter stay at the university clinic. From there, she was transferred to the psychiatric clinic of her home canton (political subdivision), where she enjoyed great freedom.

Afterwards, she worked with children in institutions of the Anthroposophical Society, but aside from three years as a day care worker, she did not experience actual employment. Her life had always been difficult, and only music and love for animals had added a harmonic note to it.

She had had satisfactory relationships with men; one had lasted for 20 years. At age 31 she had a pregnancy and by mutual agreement, she had an abortion and had her tubes tied at the same time. Although she had not experienced conscious guilt, she suffered great inner tensions as a result.

Her relationships to women often ran a dramatic course. Women supposedly had accused her of the "Evil Eye," and in her little village, she was threatened and pursued by village folk.

Actually, her life had always felt overshadowed. She always felt inferior and often harbored intentions to commit suicide. Heavy indefinable feelings of anxiety plagued her; anxiety and panic were the undercurrent of her life. As early as age 17, she was haunted by the idea that people in the street looked at her and rejected her. Compulsive mechanisms tormented her in the following ways: she felt compelled to avoid certain colors, numbers and words; she could only walk comfortably on curbstones; and she could only place certain objects to her right side, others only to her left. During later years, she recovered somewhat from these compulsive behaviors. To this day, however, she still can not fall asleep without having turned on three light bulbs, and she wakes up depressed and with headaches in the morning. As a result, she has become dependent on medication and has developed a kidney ailment.

Today, the sixty year old woman, who looks much younger, lives on public assistance, feels unfulfilled and under constant neurotic tension. Although mother and daughter did not live together, until the mother's death in 1981 they maintained a mutual fascination and a love-hate relationship.

Her nightly dreams torture her. Of the dreams recorded and written down during the period of 4½ years, only three recent ones are neutral or faintly positive. A dream recorded by the patient in October, 1978, is presented here in her own words:

> *"Morning twilight. Grey overcast sky. I am walking through small, narrow and crooked alleys. Left and right of me, stone walls strive upward. Dark-gray concrete, small windows mounted high. No window panes. Like rat holes. An oppressive scenery. Gray the light, gray the houses, gray the sky. Not a soul around. Suddenly life enters the picture. At first I see it creeping toward me from one side, then from the other, small rivulets, no wider than a child's arm: blood. Dark, sticky blood. Then the rivulets get wider, they turn into little streams. From all sides it flows towards me, it flows over my feet. Desperately I try to avoid it, I try to run away. But in vain. At last the stuff fills all the alleys. Then I wade in the sticky red juice, in it up to my ankles. In horror, I cannot emit a single sound, am not even able to scream for help. Also, nobody would hear me, because the area seems as if it's abandoned. The way before me begins to get steeper and steeper, the alleys get narrower and narrower. While crying I run on, uphill, always uphill. Surrounded by this horrible, sticky stuff, which hinders my walking, which already washes around my calves, as if somewhere high above, a dam broke. As if a waterfall of blood was gushing down to the depths. Then I wake up."*

Many times demonic spirits in the form of birds, beasts of prey, vermin and unreal human forms occurred in her dreams. The dreams often left scratches, pustules and dark red spots, some of which were still visible at the time of therapy. They appeared to be psychosomatic parallels to the dream events, and not artificially caused injuries. Although she loved plants, all died under her care. They turned brittle, changed to a dark brown color and shriveled up as if acid had been poured over them. Experts stated they had never seen anything similar. This phenomenon also yields to a psychological interpretation: aversion, and even hate toward the father, who was known for having a "green thumb" and being successful in growing plants, could have caused a counter-reaction. On the other hand, the opposition to the parents, especially for daughters to the father, can weaken the ego, for the personality of the father represents God the father, the cosmic shelter. Therefore, it seems unwise to me when inexperienced mental health workers demand rejection and separation from the parents since it shakes every "primal foundation." An ego weakened in such a way — as was established by Wickland's research — is easily taken over by alien spirits.

Actual infestations increased during the past 10 years and often occurred at short intervals. They especially affected appliances of any kind, but also clothes and household items.

During a walk through the city, a jade ring on her finger suddenly cracked with a small bang. She liked it very much, but had not worn it very long. [It should be noted here that in the presence of persons gifted as mediums, it is not unusual that crystal vases burst. I myself had experienced and analyzed this phenomenon in the presence of my (now deceased) wife. At that point in time, no tension existed between us, not even a minor disagreement. Psychologically, such an event is explained as a result of unconscious tension. The unconscious is a well- known "garbage can" for the inexplicable. An objective interpretation is just as impossible with this explanation as with the assumption of the influence of non-material spirits. Neither can be proved.]

I make this judgment in this case because I was able to get to know this patient psychologically during 5½ years of care and management. At times, it seemed to me that a certain desire to show off encouraged the patient to exaggerate or even to invent her dreams as well as the description of paranormal events. In order to clarify this, I often encouraged M.G. to repeat details of her experiences — since "one who lies, needs to have a good memory" but I noticed only minor deviations from the original narration. Therefore, it can be assumed that the dreams, which showed a typical structure of dreams, as well as the paranormal phenomena, represented genuine experiences.

The dreams reflected a quite pronounced destructive and demonically besieged unconscious without hope. It was as if the personality were overshadowed by a curse reaching into deeper levels, for even the dreams which began positively turned into the opposite. During my long experience in psychological- psychiatric therapy, I had never encountered such a dark series of dreams.

The life of the patient shaped itself in a similar way. In spite of her extraordinary musical talent, she could never make use of it. Her intellectual abilities in the linguistic area, to judge from her written expressions, are obvious. Few German-Swiss, I would judge, are capable of expressing themselves in this almost flawless written way without having had a higher education. Today, at 60 years of age, she is physically attractive, and thus her statement that she once was very pretty appears credible. Nevertheless, everything in her life went wrong. M.G. today, as mentioned before, is quite lonely, unfulfilled and dependent on public welfare. Again and again, she is shaken by fever, and she suffers from a number of different diseases.

With the diagnosis of psychopathy with a shared delusional system ("sensitiver Beziehungswahn"): paranoid thoughts actually occur. Academic psychiatry would easily find a label for this case, but for the parapsychologist it is significant that M.G. is sensitive and gifted as a medium. She reports events which she knew of in a clairvoyant or prophetic way. Her statement that she was explicitly cursed — at least by her mother — was made spontaneously as part of her description of her earlier history at a time when she did not know my interests.

The combination of a curse and mediumistic ability can be one of the basic prerequisites for possession. This became apparent in M.G.'s case in the relatively few attacks of rage and psychic states of emergency, as in the truly possessed; and today manifests as *infestatio*, which, for the external world, is the most inconspicuous form of possession. The possessing spirits were obviously unable to conquer her naturally differentiated ego, but transferred their activities into the environment, especially into her own apartment, which, psychologically speaking, is symbolic of her soul.

In order to gain a better insight into the type and form of the infestations, ten events, as they were described by M.G., are reproduced here.

1.)

"I own a color television. It is the third of the same kind within a few months. The first one functioned exactly three days, then it went crazy. The second one reacted in the same way. The third one — I have had it now for four months — showed the same irregularities within a short time. I don't understand it. Especially since it is a brand-name set bought in a well-known specialty store. Nevertheless, time and again it behaves disgustingly. It hums; worse, it emits an unbearable, penetrating whistling tone, often throughout the whole program. Then again the pictures are unstable, they move, as if pushed by a hand, from the bottom to the top, they change from color to black and white in the middle of a program, only to suddenly return to color again. I asked an expert to check our antenna. It seems to be intact. I asked a technician from the store where I bought the TV set to come in. He checked the whole TV and treated it with a spray. Yet the same evening, everything began again. The expert said: whistling is impossible in these TV sets. The spray he used did not help."

2.)

"It began ten years ago. For a few months I had been the owner of a

lovely, very expensive compact stereo system. It was shortly before 8 o'clock in the evening, when I returned home from work. For 13 years I have lived alone in a small one-room apartment at the edge of town. At the time, I stepped through my apartment door, locked it, took off my shoes and went toward my stereo equipment. Carefully I pressed the knob to turn it on and it began to work for about two minutes. Then suddenly there was an outrageous bang. Within the appliance it began to hiss and to bubble. Light, stark glaring light, intensive light seeped through the different openings. Suddenly the whole room was filled with the smell of burning. Then it was over. Externally the apparatus looked as always, completely intact. But it didn't function any longer. The next day I brought it to the company for repair. In their repair shop they established that the appliance was completely charred inside. Not a single individual part could be recognized. The apparatus was as empty as an empty box. Even the built-in safety devices were burned out, gone, as though they never had existed. How this could have happened was a mystery to everybody. The fuses in my apartment could not have been the cause. They remained undamaged. And all electric devices functioned as always without a flaw. The apparatus itself had only been in use for a few months, it had been bought at a first-class company and was in excellent condition at the time I received it. There was absolutely no cause which could explain such an event. Since the experts entrusted with this case could not explain it at all, the apparatus was sent to the manufacturer. Now, specialists concerned themselves with it. But they, too, could not get anywhere. It was the first time they were confronted with such a case. They said that what had happened was actually impossible. The case remained a puzzle. They equipped the apparatus with a brand-new interior and sent it back to me. Since then it has refused to work on several occasions. The damages were of very different natures. But every time, the whole set had to be returned to the shop for repair."

3.)

"The next incident was just as puzzling. Again I was coming home from work. . . . I own a stove with two burners, one large and one small for fast cooking. I turned on the switch, as usual, to the highest setting. First nothing happened. Then suddenly there was a bang, and the little stove began to crack and hiss. When I brought the stove to a repair shop, we all believed it to be a minor malfunction. But the next day I received a call. A woman was on the telephone. On instructions from her company, she asked in all seriousness whether I had experimented with the appliance before it malfunctioned. To me this was a superfluous question, because I treat anything which has to do with electricity with utmost respect. I would never dare to experiment with electric equipment. But the facts could not be overlooked. Inside the little stove, it appeared, everything was wantonly scrambled. I only partially understood what it was exactly. A mix-up of wiring was

mentioned. One thing remained bitter reality: had I turned on the big burner, instead of the smaller for fast cooking, there would not have just been banging and hissing. The event remains a puzzle to this very day. I myself am excluded as far as the "experimentation" goes. Burglars, perhaps? But who would have an interest in doing this, and in addition, endanger himself by experimenting with someone else's stove? That would be absurd."

4.)

"It was about 8 years ago. It happened sometimes, not very often, but still a few times over several months, when strange objects found their way onto my bed. Strange, because they were completely out of place there, and strange, too, because I could never explain how they got there in the first place. Most often small things, like pieces of wire, with or without insulation, but also screws and nails, lay openly on my bed, sometime in the evening when I returned home from work. Sometimes separately strewn across the bed, sometimes in small piles, small unpretentious remains of some kind of crafts activity. Since I use neither wire nor insulated wire (I do not own either), and I do not work with screws — at most, I may pound a nail into the wall to hang a picture (and I keep my nails carefully locked away), I am totally unable to explain the appearance of these objects in such an unusual place. First, I believed in intruders — a joke. This appeared to be the most logical, since I live by myself. The problem with this explanation is only that no one other than myself possesses the key to my apartment. Additionally, in connection with other no less strange events, I had recently had a new, expensive, solidly built security lock installed on my apartment door. The whole story made no sense at all. Nevertheless, this strange haunting continued for over a year. Then suddenly everything disappeared as quietly and as unobtrusively as it had begun. But to this very day, the events have not been explained."

5.)

"I own a cute Swedish nightgown. It is half length and is buttoned by four buttons on the front. I have to mention expressly, that these buttons are tightly sewn to their places. I am sure of that, because I check them from time to time. A few weeks ago something very peculiar happened. I was lying in my bed reading a book. Suddenly I felt a faint movement over my breast. Almost casually I looked down at myself. And there, next to me, on the mattress, was the second button from the top. And it hung, and this appears to me noteworthy, on a completely intact double thread. Not even the two knots necessary for this showed signs of damage. In other words, the button could not have come loose under normal conditions. When I looked closer at the damage to the nightgown, I found nothing but a small circular hole. It looked as

though someone had detached the button and the thread belonging to it out of the fabric by using a tiny pair of scissors. I was reading during the time this happened. So I could not have done this. Or did I? But how?"

6.)

"I mentioned the once so puzzling loss of my heater in an earlier report. I also mentioned that the company which was involved replaced it for me. For 10 days, this new heater was acting crazy in a strange way. When it happened for the first time, I believed in a deception of my senses. But then the whole event repeated itself a second and a third time. Now I am completely mixed up. At last, the sun began shining outside, the average daily temperatures happily began rising, and the nights were correspondingly mild. But one evening, the heater began to turn itself on. To judge by the slight hum, it was on the highest setting. But I had not touched it. And nobody else was in the room. The heater hummed quietly on. And now the best of all: it was running, appeared to be set, but it did not heat, because it really couldn't. The switch during the last few days was set on zero. I checked all connections. I checked all fuses, all other appliances. Nothing there that should have provided a reason for concern. Suddenly, after about one minute, the hum stopped and the heater appeared to be turned off again. Two days later, the haunting repeated itself. A day after that, during the night, the darn thing started anew. Always only for a short time, and always without emitting heat. But it was running, this was clear, although nobody had moved the switch. A strange situation."

7.)

"When I return from shopping, I habitually check all my receipts as well as my change. Usually this takes but a few minutes. Afterwards, I put the receipts in a place especially reserved for them. This time I did so as usual. Then I forgot about it, took off my coat and went to bed early, as usual. Not to sleep, but in order to read. It was about 10 p.m. at night when I suddenly felt something rubbing over the naked skin of my stomach. Something scratched and tickled. I unbuttoned my nightgown. Bewildered, I stared at the yellow piece of paper. A receipt. The same receipt which I had carefully put away a few hours before, and not under my nightgown, but in the specially reserved place for it, a cardboard box. And to prove that I had put it away, I would put my hand in a fire. That I knew absolutely for certain. In such matters I am very conscientious. But now this damned thing was lying on my naked stomach under my nightgown. Just like that. As though invisible hands had put it there. Full of repugnance, I jumped out of bed and shook myself, as though I had to shake off a spider. How, I asked myself, was this at all possible? I myself surely had nothing to do with this idiotic

hocus-pocus. This I was sure of. It could not have gotten there accidentally. Because I had put the receipt away before I had even taken off any of my clothes."

8.)

"It is my habit to prepare about one half liter of a vitamin broth daily. This I drink in small sips during the day, or when I do not want to sleep but read, also during the night. The stuff contains a block of mineral salts, trace elements and, as I said, vitamins, all in the form of powder pressed into a rectangular sachet. For preparation, I open the sachet with a pair of scissors, pour the contents into a pitcher, add warm water and stir the pulp into a tasty drink. That would be the same procedure in this case. I put the empty pitcher on the table, put the powder into it (the empty sachet, proving I had done this, was on top of the garbage bag) and put it aside. I would add the water when I needed the drink. After about one hour this was the case. I took the pitcher — but the pitcher was empty — completely empty. And it appeared nicely cleaned out, as though I had not yet had it in my hands. What was going on? How could such a thing be possible? The powder simply was gone, had literally disappeared in thin air. The weirdest part of the whole story is that this was not at all the first time it happened. It has already happened that certain objects, usually little unimportant things, literally vanished in front of my very eyes, only to be found in a completely different place a few hours later. Often I get the feeling I am not quite right in my head. Everything appears to be so senseless."

9.)

"Two times I experienced how a completely new (not yet worn) piece of clothing, without visible cause — so to speak, by invisible hand — suffered great damage. This happened with a woolen sweater. I had bought it for a lot of money in one of the best stores. And since this beautiful garment had been so expensive, I first put it into my closet, carefully protected by a transparent plastic cover. About three weeks later, when I took this sweater out of the closet, I hardly recognized it. The whole right sleeve, from the shoulder down to the cuff, was colored black. The stuff looked like tar or lubricating oil, but did not have a smell. I have to add that I never had vermin in my apartment and I do not expose my clothes to uncleanliness. And since I live alone, outside action by others is out of the question. I myself, as I said, had not worn this garment to this very day, but nevertheless it now looked as though someone had pulled its right sleeve through a bucket of coal. At this moment I began to seriously doubt my own reason, and I thought that I myself might be causing these things; for example, that perhaps I did such detestable things at night in my sleep. Naturally, I returned the sweater to the store that very day. But they could not explain the event

either. The damage was then assessed by experts in a dry cleaning facility. Result: It was neither lubricating oil nor tar nor coal dust nor anything. The stuff was unidentifiable."

10.)

"I own a beautiful measuring cup (500 ml) which belongs to my set of glass china. It actually serves more as a decoration (because it looks so nice) than as a utensil. A few days ago, early in the morning, I found this little glass container to be damaged, when it had been placed safely in a corner of my cooking area, completely protected from accidental movements. I had not used it at all lately, and I swear it had been completely intact. On the lower part of its solid glass handle a triangular piece was missing. The whole thing looked as though someone had carefully removed a piece of it. So carefully, that the damaged area feels neither jagged nor broken, but absolutely smooth, and it also looks smooth. In order to do something like that, I assume one would have to use a special tool. The fact that I live by myself, and this happened during the night, makes it twice as mysterious. Who or what had anything to do with this container — at the time when everything is asleep? I can not explain this at all. It is also strange that I can not find the piece of glass which was broken out of the cup. From the very beginning, it could not be found. As if it dissolved in thin air."

The patient has a somewhat "demonic" air. As mentioned before, she was always accused of having the "Evil Eye." Even today, her eyes have something restless, flickering and then again staring. Female sensitivity recognized this more easily, and therefore it became difficult to make friends with persons of the same sex, and she succeeded only in exceptional cases. With men, who generally look more at the external, contact appeared to be made more easily. In the last five years, however, her sexual needs have receded so much that she has no more close relationships with men, who always also wanted sexual contact.

Unusually often, her voice is high-pitched and then seems rather shrill. This is not rare in unbalanced persons, thrown to and fro, but also describes a characteristic of which witches have always been accused. With obvious satisfaction, M.G. reports of her ability to influence persons and their appliances. For example, if she feels angry toward someone, she spontaneously wishes for him to have an accident or an illness, which often occurs within a very short time. Recently, the following incident took place: she felt angry about the unpleasant way another tenant was using the washing machine. So she intensively thought: "The washing machine shall stop dead!" This supposedly took place spontaneously. The tenant came angrily out of the laundry room and called for the caretaker. A mechanic came three times but could not do anything. A plumber came and regulated the water pressure, which resulted in an overflow of water at the templates, which nobody could explain. When it again was the patient's turn to use the machine, it roared, screeched and rumbled so much that the lamp in her room was agitated. So her evil wish boomeranged. I suggested that she should repair the washing machine again with her mental power, but M.G. responded that this was impossible for her. She needed to be in an immediate, strongly affective state of agitation in order have an influence.

M.G. has been bothered time and again by infestations, and ends up in depressive states, but she also, while relatively lonesome, directs a theater of life from which she obviously finds it difficult to separate herself. This also includes the consultation with her psychiatrist, which, however, must be limited for other reasons. The exorcism — at least according to the patient — reassures her for a certain time, but only recently have significant changes taken place. Possession or related conditions often require many exorcisms and prolonged psychological counseling. At least the tormenting, in fact, horrifying, dreams are now absent. The infestations, too, have decreased considerably in frequency and severity. Remarkable psychoplastic influences on objects and appliances now seldom occur. Earlier, for example, the small infestations, such as knocking on doors and walls, inexplicable ringing of the door bell, and suddenly occurring and disappearing repugnant smells, took place much more often. However, immediately after the death of her mother in July, 1981, Oscar Wilde's book, *The Canterville Ghost,* fell out of the patient's book case in a paranormal way, landing 1½ meters away diagonally across the room.

Part of the treatment involved pointing out how the practice of much black magic, and even malevolent thoughts, fall back onto their originator. The infested patient has become more careful in this respect but still enjoys her barely concealed successes caused by magical thinking. Nevertheless, extraordinary changes toward the positive have taken place in the life of this woman.

Miss H.N.

Miss H.N., whom I have known for six years, grew up in orderly circumstances in a rural area. Her intelligence is above average, but even as a child she was unusually sensitive. Her family history included cases of mental disturbances; therefore, her previous psychiatrist had understandably sought to explain all the patient's experiences as a disturbed inner life. She was introverted, shy, and no raving beauty, but in spite of an active sexuality, had difficulties finding a partner and was almost always lonely.

We know that she and her playmate, at the age of 5, were pursued by a woman considered to be a witch, all the way to her parents' house, where the witch continued to stare hatefully at them through the window. Witches exist, and children always prove to be more sensitive than adults, who have been made insecure about reliance on their intuitive functions. In the case in question, bewitchment would be difficult to prove, but it also cannot be completely excluded. Soon afterwards, in fact, the first psychological difficulties appeared. The child was seriously tormented by nocturnal anxieties, and until long after puberty, felt herself to be a person who attracted negativity and unjust treatment, which was incomprehensible to her.

Her basically depressed mood and compulsion to commit suicide were sometimes relieved by increased feelings for life, rich experiences in her relationships to animals, and love for literature.

The patient was referred to me by her physician, because she complained of paranormal phenomena. This also included incomprehensible symptoms in her body. The growth of her fingernails would stop for several weeks; then began to grow at the rate of 1 mm per day. Her hair, especially on her body, but also on her head, had suddenly bent and stuck out in an unnatural way, and the lashes of her eyes were deformed. She experienced sudden knife stabs in her throat, but the pain would subside immediately thereafter. She often felt dangerously strangled, but then felt released immediately afterwards. When she experienced difficulties swallowing, she often successfully overcame this by saying: "Retour, God willing" or "Retour, Köbeli." (Köbeli is a Swiss nickname for Jakob.) She does not designate her former physician, against whom she made many paranoid accusations, as "Köbeli," but rather an invisible spirit. She had formerly believed herself to be controlled and influenced by a physician who had fascinated her. This ambivalent perception, although psychologically understandable, was difficult to treat, but in the course of years a noticeable calming set in. Since influences by transcendental spirits on the body and environment of a person are far removed from our thinking today, such events remain incomprehensible, and may cause an afflicted patient to develop a paranoia against living persons.

Miss H.N. nevertheless often had the feeling that an incorporeal being was standing behind her and influencing her. Such phenomena are known to psychiatric experience as schizophrenic physical sensations, but are also found in those possessed. Miss H. N. told me that she had been characterized as such by the South African missionary Dr. Steeger, an expert in this area. The patient often complained of unbearable pressure in her ears, and she described this in the way they were experienced by the researcher of paranormal tape recorded voices, W. Dreiss.

The numerous phenomena in the environment of the patient were extremely similar to the phenomena of infestations. To present the whole series of events would produce too extensive a list, but individual written descriptions are characteristic:

> *"What surprises my apartment contained! I discovered my clothes to have seams torn open, zippers partially taken out and attached to other garments. In countless cases, the zipper could hardly be closed any longer. What was still untouched in my apartment? Chairs fell apart, parts of the table were missing, a piece of leather from a chair disappeared."*

All of this was only a part of the many inexplicable damages.

In the case of H.N. also, fringes of the carpet were eaten away or appeared as if they had been cut away. At first she thought that mice might have done it, but since she had never seen them and no other damage by mice took place, she concluded that behind "her mousey" must hide a spirit.

The patient, seeking help, refused exorcism, but was thankful to be taken seriously instead of described as mentally ill. She learned that not everything which happens to us can be laid to the account of living beings, and began to consider as more and more likely the possibility of the influence by transcendent beings.

Mr. R.

A distinguished, elderly businessmen consulted me as a parapsychologist — not as a physician — because of inexplicable experiences which had afflicted him during the last three years in both of his businesses. The businesses were located far apart from each other. It began when the bit of his Kaaba key for the alarm system (which he showed to me) had acquired two strange sharp-edged bends. He could not understand this, but such bends happen relatively often in cases of infestations.

Three months later, he had piled up goods in one of his adjoining rooms. Several times the goods were not piled on top of one another any longer, but were carefully placed next to one another on the floor, which appeared completely nonsensical and could not be explained by anyone.

In the presence of an employee one evening, he heard a "bang" in the back room. When they checked, they found an ashtray, made of molded glass, had broken into two pieces. One part was still lying in the original place, the other was located 30 cm away with three partially smoked cigarette butts which had not fallen out.

A few months later, he heard a loud rumbling on the upper floor. He was on the lower floor and noticed dust swirling down from the ceiling. When he checked, he found a heavy roll of wrapping paper, which had been stacked normally, lying on the floor of a relatively removed adjoining room.

On the window ledge of the balcony which belonged to the store stood a large and a smaller pot of flowers. He had watered the flowers the day before. The next day he noticed that the smaller pot was lying on the floor, 60 cm away from the ledge. The plant was hardly loosened in the unbroken pot. In one of his display cases, he hung watches. The centrally-placed watch had inexplicably come loose from its nail which had remained in its place. On the uppermost tray, and only on this one, all price marks were placed upside down.

Individual watches vibrated in the presence of witnesses, when other watches, placed next to them, did not vibrate. The businessman had the impression that the vibrations got stronger when he looked at them. Incomprehensible things happened to the arm bands of watches. One which shortly before he had placed ready for attachment, was found already mounted when he returned a little later. Nobody had been in the room during that time.

He had just used the service elevator. To his astonishment, the moment he left, it immediately began to travel down again, but nobody else had been in the house. Lamps suddenly did not work, and then functioned again. Light bulbs rang like alarm watches. The pocket calculator exhibited several false results, but worked correctly again the next day.

According to him, he was trying to break off his problem-ridden relationship with a girlfriend. After every attempt to do this, the phenomena began. A few weeks earlier, an exchange between the two had had a negative outcome for both. Afterwards, a mutual friend, who was aware of the situation, noticed upon her return home that a red house plant, which stood on a small platform lower than the couch next to it, was split in two. One part of the plant was still upright in the pot; the other part, still connected to its roots, was lying bent on the couch. The plant always spreads dusty red pollen, but mysteriously, none of it was found on the couch. The businessman also told about prophetic and clairvoyant abilities, which he believed he had always possessed.

Here the animistic-parapsychological interpretation is possible. Tensions were obviously present, but are not of an extraordinary kind. The occurrences did not always show a negative — and in no case an actual demonic — character. They appeared more like mischief, which, strange to say, finally affected someone only peripherally involved.

The event primarily has the character of an infestation. Whether transcendent spirits are playing a role can not be proved or disproved.

Miss O.

The girl, still young and pretty, looked foreign in her environment, but only vague information hinted, according to Miss O., that she was part gypsy. Adopted shortly after birth, neither she nor her adoptive mother could get information about her origin from official sources.

Even as a child, she was accused of having the "Evil Eye," and though innocent, she was beaten time and again by schoolmates without ever receiving help from the teachers. As an adult, too, wherever she appeared, she aroused attention, even anxiety, which was inexplicable to her. In recent months, this phenomenon had increased to an extraordinary degree.

She experienced her first prophetic dream (which showed her ability as a medium) at age 12. She dreamed that in one of the houses in her neighborhood a gas oven had exploded, the house had caught on fire, and only the youngest member of the family was able to save his life by jumping out of the window; all the others died. She woke up completely frightened, and went to the kitchen to drink something. Immediately thereafter, at 3 a.m., the events of the dream, in every detail, became reality.

Something similar happened to her at age 17. In her dream, she saw a serious accident at a well-known place on the way to her workplace. The next day, she did not take her motorcycle as she usually did, but walked to work. When she came to the place, the accident occurred as she had seen in her dream and took the life of a young man. The dream recurred in a similar form six months later. Again, she walked the next day, and witnessed an accident at the same place. This time a bicyclist was fatally injured.

Especially in recent times, many strange events have happened. For example, when on a car ride with her friend, they stopped for a very short time. A car radio cassette, placed on the passenger seat, could not be found when they got back in, in spite of an intensive search. She bought a new one, but six weeks later she found the old one in her glove compartment which they had carefully checked at the time.

Car radio cassettes with which the girl has a special connection disappear — she states — all the time, and then re-appear. Cassettes which do not belong to her suddenly are lying in her glove compartment.

In the apartment of her mother, when she happens to stay there, glasses, various pieces of silverware, and a tear gas pistol disappeared. While she was there, electric fuses burned out, light bulbs failed, and occasionally burned again for a short time. The television set started all by itself. Doors open by themselves when she wants to go into another room and close afterwards with no action on her part. At night, the mother herself heard the sound of dragging feet or the noise of crows, when none were near. During the night from the 2nd to the 3rd of May, 1983, Miss O., while fully conscious, heard knocking and high whistling tones coming from the stairway of the house; in addition, she heard dialogues which she can remember verbatim. This is comparable to the information from those harassed by tape recorded voices.

Often, when she is at her parents' home, pictures come loose from their mounts and vases which earlier had been intact, suddenly show notches — damage which no one is able to explain. Many times, objects were apported from one house into the other or to the car, and some were also deported again. This was also inexplicable.

In her own apartment, she once had prepared a hayflower bath, lay down for a short rest, and fell asleep for one hour. When she awoke, the wooden bucket, including its contents, was gone, and could not be found within the whole house. This, too, remained incomprehensible.

A few weeks ago, she looked at the fuse box in a department store and thought to herself: "That would be funny if the electricity failed." Promptly, a blackout for over one hour took place. In the same department store, several toy cars could be made to run by remote control. One was supposedly defective and not in use. Nevertheless, apparently by the power of her thoughts, it ran again. One is reminded of the countless watches, which, although proven to be defective, were made to function again by the influence of the so called "Geller Effect," an occurrence which I was able to observe myself.

She also succeeded in bending spoons and afterwards in returning them nearly into their original shape, but she never had luck with this in the presence of others or her friend.

In addition to apport phenomena (materializations?) of currency (which she could not influence with her will, however), some bills have disappeared out of safe containers — once, together with two pieces of gold. Once, under the impression of such events, she jokingly said to her friend: "I hope father's car does not disappear" (it was locked in the garage, and her father had the key and was away from home in a second car) and a short time later it actually was not in its place any longer, and returned, locked up, only an hour before the father came back. It is not easy to believe such stories. However, it has to be remembered that events of this kind happen independently of the laws of time, space and matter; and in principle, the size of an object plays no role.

Positive events took place, too. She seems to possess considerable powers of healing. A year ago, lumps developed in her breasts, which the physician in a laboratory test determined to be cancer growths and she was scheduled for surgery. She mentally concentrated on healing herself, in which she succeeded after one month. Since then, she has practiced mental healing. She has been able to lower her friend's fever, to heal her mother's migraine headaches, and also to positively influence sick animals. Her goal is now to become a psychic healer.

A peculiarity of Miss O. is described by her friend, who states that she can fall asleep unusually fast, and she can not be awakened. On holidays, she spends up to 16 hours in leaden sleep. (In the *Rituale Romanum,* this is described as a symptom indicative of possession).

Miss O. describes the character of her adoptive mother as that of an exceptional woman. Clad in black, she regularly travels to her home town 200 km away, and it is suspected that she visits demonic cults there. A cabinet containing exclusively black clothing stands in the mother's bedroom. It could be possible that both women, who secretly fear one another, cause an accumulation of powers.

Parapsychologically, this case is highly interesting. Whether the paraphenomena are a result of the girl's own psychopotential or whether transcendent spirits are attracted by her or her mother's abilities as mediums, remains unresolved.

The boundaries of these possibilities and the particular forms in which they occur are fluid. Miss O. exhibits peculiarities of character — not described here — which clearly are of demonic nature. Although the paranormal is many times constellated by her willful initiation, on the other hand, she also feels considerably troubled.

Perhaps the interplay between a "psychoactive" and an infested personality takes place here. Both types of phenomena originate in similar mental roots and conform to the same laws. As in the case of poltergeists, apportations, deportations, psychokinesis and psychoplastic events take place in colorful succession. Through the facts presented above, the psychogenesis of poltergeist phenomena is brought up for discussion again. Are they paranormal energies, controlled by humans in differing degrees? Or is additional energy, provided by motivated spirits, required? The phenomenon of possession indicates the latter version, but without clearly negating the "animistic" hypothesis. Rigid battle lines should be avoided in any case.

19. WITCHCRAFT AND POSSESSION

Witchcraft (or sorcery) is considered to be one of the causes of possession. It has many characteristics similar to telepathy. Telepathic impulses affect the ethereal sensory centers of the receiver and often, though not always, are based on an emotional arousal of the sender. In my opinion, the ethereal planes of the mental- and astral body are thereby affected. This would explain how the contents of transmitted thoughts reach awareness in the percipient. During transmittal by magic, which has a much stronger emotional component and often occurs during a state of half-trance, it is particularly the ethereal plane of the pictorial body — or the etheric body — of the victim which is affected. The contents of the transmission seldom reach into the consciousness of the victim, but can affect him physically and cause numerous organic disharmonies. Such disturbances can even lead to death. Unfortunately, the effects described cannot as yet be objectively verified with contemporary experimental designs, and thus remain hypothetical.

In telepathy, as well as magic, successful transmission presupposes openness as well as mediumistic ability on the part of the person afflicted by magic. In the perceptions of Voodoo, not everyone is vulnerable to magic. A person with stronger mental powers and spiritual strength — we would say someone possessing a strong ego — is invulnerable.

Magic also cannot be explained by natural science and has been ignored as superstition. Naturally, not everything which is branded as magic is objectifiable. Paranoid and slovenly thinking leads to many misconceptions, but one who concerns himself with this area in an unbiased fashion, and who considers the practices of non-intellectual cultures, comes to understand that magic is an aspect of reality.

Within parapsychology two possible explanations are being discussed: *first, by way of ethereal flows of energy, the corpus subtile — as mentioned before — and especially the etheric body of the victim is affected and, from there, his physical functioning is pathologically affected.* Such flows of energy can be mobilized by the sender during times of extreme negative arousal. We need to think this way about the proven effectiveness of the *curse,* which is considered to be one possible cause of possession. The emotional excitement of the person who invokes the curse must be very strong and requires a certain immediacy. A weakening of the emotional ethereal body *(corpus astrale)* by a curse in early childhood seems a possible explanation, since I am thinking of a telepathic influence on the early childhood psyche in the sense of a weakening of the ego, which manifests itself later, and permits the entrance of possessing spirits. The delayed influence of the curse seems to be best explained in that way.

When magic is employed in the case of a merely aggressive attitude which previously existed, or especially on behalf of a third person, its emotional immediacy is greatly reduced and the force of the energy flow is usually too weak. It then requires a magical action and ritual, not only to increase its strength, but also to decrease the ego-dependency of the magician, which allows ethereal sources of energy to flow out with more direction and more easily. A decrease of ego-dependency takes place during the trance. This flows into the multi- dimensionality of life, while the state of consciousness only acts in three dimensions, plus the fourth dimension — time. During the state of trance, a person, without difficulty, grows into the metaphysical, into wholeness, where thought and matter are one and the same. This makes an analogical event possible, which — in the understanding of natural science — produces non-causal effects which we know about within the field of esoteric astrology. The *causa* (cause), in the astrological sense, is a cosmic representation in multidimensional space.

With regard to magic, we have to assume the existence of a common layer between spirit-soul and matter, which belongs to both entities, and which is incomprehensible within the framework of natural science. This layer is the connecting link but remains hidden from our external senses. Possibly we are dealing with an imaginary plane of encounter, where, in the tantric teaching of the five bodies, a still ethereal body (Prana) changes into *physis* (material substance) at a point where its degree of density begins to be perceptible by our external senses.

Into this joint layer leads the so-called *"Abaissement du niveau mental"* (Levy-Bruhl), which in reality is no *"abaissement,"* i.e. no "sinking down," but an immersion into and a return to an ethereal and therefore non-material world. Every curse, all magic, all possession and every exorcism originates in this common layer.

Destructive magic can lead to illness or even death, without any direct symptoms of possession being present. It is the result of a mental- psychic influence on the victim, and sometimes also the effect of bewitched objects given to the bewitched person who has no knowledge of their damaging influence. The Huna teachings interpret their effect by assuming that so-called "Aka threads" of the mental content of a thought adhere to the object and in this way can transfer themselves into the material reality of the victim.

I would assume that the mental archetypical, such as hate, jealousy, etc., determines the direction of the event at the time of the influence on the body, while the emotional provides the energy.

Second, as a further possible influence, the participation of demonic spirits has to be considered. A call to them takes place within the magic ritual, which acts as a summons to negative, ethereal spirits. It is also conceivable that such spirits may also interfere without being called on, utilizing the victim's weakness of ego, caused by the magician. In that case, then, we are actually dealing with harassment or possession, which assists the intentions of the magician. Those who reject magic as superstition, lack knowledge and experience in these existential areas and realms of investigation.

20. SUMMARY AND CONCLUSIONS

"L'intellectuel est le célibataire de la verité"
["The intellectual is the eunuch of truth"]

This clever saying by Jean Carteret illuminates quite accurately the picture of science in our modern world, which probably faces major changes in the coming decades. Sole attention given to the intellect and natural scientific methods derived therefrom, leads to an unmistakable sterility of perspective, which future generations will no longer accept.

The eunuch lacks the full range of human experiences, especially those of marriage and raising a family. Similarly, one who holds a concept of the world restricted only to matter can not conceive of the richness of the spiritually acting forces affecting this world. How can a physician or a psychiatrist trained only in causal analytical concepts comprehend the entirety of the human soul, which as a non-material quantity, is located just as much in the transcendent as it is in the material world?

The phenomenon of possession belongs to the primeval experiences of mankind, encountered on all continents. A scientist who has not experienced possession will categorize the phenomena as superstition. Also, spectacular cases are rare, and the great majority of our city dwellers are either not aware of them or associate them with mental illnesses. Someone who is open to the problem, and who like Van Dusen has worked for years in psychiatric hospitals, is capable of recognizing the cases of possession which occur relatively frequently. Unfortunately, it is not easy to determine whether many neuroses which are resistant to other types of psychological therapy, may be cases of possession by some entity. This is especially difficult in minor disturbances, which can, however, be very difficult to deal with. This problem, too, will continue to be a matter for discussion and debate.

That polarities, such as good and evil, reflect the nature of human experience and existence, should be kept in mind. Since persons influenced by positive forces seldom seek psychiatric help, it is obvious that we deal more extensively with negative aspects of this phenomenon. This should not, however, lead us to ignore or discount the role of positive influence in the case of many healers, artists, composers, inventors, etc.

It should be emphasized that critics who lack any experience of their own and are trained only in the traditional sciences will have no valid basis for evaluating the phenomena of possession and exorcism, but some will do it anyhow. Their belief in the widely accepted "knowledge" provides enough motivation. I would like to provide some food for thought: *"In order to reach the source, one has to swim against the current."*

In summary, what can we say that we now know about possession and its lesser forms of harassment and infestation? Since most of the dramatic cases have been drawn from earlier times when it is presumed there was a greater naiveté about mental functioning, it is easy to dismiss or neglect the true significance of the observed cases. Yet we see that actual possession, with virtually identical features, is still observed today, even if with less frequency. As happens not infrequently in the area of personality pathology, once a pattern is observed and clearly described, a large number of other investigators begin to observe it also. Perhaps there are many more cases of actual possession today than we believe, but they exist undiscovered due to unwillingness to entertain such "far out" hypotheses.

Although the existence of a hierarchy of spirits and demons can only be speculatively documented at this time, the pattern of manifestations seems clear. In possession, dramatic modification of physical forms is present, with physical manifestations which defy apparent limits of reality — voice and personality changes, foreign substances found in or propelled from the body, and intense dislike for religious icons and statements expressed by some disturbed persons.

Some tentative conclusions seem warranted, although distinctive cases of outright possession in our modern era are few, possibly because most people are not actively looking for them:

1. With regard to the persons involved, where paranormal events are considered to be caused by a bioenergetic field of energy of a consciously or unconsciously restless and perhaps insecure person, my 50 years of experience lead me to conclude otherwise.

2. The persons afflicted always seem to possess mediumistic sensitivities. This, I believe, is pertinent, but the ability as a medium is not a sufficient cause in itself.

3. For lesser causes of possession (hauntings or infestations), some sort of magic spell involving witchcraft appears to be involved. Witchcraft apparently is the source of energy for the demonic spirits, although the form and extent of the effects seem to be due to the spirits themselves.

4. Demonic spirits, whether angel demons, "poor souls," or whatever kind, must be around and wish to make themselves known.

These conditions, combined in some way, are both necessary and sufficient to bring about some cases of possession. It also seems that the three types of possession always deal with the same basic event — the condensation of ethereal matter into more dense matter, as well as its psychoplastic deformation.

Some distinguishing characteristics of the more extreme cases of actual possession (as contrasted with harassment or infestation) exist in the following:

A. Possessed persons, when contrasted with other clinical states such as schizophrenia, manifest normal personality patterns between attacks.

B. Some sort of weakening of the ego is involved to permit the possession. This may exist in the ongoing personality makeup, as in multiple personality disorders *(Allison* and *Crabtree),* or possibly in some cultures as a result of magic spells.

C. Possessed individuals have amnesia for the attacks, whereas lesser forms of possession (harassment, infestation) do not cloud the memory of the afflicted.

D. Effects on the body and environment of possessed persons are often selective and bizarre. A large number of unusual objects have been removed from the bodies of possessed individuals and inexplicable objects and "controlled" burning have occurred. Such phenomena are never experienced by schizophrenics.

It should be added that there is much evidence that the effectiveness of an exorcism is related to the cultural or religious beliefs of the possessed and therefore the methods and rituals should be tailored to the personality of the person to be exorcised. For example, if the possessing entity has a strong anti-religious bias, it is likely to vigorously resist if the attempted exorcism is couched in religious terminology.

Dr. Carl Wickland's extensive experience as psychiatrist in mental hospitals led him to conclude that many persons judged insane were more likely to be possessed — not necessarily by evil entities, but by lost or confused "earthbound souls," who, not realizing they were "dead," had taken control of emotionally unstable persons, causing extreme confusion and disorientation.

I can understand the individual advocate of natural scientific orthodoxy, but such a person should learn that in the course of time, no concept of the world has lasted forever. Each must submit to rhythmic currents, which perhaps may turn them 180 degrees. "Everything flows" *Panta rhei!* (Heraclitus).

Every pertinent dialogue is desirable. One's own mistakes will also be resolved that way, and most important, the problem is presented for discussion rather than being ignored or hushed up.

The main purpose of this book is to stimulate interest in and dialogue about the phenomenon of possession as an important concept in understanding human behavior.

BIBLIOGRAPHY

Allison, Ralph, M.D. & Ted Schwarz, 1980. *Mind in Many Pieces*. Rawson, Wade, New York

Crabtree, Adam. 1985. *Multiple Man: Exploration in Possession and Multiple Personality*. Collins, Publishers, Toronto & Praeger, New York

Ebon, Martin, (Ed.) 1974. *Exorcism: Fact Not Fiction*. New American Library, New York.

_____1974. *The Devil's Bride: Exorcisms Past and Present*. Harper & Row, New York.

Guirdham, Arthur. 1972. *Obsession: Psychic Forces and Evil in the Causation of Disease*. Neville Spearman, London.

Fiore, Edith, Ph.D. 1987. *The Unquiet Dead: A Psychologist Treats Spirit Possession*. Doubleday, New York.

Nauman, St. Elmo, Jr. Ph.D. (Ed.) *Exorcism Through the Ages*. Philosophical Library, New York.

Oesterreich, T.K. (tr. D. Ibberson) 1966. *Possession: Demoniacal and Other*. Lyle Stuart Inc. Secaucus, NJ.

Ramos, Maximo D. 1971 *Creatures of Philippine Lower Mythology*. University of the Philippines Press, Manila.

Rodewyk, Adolf (tr. by M. Ebon) 1985. *Possessed by Satan*. Doubleday, New York.

van Dusen, Wilson. 1972. *Natural Depth of Man*. Harper & Row, New York.

_____1972. *Presence of Spirits in Madness* (booklet). Swedenborg Foundation, Inc., New York.

Wickland, Carl A., M.D. 1924. *Thirty Years Among the Dead*. National Psychological Institute, Los Angeles. Reprinted 1978 by Spiritualist Press, London. Also shortened version by Amherst Press, Amherst, Wisconsin.

Books about Positive Aspects of Possession

Brown, Rosemary. 1971. *Unfinished Symphonies*. William Morrow & Co., New York.

_____1974. *Immortals at My Elbow*. Bachman & Turner, London.

Chapman, George. 1973. *Extraordinary Encounters*. Lang Publishing Co., Aylesbury, England.

_____1978. *Surgeon From Another World*. W.H. Allen & Co., London

Fuller, John G. 1974. *Arigo: Surgeon With the Rusty Knife*. Thomas Y. Crowell, New York.

Hutton, J. Bernard. 1966. *Healing Hands*. W.H. Allen & Co., London.

Prince, Walter M.D. 1966. *The Case of Patience Worth*. University Books, New York.

Related Books

Alexander, Marc. 1982. *Haunted Houses You May Visit: A Ghostly Guide to Britain's Stately Haunted Homes.* Sphere Books, Ltd., London.

Beard, Paul. 1966. *Survival of Death.* Pilgrims Book Services, Tasburgh, Norwich, England.

Bradley, Rob't A., M.D. & D. Bradley, 1967. *Psychic Phenomena: Revelations and Experiences.* Parker, West Nyack, New Jersey.

Bull, Titus, M.D. 1932. *Analysis of Unusual Experiences in Healing.* London.

Chesi, Gert. 1981. *Faith Healers in the Philippines.* Perlinger, Woergl, Austria.

Delacour, Jean-Baptiste. 1975. *Apage Satana.* Ariston-Verlag, Geneva.

Dethlefsen, Thorwald. 1976. *Voices from Other Lives.* H. Evans & Co., Inc. New York.

Eddy, Sherwood. 1959. *You Will Survive After Death.* Holt, Rinhart & Winston, New York.

Fodor, N. 1966. *Encyclopedia of Psychic Science.* University Books, New York.

Fuller, John G. 1985. *The Ghosts of 29 Megacycles.* Souvenir Press, London. (also in paperback, 1986. New American Library, New York)

Hickman, Irene, D.O. 1983. *Mind Probe–Hypnosis.* Hickman Systems, Kirksville, Missouri.

Inglis, Brian. 1985. *The Paranormal: An Encyclopedia of Psychic Phenomena.* Granada, London.

Juergenson, Friedrich. 1967. *Sprechfunk mit Verstorbenen.* Bauer Verlag, Freiburg, Germany.

Kelsey, Denys, & Joan Grant. 1967. *Many Lifetimes.* Doubleday & Co., New York.

Meek, George W. (Ed.) 1977. *Healers and the Healing Process.* Theosophical Publishing House, Wheaton, Illinois.

Mitchell, Edgar D. (Ed. John White) 1977. *Psychic Exploration.* G.P. Putnam's Sons, New York.

Peck, M. Scott, M.D. 1983. *People of the Lie: The Hope for Healing Human Evil.* Simon & Schuster, New York.

Prange, Erwin. 1973. *The Gift is Already Yours.* Logos International, Plainfield, N.J.

Raudive, Konstantin. (tr. N. Fowler). 1971. *Breakthrough: An Amazing Experiment In Electronic Communication with the Dead.* Colin Smythe, Ltd., Gerrards Cross, England, and Taplinger, New York. (Also in paperback, Lancer Books, New York.)

Russell, J.R. 1972. *Witchcraft in the Middle Ages.* Citadel Press, Secaucus, New Jersey.

Scott, Beth & M. Norman. 1985. *Haunted Heartland.* Warner Books, Inc. New York.

Sherman, Harold. 1967, *Wonder Healers of the Philippines.* DeVorss & Co., Los Angeles, California.

Stevenson, Ian, M.D. 1966. *Twenty Cases Suggestive of Reincarnation.* American Society for Psychical Research. New York.

Uphoff, Walter H. & Mary Jo Uphoff. 1980. *New Psychic Frontiers; Your Key to New Worlds.* (3rd edition) Colin Smythe, Ltd., Gerrards Cross, England and New Frontiers Center, Oregon, Wisconsin.

Whitton, Joel, M.D., Ph.D. & Joe Fisher. 1986. *Life Between Life.* Warner Books, New York.

Wilson, Colin. 1981. *Poltergeist, A Study in Destructive Haunting.* New English Library, London.

INDEX

A

Adam, Attorney **154**
Aeschuylus **24**
Agpaoa, Tony **55-56**
Alkmaion **10**
Allison, Ralph **xvi, 89, 177**
Alt, Rev. Fr. **128-129, 131**
American Association: Electronic Voice
   Phenomenon **144**
Archetypes of good and evil **25**
Arigó, Ze **xiv, 43, 74**
Aristotle **10, 19**

B

Baettig, Victor **144-145**
Baenziger, Andreas **78-79**
Bayless, Raymond **143**
Bibliography **179**
Benedetti, Baetano **85-88**
Bender, Dr. Hans **51, 144, 154**
Blacher, Karl **90**
Blasius, Walter **11, 18**
Blasius, Wilhelm **10**
Bleuler, Eugen **4**
Bleuler, Manfred **4**
Bleuler Research Center **4-5**
Blumhardt, Johann Christoph **3, 29,**
   36-37, 49-50, 53, 55, 71-88, 100,
   111, 114, 142
Bodini, Johann **3, 101, 105-106, 110, 112**
Boddhisattva **41**
Bodhisattvas **132**
Boehme, Jacob **49**
Bohr, Niels **26**
Bonner, Gilbert **145**
Bozzano, Ernesto **78**
Braendel, David **105**
Bradley, Robert A., M.D. **xv**
Bramely, Serge **117, 120-121**
Buddha **7, 40, 132**
Buddhism **60, 132**
Bull, Titus, M.D. **25, 66, 138**
Buschbeck, Hanna **145**

C

Cabala **14, 46**
Calvin, John **53**

C

Capuchins **4, 123**
Cartaret, Jean **174**
Carus **10, 19, 70**
Cartesian **87**
Cass, Raymond **145**
Cele, Germana **97, 112, 115**
Ceylon (Sri Lanka) **59, 61**
chakras **44, 64**
Chesi, Gert **57, 80, 117**
Chapman, George (Dr. Wm. Lang)
   xiv, 41, 44
Chapman, Michael **42**
chemotherapy **8**
chorea minor **106, 107**
circumsessio **35, 39, 137-138, 142, 150**
Coats, David **xvii**
Coats, Sigrid **xvii, 13**
corpus subtile **69, 84, 118-119**
Crabtree, Adam **xvi, 89, 135, 177**
Crookes, Sir William **134**
cultic possession **117, 122**

D

Daimon **24**
Dante **23**
de Freitas **43**
Delacours, Jean Baptiste **34, 76, 97,**
   137, 150-151
del Rosario, Rosita **79**
dementia praecox **31-32**
Descartes, René **2, 6-7, 10-11, 19, 23**
Dittus, Gottlieben **3, 29, 31, 35, 37,**
   48-49, 55, 71-74, 76, 79, 81, 89, 100,
   109, 111, 114, 118, 124, 151
Dittus, Katharina **75**
Dreiss, W. **144-145, 168**
Duke University **7**

E

Ebon, Martin **xvii**
Ehrlich, Frances E., M.D. **xviii**
electronic Voice phenomenon; (EVP)
   143
Ellis, David **145**
epileptic seizures **34**
Esotera **1, 20, 27**

Estep, Sarah **145**
Eugenie, Princess of Leyen **51, 72, 138**
Euripedes **24**
Exorcist, The **x, xiii**

F

Farrelly, Frank **xvii**
Faust **12-13, 15, 23, 37, 130**
Fernelius, Johannes **108**
Ferry, Jeanne **100**
Fiore, Edith, Ph.D. **xvii**
firewalking **1, 26, 82, 119**
Fleischmann, Fr. Valentin **128, 130-131**
Flores, Juanito **43**
Forschungsgemeinschaft fuer
  Tonbandstimmen **144**
Frei, Gebhard **96**
Freud, Sigmund **28-29, 67, 130-131**
Fritz, Adolfo **xv, 43**
Fromm, Erica **38**
Froeschel, Sebastian **54**
Frueh, Walter **111**
Fuchs, Luise **149**
Fuller, John G. **43, 148**

G

Gasparetto, Luiz **xv**
Gassner, Johann Josef **90**
Gehring, Peter **51, 72**
Geller, Uri **20, 50, 95-96**
Gilula, Marshall, M.D. **xviii**
Goethe, Joh. Wolfgang von **10, 13, 15,
  18-19, 23, 37, 130, 133-134**
good and evil **20-21**
Goodman, Felicitas D. **126-127, 133**

H

Haraldsson, Erlendur **20**
Harriman, Averill **147**
Harsch-Fischbach, Jules **149**
Harsch-Fischbach, Maggy **149**
Hathaway, Claude Macy **134**
Heim, Burkhard **26**
Heisenberg, Werner Karl **26**
Heitler, Walter **10, 26**
Henn, Gunter **144**
Heraclitus **10, 19, 177**
Herrmann, Rev. **128**
Herschel, William **6**

hexagram **12**
Hinze, Oskar Marcel **28, 48, 58, 111**
Hippocrates **45**
Hitler, Adolph **40, 131**
Holbe, Rainer **149**
Horia, Vintila **115**
Huna **174**
Hutton, J. Bernard **43**
Huxley, Aldous **107**

I

Illfurt, lads of **31, 95, 98, 107-108, 124**
Imago Mundi **27**
Index **181**
infestation (*infestatio*) **35, 137, 150**

J

Janos **29**
Jordan **26**
Juergenson, Friedrich **143-145**
Jung, Carl Gustav **1-2, 4, 11, 18, 20, 28,
  30, 35-36, 58, 67, 83-84, 114, 130**
  functions of cognition—*perception,
    intuition, emotion* and *intellect* **11**

K

Kaffir **144-145**
Karger, Friedbert **154**
karma **35**
Kant, Immanuel **7, 19**
Kékulé, F.A. **9**
Kerner, Justinus **113**
Kiefer, Waldemar **24**
Kirkegaard, Soeren **35, 89**
Klages, Ludwig **11, 16, 20, 46, 70**
Koch, Kurt **36**
Koeberle, Fidelio **144**
Koenig, Hans Otto **149**
Kulagina, Nelja (Nina) **96**

L

Lamoreaux, Joe **145**
Lamoreaux, Michael **145**
Lang, Basil **42**
Lang, Dr. William (George Chapman)
  xiv, 41-43
Lechner-Knecht, Sigrid **118**
Livizzano, Donato **99**
Luther, Martin **3, 47, 53-54**

M

Macumba 117, 119
MacRae, Alex 145
mae de santo 117-118, 120-121
Magdalena of Loewenberg 101-105,
 111
Magdalene of Orlach 113-114, 151
Maier, R. 19
Manning, Matthew 95
McKee, Daniel 145
Meek, George W. 99, 147-149
Menedes, Eliezer 62
Mephistopheles 23
Michel Analiese 4, 25, 34, 45, 50, 112,
 118, 125, 127-134
Michael, Johann 108
Mills, John Stuart 6
Monet xv
Monroe, Robert 155
Moerike, Eduard 13, 15
Moses 40
Motoyama, Dr. Hiroshi 25, 58, 64
Mueller, George J. 148
multiple personality 92, 135
Murphet, Dr. Howard 20

N

Nager, Katharina 5, 41, 79, 91
Napoleon 40
Naumann, St. Elmo 107
Nazis 92
Nero 40
Neumann, Therese (see von
 Konnereuth) 123-124, 132
Newton, Isaac 7, 19
Nielsson, Haraldur 72
Nigg, Walter 1-2
Nietsche 17
nirvana 41
Nowotny, Karl, M.D. 44

O

Obri, Nicole 96, 124
obsessio 68, 137, 150
Oligane, David 29, 55-56, 80
Oken 10, 19
Orbito, Alex 55, 57, 111
O'Neill, William 148
ouija boards x, xv

P

Pachita 74
pae de santos 117-119, 120
Pan, Greek god 120
Padre Pio 123-124, 129, 132
Paracelsus, Theophratus 6, 28, 48,
 69-70
paranormal weight 97
Pauli 26
Peck, M. Scott, M.D. xvi
Picasso xv
Plato 14, 19
Polycrates syndrome 17
Pope Leo XIII 45, 53
Pope Paul V 37, 45, 52
Pope Paul VI 3
Pope Pius XII 45, 52
Portman, Adolf 18
possessed nuns 109
prana 12, 44
Prange, Erwin 71
possessio 35-37, 68-69, 142, 150
Protagoras 19
psychic surgery 27, 29, 43, 49, 54-55,
 74, 79-81, 96, 111, 113, 155
Puharich, Andrija, M.D. 43, 74
Pythagoras 10

Q

Quieroz, Edson, M.D. xv, 43
Quimbanda 117, 120

R

Raudive, Dr. Konstantin 143-149
Renoir xv
Renz, Fr. A. 130-133
Resch, Dr. Andreas 154
Rhine, Joseph B. 7
Rituale Romanum 25, 36-37, 39, 45,
 52, 89, 114, 131, 137, 172
Ringger, Peter 5, 75, 77, 89-90, 109
Rodewyk, Adolf, S.J. 4, 36, 112-113,
 130
Rosenheim (poltergeist) 154
Roth, Fr. (Chaplain) 128-129
Rudolph, Theodor 144
Rýzl, Milan 98

S

sacerdotyl 52
Sai Baba 20, 41, 96

Sartre, J.P. **7**
Satyrs of Dionysius **24**
Schaefer, Hildegard **144**
Schamoni, W. **40**
Schelling **10, 19, 20-21**
Schiebeler, Dr. Werner **58**
schizophrenia **8, 31-33, 94, 118, 137-139, 145-146, 168**
Schleicher, Agnes **112**
Schmit, Fr. Leo **144, 146**
Schneider, Alex **42, 144-145**
Scharfetter, Dr. Christian **32, 59, 61**
Schreiber, Klaus **149**
Schroeder, Greta **44**
Schweitzer, Dr. Albert **51**
Seidl, Franz **144, 157**
Seiler, Tobias **101**
Senkowski, Ernst **148-149**
Seutemann, Sigrun **58**
Severson, Roger A. **xviii**
Sharpe, Mary **145**
Sheargold, Richard **145**
Siegmund, Georg **73**
Silesius, Angelus **120**
Silvio **95**
Sison, Josephina **55, 57**
Smythe, Colin **144**
Socrates **24**
Solomon's Seal **12**
Spiricom **147-149**
Sri Ganapathy Sachchidananda **1, 41, 96, 119**
Staudenmaier, Ludwig **142**
Swedenborg, Emmanuel **7, 24-25, 44, 66, 68-69**
Swiss Society for Parapsychology **ix, 5, 42, 151**
syncretism **122**
Szondy **28**

T
Tantra **25, 48**
terreiro **117, 119, 121**
Tertio, Eleuterio **55-56**
Thuerkauf, Max **9-10, 26**

Thangka **24-25**
TIME magazine **xv**
Tournier, Paul **29**

U
uchtoloni analysis **57**
Uphoff, Mary Jo **2**
Uphoff, Norman **148**
Uphoff, Walter H. **2, 148**

V
van Dusen, Wilson **66, 69, 73, 138, 175**
van Gogh, Vincent **xv**
Veilleux, Richard **75**
Verein fuer Tonbandstimmen Forschung **144**
Vinardi, Livio **75**
Nivchow, R. **7**
von Avila, St. Therese **124**
von Copertino, St. Joseph **2**
von Helmholz, H. **7, 19**
von Konnersreuth, Therese (Neumann) **123-124, 132**
von Szalay, Attila **143**
voodoo **177**

W
Wagner **23**
Watson, Lyall **99**
Welch, William **145**
Wenzel, Martin **149**
Wickland, Carl W., M.D. **xvi, 23, 26, 62, 65-66, 69, 80, 137-138, 177**
Wickland (Mrs.) Anna **65-66**
Wilde, Oscar **167**

X
Xenoglossy **37-38**

Z
Zen Buddhism **25, 64**
Zener cards **7**
Zoller, Heinrich **10**
Zwingli, Ulrich **53**
Zuendel, Friedrich **77**